Renaissance Drama

Renaissance Drama

SANDRA CLARK

polity

First published in 2007 by Polity Press

Polity Press
65 Bridge Street
Cambridge CB2 1UR, UK.

Polity Press
350 Main Street
Malden, MA 02148, USA

ISBN-13: 978-07456-3310-7
ISBN-13: 978-07456-3311-4 (pb)

A catalogue record for this book is available from the British Library.

Typeset in 11.25 on 13 pt Dante
by SNP Best-set Typesetter Ltd., Hong Kong
Printed and bound in India by Replika Press PVT Ltd, Kundli

For further information on Polity, visit our website: www.polity.co.uk

Contents

Illustrations

Preface

This book examines the drama of its period, plays produced for the public stage, in relation to those aspects of the contemporary social and cultural context which figure most prominently in it. Thus, it has seemed to me most appropriate to adopt a largely thematic approach, rather than one organized around authors. This is also for two other reasons, partly because I wanted to include as wide a range of plays as possible in order to represent the richness and variety of the early modern professional stage, and because I regard it as culturally distorting to focus on individual playwrights at a time when they were much less significant figures than they were later to become, when authorial individuality was hardly at all an issue. A high proportion of these plays was written by more than one author; and many have come down to us without any authors' names at all. Such plays can easily become marginalized when the focus is on a particular playwright and his body of work. But it is of course impossible to ignore the fact that one playwright's name has taken on such significance that it often now stands for the whole period; the titles of books such as *The Profession of Dramatist in Shakespeare's Time 1590–1642* or *The Shakespearean Stage, 1574–1642* say it all. In the main part of the book I have tried to avoid the 'conventional insulation' (to borrow a critic's useful expression)* of Shakespeare from his contemporaries by drawing on his plays where appropriate to exemplify my points in the same way as any other plays, and treating them as one element in a larger context. But I have given Shakespeare the last chapter, in which I try to assess his place in the theatrical culture of the day by looking at his interactions with other writers. I hope this diversion from the thematic and genre-based scheme of the other chapters is justified by the broader picture it provides of playwrights in dialogue with one another as a particular feature of the theatrical culture of the time.

* Ruth Morse, ' "What City, Friends, Is This?" ', in Dieter Mehl, Angela Stock and Anne-Julia Zwierlein (eds), *Plotting Early Modern London: New Essays on Jacobean City Comedy* (Aldershot and Burlington, Vt: Ashgate, 2004), p. 178.

The book is written with the needs of students in mind, and it is on this basis that I have made assumptions as to how much and what kind of information to provide. While I imagine most readers will come to it with certain preconceptions about the period and the plays, I hope to extend a knowledge of the Elizabethan theatre that may be restricted to the best-known and/or most anthologized plays by familiar writers. I have not, however, attempted to include court and closet drama, or civic pageantry. I am keen to think about the theatre as a newly established commercial institution in early modern London, and it is this consideration that has guided my choice of topics on which to focus. These plays were written to make money, and needed to engage with the concerns of their audiences, concerns which are reflected in the themes I explore. At the same time, I hope to show that plays were not purely reactive and that theatre did more than merely reflect the society which produced it. The strength of the anti-theatrical prejudice in the period testifies to a belief that theatre was culturally powerful and perhaps dangerous, at least to certain interests. Through the demonstrated skills of those marginal men, the players, it could influence the hearts and minds of its audiences and even change the ways in which they related to their society.

A note on texts   I have tried to take my quotations from those editions of play texts which students will find most useful, that is, those which are scholarly, annotated and easily available. In the case of some of the less familiar plays, such editions do not exist. I have used early editions of non-dramatic texts where available, since in my view this helps us to hear the voice of the past with less mediation. The result is a mixture of old- and modern-spelling quotations; but this seems to me preferable to wholesale modernizing for the sake of consistency. In old-spelling texts, I have silently regularized the use of u/v, i/j, and long s. A list of editions from which quotations are taken is provided.

Acknowledgments   I would like to acknowledge financial assistance from Birkbeck, University of London, towards the costs of the index and the illustrations, and also less quantifiable assistance in the form of inspiration from Birkbeck students in many classes on Shakespeare and the drama of his time. In more domestic ways, Mike Holmes has had a large part to play in helping this book on its way.

1

Introduction

The year 1576 has often been highlighted as an iconic date in the history
of early modern theatre – it was the year when the Theatre (with a capital
T) was built – 'the watershed in the affairs of the theatre',[1] after which the
era of Shakespeare, Marlowe and Jonson could begin. It was of course a
highly significant moment in the development of the English professional
theatre: the point at which James Burbage, formerly a joiner and now a
player in the Earl of Leicester's company, felt it was commercially viable
to raise money to lease land in Shoreditch, outside the boundary of the
City of London, and put up a new and expensive building in the expectation that sufficient paying customers would be attracted to justify the
investment. As it happened, he was not alone in his judgement of the possibilities for making money out of plays at this time, for another theatre,
the Curtain, was built close by, opening in 1577, and also one on the south
side of the river, at Newington Butts, the name of which is unknown. Why
did Burbage and his fellows choose this particular time to take what must
have been quite a financial gamble? As has been said, the history of professional theatre does not begin with buildings, and clearly there must have
been certain social and cultural conditions already in place which encouraged these entrepreneurs to take such a step.

This chapter will focus on commercial theatre, its role and cultural significance in London in the period. But some account of the preconditions
for the development of this theatre must inevitably include other types of
theatrical activity which existed both in London and in other parts of
England and were not necessarily designed to make money. Under the
aegis of three rather socially diverse institutions, the church, the court and
the universities, theatre had been evolving over a long period of time. Of
these, theatrical events deriving from the festivals of the medieval Catholic
church represented a genuinely popular form of entertainment which had
long enjoyed the support of civic authorities such as trade guilds who
helped organize and finance them and were integral to the life of the
local community. During the sixteenth century the crown took over the

authority to regulate the subject matter of religious plays which had formerly been the province of the church, and proceeded with the suppression of interludes and cycle plays in various areas of the country, particularly the north of England, where the great cycles of York, Chester and Wakefield had been created, until they were completely banned. The Chester cycle was performed for the last time in 1575, and the Coventry cycle in 1579. Evidently there was much support for the continuation of these plays, since local authorities continued to sponsor them once church sponsorship had lapsed with the Reformation, and the mayors of Chester and Coventry were summoned before the Privy Council in 1573 and again in 1575 for allowing the plays to be performed against the wishes of the Archbishop of York and the Ecclesiastical Commission of the North. The Chester archives contain a document in which the two mayors protest that 'they did nothing in their several times of mayoralties touching the said plays but by the assent, consent, and agreement of the Aldermen, Sheriffs and Common Council of the said City'.[2] Although it may be the case that 'a great era of amateur, community drama had been snuffed out'[3] when these plays ceased to be performed, it is noteworthy how long they did continue, given the proclamation of the first year of Elizabeth's reign which forbids all plays in which 'either matters of religion or the governance of the estate of the Commonwealth shall be handled . . . before any audience but of grave and discreet persons'.[4] And there was a period of overlap with the beginnings of secular commercial theatre, and some professional playwrights, such as Shakespeare, may well have witnessed performances of these plays in their youth.

The court had a tradition of active interest in theatricals since at least the times of Henry VIII, and it was he who instigated the office of Master of the Revels to regularize and supervise court entertainment. He enjoyed many kinds of organized revels, including pageants and tilts, and himself took part when young in an entertainment in disguise, 'after the manner of Italie, . . . [in] a Maske, a thyng not seen afore in Englande'.[5] Elizabeth, though less extravagant than her father, also enjoyed masques and musical revelry at court, which took place at various festival times during the year; and when she went on the annual progresses to visit her subjects she liked to be entertained with symbolic pageants specially devised to promote her image as Cynthia the Virgin Queen. She became increasingly interested in stage plays as such, and in the 1580s there appeared the first body of plays specifically written for court performance, by John Lyly. In 1583 she demonstrated active involvement in the commercial theatre by having her Master of the Revels, Edmund Tilney, create a company known as the Queen's Men by cherry-picking twelve of the best actors from the existing companies. Her support for the commercial theatre was vital to its success in the face of opposition from the London City fathers.

The universities and Inns of Court shared with the court something of the traditions of theatrical forms of seasonal revelry, but also in the course of the sixteenth century developed an academic drama in other ways. Humanists promoted the value of drama as a pedagogical tool which educated young men of the upper classes in rhetoric, public speaking and self-presentation, as well as in classical authors. William Gager, who wrote plays for the students to perform at Oxford, set out his intentions as follows: 'We . . . do it to recreate ourselves, our House, and the better part of the university . . . to practise our own style . . . to be well acquainted with Seneca or Plautus; honestly to embolden our path; to try their voices and confirm their memories; to frame their speech; to conform them to convenient action; to try what metal is in everyone, and of what disposition they are of.'[6] The Records of Early English Drama for Cambridge indicate a number of men preferred for government service on account of the skill they demonstrated in dramatic performances.

University and commercial theatre were in most ways totally distinct. 'No plays written for the commercial London stage were ever performed by Oxford students; no plays written by Oxford academics were ever performed by professional actors; and no professional companies ever performed within university precincts', as John R. Elliott puts it.[7] But the students who had performed plays written for them and also studied those of classical playwrights might then go on to become part of the audiences for the Theatre and the Curtain; and certainly those students of the Inns of Court, who were probably older and more sophisticated, had considerable familiarity with the commercial theatre of London, as they demonstrated in plays like Marston's Middle Temple play, *Histriomastix*, and the so-called Parnassus plays, even if they spurned it as gross and populist.

All this is evidence of a range of well-developed and well-supported theatrical activity which was vibrant at different social levels in the later sixteenth century. But most significant, perhaps, for London's perceived readiness for commercial theatre, as Burbage saw it in 1576, was the existence of a number of companies of actors already performing for money in London and elsewhere. Companies of strolling players, usually under the livery of a nobleman but earning at least a part of their living from performing to public audiences, had been in existence since the fifteenth century. In the sixteenth century these had become increasingly active. The Records of Early English Drama for Bristol show more than two visits a year to the city by professional touring companies in the 1560s and 1570s. In London in the 1570s a considerable number of companies were active: those belonging to the Earl of Leicester, which included James Burbage, and also 'others belonging to the Earls of Warwick, Sussex, Oxford, Lincoln, Pembroke, and Essex, and perhaps still others belonging to Lord Howard, Lord Rich, Lord Abergavenny, and Sir Robert Lane'.[8] There is evidence of temporary playing places in inns and taverns in London from the 1520s, but, most significantly, John Brayne, Burbage's brother-in-law, was engaged in erecting wooden scaffolding 'for interludes or plays' (over which he had a legal dispute with the carpenter) at the Red Lion in Whitechapel in 1567.[9] The Bel Savage Inn on Ludgate Hill was in use for plays from at least 1575, and in that year George Gascoigne (who had written plays for the Inns of Court) was writing in *The Glasse of Governement* as if public playgoing was a regular activity, even if not one he especially cared for. Anyone wanting to hear a jest 'or feed his eye with vain delight', he said, would find 'Bel Savage fair were fittest for his purse'.[10]

The story of theatre in Shakespeare's time is one of transformations, particularly in the use of space, 'from transient to fixed locales, from outdoor to indoor settings, from city to suburbs to provinces, from public to private theaters',[11] but also in terms of increasing professionalism. From now on, even if it is not quite true to say, as G. E. Bentley does, writing before the revelations provided in the Records of Early English Drama about theatrical activities by touring companies outside London, that most plays were 'performed in buildings planned and built for the presentation of plays',[12] it is the case that most plays were written and acted by men whose livelihood was the theatre. In 1633, William Prynne in his vitriolic attack on theatres, *Histriomastix, The Players' Scourge, or Actors' Tragedy*, refers disparagingly to 'the Profession of Play-Poets, of Stage-Players'.[13] How was the growth of these new professions achieved and received? Nowadays the drama of this period has a high cultural status, and the literary prestige accorded to Shakespeare and a few of the large number – more than 250 – of professional playwrights at work during the period has sometimes pushed consideration of the materiality of the early theatre industry into the background. But it is worth pausing to consider the factors that contributed to its creation.

The industry developed amid much hostility. Stage plays and players traditionally had a poor image, for reasons both religious and secular, which were not always clearly differentiated. Most of the early drama was itself religious in nature, and promoted particular doctrinal interests; the religious tensions that developed during the middle of the century in a

1 Map of London, from *Civitates Orbis Terrarum*, by Georg Braun (1542–1622) and Frans Hogenburg (1635–90), *c*.1572.

period of rapidly changing attitudes to what was and was not orthodox complicated the role of religious drama and left plays and players open to charges of sedition. Broader objections to plays could be boosted by the citation of scriptural prohibitions against cross-dressing, lewd behaviour and idleness; they were seen to rival sermons in popular appeal. The fear of theatre as a source of moral contamination was so strong that it extended into the idea of physical contamination. Bishop Grindal, writing to William Cecil in 1564, believed that the activities of the London players might even be responsible for the current outbreak of plague:

> By searche I doo perceive, thatt ther is no one thinge off Late is more lyke to have renewed this contagion, then the practise off an idle sort off people, which have ben infamouse in all goode common weales: I meane these Histriones, common playours: who now daylye, butt speciallye on holy-dayes, sett up bylles, whereunto youthe resorteth excessively, & ther taketh infection.[14]

The building of the Theatre and the Curtain provoked an immediate response by the church; sermons were preached at St Paul's Cross by John Stockwood against 'beastlye Playes' and the 'gorgeous Playing place erected in the fieldes' to which thousands resorted, even on the Lord's day,[15] and a flood of Puritan-inspired pamphlets and treatises followed, with titles like *A Treatise wherin Dicing, Dauncing, Vaine playes, or Enterluds, with other idle pastimes, &c, commonly used on the Sabboth day are reproved by the Authoritie of God and auntient writers.* This was written by John Northbrooke in 1577 and several times reprinted.

Secular opposition expressed itself in terms both moral and material: playgoing encouraged idleness, licentious behaviour and disorder, and the players made money from activities which did not consist of honest work. Grindal in 1564 had referred to players as 'an idle sorte off people, which have ben infamouse in all goode common weales'.[16] Twenty years later the City fathers responded to a petition by the Queen's Men for permission to perform within the city over the winter season by pointing out that 'It hath not ben used nor thoughte meete heretofore that players have or shold make their lyving on the art of playing, but men for their lyvings using other honest and lawfull artes, or reteyned in honest services, have by companies learned some enterludes for some encreasce to their profit by other mens pleasures in vacant time of recreation.'[17] There was much prejudice against the theatrical profession as 'a new and hitherto unrecognized form of employment'[18] which could not be easily accommodated within the structures of a conservative and status-conscious society. Professional players occupied an ambiguous position, somewhere between the licensed retainers of aristocratic households from whose ranks they had evolved and to the protection of which they sometimes had recourse, and the 'Rogues, Vagabonds and Sturdy Beggars' with whom the Act for the Punishment of Vagabonds of 1572 sought to identify them.[19] Antagonism to them did not cease to find expression throughout the period, as Prynne's *Histriomastix*, printed in 1633 amply testifies, but during the reigns of Elizabeth and her two successors, they found powerful defenders and their status rose considerably.

Noble patrons were a significant factor in the development of the profession; their influence bore on its control, its protection in the face of antagonism, particularly from the City authorities, and on its growth in prestige. The 1572 act required all troupes of players to be licensed by noblemen of the rank of baron or higher if they were not to be treated as vagabonds, and although this was in a sense restrictive it also had the positive effect both of consolidating the troupes that did remain and of confirming the status of the noblemen who patronized them.[20] And even if the relationship between troupe and patron was no longer that of paid household servants to their employer, the players still needed their lord, as the petition of the same year by the Earl of Leicester's men to be retained by him makes clear: 'not that we mean to crave any further stipend or benefit at your lordship's hands but our liveries as we have had, and also your honour's licence to certify we are your household servants when we shall have occasion to travel amongst our friends as we usually do once a year, and as other noblemen's players do and have done in time past, whereby we may enjoy our faculty in your lordship's name as we have done hithertofore'.[21] As the Queen's favourite, Leicester was a uniquely powerful man and also an unusually involved patron. The royal patent awarded to his troupe in 1574, permitting them 'to use, exercise, and occupy the art and faculty of playing comedies, tragedies, interludes, stage plays, and such other like . . . as well within our City of London and liberties of the same as also within the liberties and freedoms of any of our cities, towns, boroughs etc',[22] was, as Bradbrook says, 'the first social gesture of recognition towards the art of the stage'.[23]

The player's claim to social legitimacy through the offices of his patron was sometimes seen as a cover for the baseness of his profession, as in the satirical 'Character of a Common Player' (1615): 'howsoever he pretends to have a royal master or mistress, his wages and dependence prove him to be a servant of the people'.[24] But in the period up to 1603, which saw a constant struggle between the City authorities and the players, the support of noble patrons was vital to the players' professional survival. The Queen was not a neutral party, and the players, when threatened with suppression, could credibly draw on the idea that they needed to perfect their public performances 'the better to content her maiestie' when called upon to appear at court.[25] She was interested enough in theatre to have her own troupe of players formed, bearing her name, and the man delegated to appoint the players was Sir Francis Walsingham, a political ally and also a relative by marriage of Leicester, who well understood the propaganda value and political uses to which theatre might be put. A recent study of the Queen's Men suggests that it was a company 'designed to increase the prestige of their patron throughout the land, to harness the theatre in the service of a moderate Protestant ideology, and to add a vivid group of travellers who might serve the [Privy] council's needs for secret information about recusants or foreign visitors in more than one way'.[26] These considerations may also be relevant to the fact that when James VI and I acceded to the throne in 1603, he lost no time in issuing a royal patent to enrol 'the company of actors formerly known as the Lord Chamberlain's Men as Grooms of the Chamber within his personal household and to be known henceforth as the King's Men'.[27] Soon afterwards he took over two further companies to become the Queen's Men and Prince Henry's Men.

This action can be diversely interpreted, as protective or as restrictive, even as a step towards 'the "absolutism" traditionally associated with

James and the Stuarts in general', although this latter view has been strongly challenged.[28] But it certainly constitutes formal acknowledgement of the existence of the relationship between the court and the major companies, and did increase the 'sheer royal "consumption" of drama'.[29] It is indicative of the rapidly changing status of the acting profession, accompanied by players' applications for coats of arms (subject to mockery in Shakespeare's case), Jonson's publication of his collected plays in a folio volume entitled 'Works' in 1616, and the King's Men's move into the indoor Blackfriars theatre in 1608. James Burbage had bought the buildings, conveniently situated within the city walls, though within a Liberty (a district exempt from the jurisdiction of the City fathers), and converted them into a theatre in 1596, but objections from influential neighbours against the erection of a public playhouse prevented its use for adult players until twelve years later. The Blackfriars was used for child companies from 1600 until 1608; it was a so-called 'private' theatre with indoor facilities, unlike the Theatre, the Curtain, and the Bankside playhouses, and could charge higher prices, thus attracting a more select kind of audience. As the first private playhouse in which an adult company regularly performed, it was another mark of the rise in status and acceptability of the profession. The residents of the area tried constantly to have it closed, citing the traffic jams caused by the coaches of well-to-do theatre-goers, but to no effect. The King's Men used it continuously until the closure of the theatres in 1642. The stability and organization of this company is also of significance. The personnel of the company was unusually stable, with few actors moving to other groups, and recruitment was largely from within its own ranks; not only did it retain the use of the Blackfriars theatre over many decades, but from 1599 it also owned the Globe, built partly out of timbers removed by night from the dismantled Theatre in Shoreditch. The Globe was financed and built by a consortium formed by the Burbage family and the leading actors of the Lord Chamberlain's Men, including Shakespeare, who became shareholders ('sharers' was the contemporary term) in the company. Thus the Globe, rebuilt in 1613 after the first building was destroyed by fire, became 'the first London theatre built by actors for actors'.[30] The consortium managed the theatre and chose its repertoire; Shakespeare's share of the profits contributed more to his wealth than did his income from writing plays. Its clown, Will Kempe, and its leading actor, Richard Burbage, became the celebrities of their day.

Acting in the period became a trade, and one that in general was never held in high esteem. There were exceptions: Kempe in his time with the

Chamberlain's Men (1594–9) was a much bigger name than Burbage or Shakespeare, and he could use his personal popularity to draw huge crowds to witness the dance from London to Norwich, recorded in his pamphlet, *Kempe's Nine Days Wonder* (1600), which he undertook as a kind of publicity stunt, resulting from a wager, when he quit the company in 1599. Apparently he was such an attraction that by 1598 you could hear all over London 'whores, beadles, bawds, and sergeants filthily chant Kempe's jig'.[31] His predecessor as a clown, Richard Tarleton, was even more famous, and went down in popular legend as a 'wondrous plentifull pleasant extemporal wit'[32] though he was also a writer of plays and ballads and a Master of Fencing; after his death his picture was hawked around the streets of London;[33] Sir Philip Sidney was godfather to his son. Richard Burbage, too, moved in high circles, and was a friend of William Herbert, third earl of Pembroke, who attended his funeral; a lengthy funeral elegy for him celebrates him as 'England's great Roscius', whose talent honoured his country, and there was said to be more mourning for him than for Queen Anne, who died the same year.[34] The character of 'an excellent actor' from *The Overburian Characters* (1615) is thought to have been based on him. The actor is praised for moral and aesthetic attributes; and his art is seen as essentially lifelike, as an extension of nature:

> Whatsoever is commendable in the grave orator is most exquisitely perfect in him: for by a full and significant action of body he charms our attention: sit in a full theatre and you will think you see so many lines drawn from the circumference of so many ears, whiles the *actor* is the *centre*. He doth not strive to make nature monstrous, she is often in the same scene with him, but neither on stilts nor crutches . . . By his action he fortifies moral precepts with example; for what we see him personate, we think truly done before us . . . he adds grace to the poet's labours; for what in the poet is but ditty, in him is both ditty and music . . . All men have been of his occupation: and indeed, what he doth feignedly, that others do essentially.[35]

In the same year as this was published Sir George Buc, Master of the Revels, wrote of the theatre as a polished art, one of the attractions of London:

> The most ancient kind of poetry, the dramatic, is so lively expressed and represented upon the public stages of this city, as Rome in the age of her pomp and glory never saw it better performed.[36]

Buc may not be writing entirely disinterestedly, since his office made considerable profits from licensing performances, but still it is a huge step for professional theatre, from civic pollution to civic asset. However, prejudice

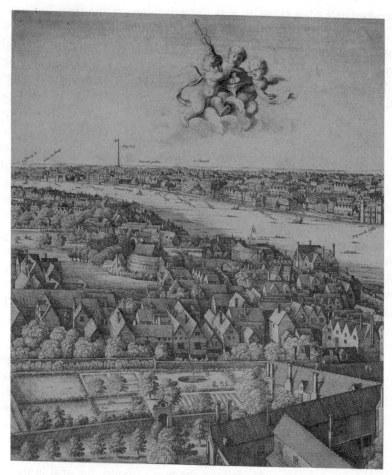

2 Wenceslas Hollar, view of London from Southwark, c.1670.

against the theatre did not die away, since it reflected broader anxieties over the rapid social changes taking place during the period. It has been suggested that, by their very nature as wide-ranging anatomies of absurdity, anti-theatrical polemics such as Stephen Gosson's *The School of Abuse, containing a pleasant invective against poets, pipers, players, jesters and such like caterpillars of a commonwealth* (1579), Philip Stubbes's *The Anatomy of Abuses* (1583), or *This Worlds Folly. Or a Warning-Peece discharged upon the Wickednesse Thereof* by I. H. (1615) did not view the public theatre in the period 'as an isolated phenomenon, but as part of an ensemble of cultural and social changes disturbing enough to warrant various forms of intervention and management'.[37] The ways in which the drama itself relates to these changes will be considered in subsequent chapters.

Defenders of theatre, such as Thomas Heywood in *An Apology for Actors* (printed 1612 but written earlier), drew attention to the effects of playgoing on spectators; for him they were moral and exemplary, for example, encouraging patriotic responses:

> What English blood, seeing the person of any bold Englishman presented, and doth not hugge his fame, and hunnye at his valor, pursuing him in his enterprise with his best wishes, and as beeing wrapt in contemplation, offers to him in his hart all prosperous performance, as if the Personator were the man Personated, so bewitching a thing is lively and well-spirited action, that it hath power to new-mold the harts of the spectators, and fashion them to the shape of any noble and notable attempt.[38]

Anti-theatrical polemicists viewed the playgoer's response to the spectacle, and to the actor's mimetic virtuosity, quite differently, fearful of the strong emotions aroused. John Rainoldes in *Th'Overthrow of Stage-Playes* (1599) was particularly concerned by the sexual stimulation of seeing boys in women's parts, persuasively acting like whores and inflaming improper passions in their audiences:

> If amatory pangs be expressed in most effectual sort: can wise men be perswaded that there is not wantonnesse in players partes, when experience sheweth (as wise men hath observed) that *men are made adulterers and enemies of all chastity by coming to such playes?* That *senses are moved, affections are delited, heartes though strong and constant are vanquished by such players?* That *an effeminate stage-player, while he faineth love, imprinteth woundes of love?*[39]

Such accounts of audience response, entirely dictated by the writers' agendas, cannot be taken at face value. But what can we piece together of actor–audience relations in reality? Who went to the theatre, and what did they think of what they saw? Are there ways in which early modern theatre-going might challenge and change audiences' attitudes to the society in which they lived?

To begin with, it is probably fair to assert that a higher proportion of the local population attended the theatres than is now the case. Andrew Gurr reckons that around 15 to 20 per cent of all those living within reach of the Shoreditch or Southwark playhouses were regular playgoers,[40] although others have put it somewhat lower. In broad terms, audiences were socially mixed, and the penny which paid for standing room in the yard in the public theatres was only the price of a quart of cheap beer. It was, in Martin Butler's words, 'a singularly inexpensive form of entertainment'.[41] Before 1599, when there were only public playhouses available, audiences were socially very mixed. Sir John Davies's epigram 'In Cosmum', written about 1593, describes a diverse crowd of playgoers leaving the theatre at the end of the performance:

> For as we see at all the play house dores,
> When ended is the play, the daunce, and song:
> A thousand townsemen, gentlemen, and whores,
> Porters and serving-men together throng.[42]

Butler lists what he calls 'a splendidly varied panorama of the under-privileged',[43] for whose presence at the theatre there is contemporary evidence. But in 1599, when the indoor theatres reopened after a period of closure, Gurr credibly speculates that the number of gentry attending the public theatres began to decline, and the two types of theatre began to attract different audiences.[44] Admission to the indoor 'private' theatres, which had no standing space, was sixpence minimum, so that their audiences were likely to be from the wealthier classes, largely excluding apprentices and serving-men. Social polarization developed. The Blackfriars became 'unquestionably the most reputable playhouse of the whole later period'.[45] By contrast, the outdoor Red Bull theatre in Clerkenwell, where Webster's *The White Devil* failed in 1610/11, became known as the place for 'clownery, clamor, and spectacle',[46] and did not provide the 'full and understanding auditory' which the playwright required for the appreciation of his work.[47] Webster probably had better luck with *The Duchess of Malfi*, which was, as the 1623 title page tells us, 'presented privately, at the Blackfriars, and publicly at the Globe, by the King's Majesty's Servants'. The repertoires of the public and private theatres were not always separate, but their audiences were; the cachet suggested by the term 'private' had social reality, theatre-building in the latter part of the period concentrated on the indoor theatres, which made much more money, and the division between the two types of playhouse, 'aristocratic hall and plebeian amphitheatre', became increasingly pronounced, and by 1639 'nearly complete'.[48] Gurr's analysis of the situation from 1630 suggests a social hierarchy: the Blackfriars is at the top, with the Cockpit, an elite hall theatre in Drury Lane, and the Globe (because of its use by the King's Men) as alternatives; there was a smaller hall theatre, the Salisbury Court, in Whitefriars, which came next; then followed the other Bankside theatres, the Swan and the Hope, and finally, the remaining amphitheatres in Shoreditch, the Red Bull and the Fortune.[49]

Evidence of the nature of audience response to the plays is fragmentary, fortuitous, piecemeal, subjective – extremely various and impossible to summarize. We can tell to an extent what plays were popular, *The Spanish Tragedy*, for example, and *Mucedorus*, but not why. What we can be certain of, however, from a variety of sources, is that plays were expected to move their audiences to strong responses, and did so. It was a pillar of the anti-theatricalists' position that plays depicted all sorts of bad behaviour, which spectators were readily induced to imitate. John Northbrook claims in his *Treatise wherein . . . Dicing, Dauncing, Vaine Playes . . . are reproved* that

> If you will learne how to be false and deceive your husbandes, or hus-
> bandes their wyves how to play the harlottes, to obtayne one's love, howe
> to ravishe, howe to beguile, howe to flatter, lye, sweare, forsweare, howe
> to allure to whoredome, how to murther, how to poison, howe to disobey
> and rebel against princes, to consume treasures prodigally, to move to
> lustes, to ransacke and spoyle cities and townes, to bee ydle, to blaspheme,
> to sing filthie songs of love, to speake filthily, to be prowde, how to mocke,
> scoffe, and deride any nation . . . shall you not learne, then, at such enter-
> ludes howe to practise them?[50]

Defenders of theatre, like Thomas Heywood, also argued that plays could inspire imitation, but on the basis that what they had to teach was moral conduct. Hamlet's view, that those with bad consciences might be moved to confess and repent their sins by the power of theatrical spectacle, might have been based on the incident recounted in *A Warning for Faire Women* (1599). Here, the characters are discussing how, by God's provi-dence, secret murders are always eventually discovered; Master James tells how

> A woman that had made away her husband,
> And sitting to behold a tragedy
> At Linne a towne in Norffolke,
> Acted by Players travelling that way
> Wherein a woman that had murderd hers
> Was ever haunted with her husbands ghost:
> The passion written by a feeling pen,
> And acted by a good Tragedian,
> She was so mooved with the sight thereof,
> As she cryed out, The play was made by her,
> And openly confesst her husbands murder.[51]

Heywood cites the same incident, naming the play as *Friar Francis* and the players as the Earl of Sussex's men, who, according to Henslowe's *Diary*, had performed it in London in 1593. Such evidence can only be apocryphal, but it testifies to the belief in the effects theatre might produce on its audi-ences. As Jeremy Lopez puts it, 'If both the Puritans and their adversaries were willing to believe that a play could affect reality and the lives of its audience, it seems more than safe to assume that this is the kind of assumption playgoers would have brought with them to the playhouse.'[52] Simon Forman, a doctor, astrologer and wise man, who lived in London and was a keen theatregoer, provides some of the few eyewitness accounts that exist of a contemporary playgoer's reactions to specific productions in his 'Book of Plays and Notes Thereof'. Although tantalizingly short on aesthetic evaluation, Forman's records of seeing *Macbeth, Cymbeline,* and *The Winter's Tale* at the Globe in 1611 show that what he took away from the experience was primarily details of the story, but that he was also concerned to derive a moral lesson from it. His description of *The Winter's Tale* concludes, 'Beware of trusting feigned beggars or fawning fellows.' He also saw a production of *Richard II,* though not Shakespeare's play. He describes the Machiavellian behaviour of the Duke of Lancaster, Bolingbroke's father, who hanged a man that told him his son would become king. 'This was a policy in the commonwealth's opinion, but I say it was a villain's part and a Judas kiss to hang the man for telling him the truth. Beware by this example of noblemen and their fair words, and say little to them, lest they do the like by thee for thy goodwill.'[53]

Less studied, and more emotional, responses are sometimes recorded. Nashe seems to have a performance of *Henry VI, Part 1* in mind when he refers to brave Talbot triumphing again on the stage, 'his bones new embalmed with the teares of ten thousand spectators at least (at severall times), who, in the tragedian that represents his person, imagine they behold him fresh bleeding!'[54] An anonymous commendatory verse prefacing the printed text of *The Duchess of Malfi* (1623) praises Webster for the pathos of his heroine:

> Thy epitaph only the title be –
> Write, 'Duchess', that will fetch a tear for thee,
> For who e'er saw this duchess live, and die,
> That could get off under a bleeding eye?

Audience disapprobation could also be forcefully registered. Evidently Fletcher's pastoral tragicomedy, *The Faithful Shepherdess* (1608/9), failed totally at its first performance. The ambitious playwright, encouraged by his supporters, published it soon after, together with his own rather supercilious address to the reader and a raft of commendatory verses, in which the authors, Chapman, Jonson and Beaumont among them, make it clear that the collective response of an ignorant audience was responsible for the play's poor reception. Jonson was intensely scornful of such undiscriminating spectators:

The wise, and many headed Bench, that sits
Upon the Life, and Death of Playes, and Wits,
(Composed of gamster, Captaine, Knight, Knights man,
Lady, or Pusill, that weares maske or fan,
Velvet, or taffeta cap, rank's in the darke
With the shops Foreman or some such brave sparke,
That may judge for his sixpence) had, before
They saw it halfe, damd the whole Play.[55]

Field, in another commendatory verse, refers to the audience as 'the monster' who 'clapt his thousand hands, / And drownd the sceane with his confused cry'. The will of the people surprised a foreign visitor, Antonio Galli, visiting the Curtain in 1613, when the title of a play for the next day was suggested but the people called for something different.[56] Edmund Gayton, writing in the interregnum, recalled what might well happen at one of the rougher theatres if the crowd became displeased:

The players have been appointed, notwithstanding their bills to the contrary, to act what the major part of the company had a mind to. Sometimes *Tamerlane*, sometimes *Jugurtha*, sometimes *The Jew of Malta*, and sometimes parts of all these; and at last, none of the three taking, they were forced to undress and put off their tragicke habits, and conclude the day with *The Merry Milkmaides*. And unless this were done, and the popular humour satisfied (as sometimes it so fortun'd that the players were refractory), the benches, the tiles, the laths, the stones, oranges, apples, nuts, flew about most liberally: and there were mechanickes of all professions, who fell everyone to his trade, and dissolved a house in an instant, and made a ruin of a stately fabric.[57]

There are no records of any theatre being demolished in this way, and Gayton was referring to Shrove Tuesday misbehaviour, but Bacon, in *The Advancement of Learning*, had earlier observed that the power of theatre comes from its appeal to collective emotions: 'Certain it is, though a great secret in nature, that the minds of men in company are more open to affections and impressions than when alone.'[58] In a society where people had few opportunities to gather in large heterogeneous groups, except at sermons, plays or animal baitings, crowd reaction was an exciting phenomenon, but also one which aroused anxiety. Jonson's Induction to *Bartholomew Fair* acknowledges how easy it is to 'censure by contagion' (Induction, 100). Hamlet in his advice to the players voices a playwright's awareness of the dangers of working for a facile response from 'barren spectators' which, counterproductively, will 'make the judicious grieve, the censure of the which one must in your allowance o'erweigh a whole theatre of others' (3.2.25–7). But this, perhaps, is an elitist viewpoint; Hamlet enjoys theatre, might be a good amateur actor, and understands theatre's power to move performers and spectators alike, but he does not have to make his living from it.

Marlowe sought to distance his drama from the common currency of the 1580s playhouse and to elevate and move it on 'from jigging veins of rhyming mother-wits,/ And such conceits as clownage keeps in pay', but all playwrights wrote with a consciousness of their audience and their need for its approval. It has been suggested that 'more than any other drama, early modern drama talks about and openly solicits applause'.[59] The metatheatricality of this drama, its constant reminders to the audience of their status as audience, is another aspect of this. Plays of the period refer to, and sometimes represent – through the device of the play-within-the play, playhouse practice; they represent living actors and playwrights, and, for instance, in the so-called 'war of the theatres', debate the current state of the theatre. 'All the world's a stage' was one of the great commonplaces of the period, and comedies of London life in particular explore 'a society that represented itself . . . insistently as a stage full of actors'.[60] In Beaumont's *The Knight of the Burning Pestle* (1607) the Citizen and his wife clamber eagerly onto the Blackfriars stage, unaware of the faux-pas they are committing in trespassing on territory that was usually reserved for gentlemen. The wife cheerfully excuses herself:

> By your leave, gentlemen all; I'm something troublesome. I'm a stranger here; I was ne'er at one of these plays, as they say, before; but I should have seen 'Jane Shore' once; and my husband promised to carry me to 'the Bold Beauchamps' but in truth he did not. I pray you, bear with me.
> (1.1.60–6)

In Jonson's *The Devil is an Ass* (1616), Fitzdottrell, who is a foolish gentleman and a keen playgoer, also takes to the stage in the Blackfriars, boasting to his wife of how he will display himself there in his new cloak:

> Here is a cloak cost fifty pound, wife,
> Which I can sell for thirty, when I ha' seen
> All London in't, and London has seen me.
> Today I go to the Blackfriars Playhouse,
> Sit i'the view, salute all my acquaintance,
> Rise up between the acts, let fall my cloak,
> Publish a handsome man, and a rich suit,
> (As that's the special end why we go thither,
> All that pretend to stand for't o'the stage).
> (1.6.28–36)[61]

Such self-conscious references draw the audience into the play, developing a body of shared experience that works towards the creation of a common culture of theatregoing. Other techniques, essential to the dramaturgy of the early modern stage, that function to share meanings with the audience are the soliloquy and the aside. Both provide the opportunity for moments when the character speaking can acknowledge the presence of the audience, implicitly claiming a role both within and outside the fiction. Sometimes this is so selfconsciously done as to draw attention to the rift in the narrative surface. In Heywood's *A Woman Killed with Kindness* (1607), for instance, Anne Frankford breaks off a short soliloquy expressing her remorse at having destroyed her marriage by committing adultery to extend the lesson she has learnt to the women in the audience:

> Oh, women, women, you that have yet kept
> Your holy matrimonial vow unstain'd,
> Make me your instance when you tread awry;
> Your sins like mine will on your conscience lie.
>   (4.4.139–42)

But the dual role can be maintained with no loss to the fiction. Iago, having manipulated Cassio into a demeaning and drunken confrontation with Montano, counsels him to solicit Desdemona as a means to getting his job back, and then turns triumphantly to the audience to share the success of his plan:

> And what's he then that says I play the villain,
> When this advice is free I give, and honest,
> Probal to thinking, and indeed the course
> To win the Moor again?
>   (2.3.310–13)

Here, the character's role within the narrative as a boastful and intellectually superior plotter combines with his status outside it as Vice and Machiavel to create the sort of theatrical moment peculiar to the conditions of the early modern stage, when the audience is momentarily invited to share the consciousness of the character within the fiction.

Muriel Bradbrook refers to the 'gradation between frank appeal *ad spectatores* and the subtlest nuances of Shakespearean dramaturgy' as one of the achievements of the language of this theatre.[62] She also considers that 'there was no question of the characters stepping "out of the picture" for they were never in it'.[63] But the acceptance that this was essentially a non-naturalistic theatre does not preclude an audience's concern with some forms of realism, and a desire to enter into the dramatic illusion.

Acting styles need not always have been broad, swashbuckling, huffing, 'stalking and roaring'.[64] Hamlet expresses contempt for the exaggerated acting of a 'periwig-pated fellow' who will 'tear a passion to tatters, to the very rags, to split the ears of the groundlings', and there is plenty of evidence that audiences liked 'natural' acting, even if, as critics often remind us, the term bore different connotations for the Elizabethans from those of post-romantic times conditioned by concepts of scientific naturalism. Soliloquies might act as primarily expositionary devices in which the speaker gives the audience necessary information, or they could address the audience directly, but they might also represent the kind of thinking aloud indulged in by an isolated individual who needs to unburden himself in solitude. 'Personate' in the sense of assuming or representing the character of another, appears as early as 1599, in Marston's *Antonio and Mellida*, when Alberto asks, 'Whom do you personate?' Marston was notoriously adventurous in his vocabulary, as Jonson jeeringly noticed, but this usage does indicate the development of a new attitude to stage representation, a sense that 'drama is turning to the depiction of individuals, characters with a particular "identity" or inner self'.[65] Contemporary responses to the acting of Burbage indicate that he moved his audiences through his power to create an illusion through characterization. The author of the anonymous funeral elegy praises this ability:

> Oft have I seen him leap into the grave,
> Suiting the person, which he seemed to have,
> Of a sad lover, with so true an eye
> That there I would have sworn he meant to die.
> Oft have I seen him play this part in jest
> So lively that spectators, and the rest
> Of his sad crew, whilst he but seemed to bleed,
> Amazed, thought even that he died in deed.[66]

Henry Jackson saw a production of *Othello* by the King's Men at Oxford in 1610, and was overcome by emotion at Desdemona's death scene: 'But truly Desdemona, having been killed by her husband before our eyes, although she pleaded her cause superbly throughout nevertheless she moved [us] more after she had been murdered, when, lying upon her bed, her face itself implored pity from the onlookers.'[67] Jackson's comment suggests that the acting (by the boy player) was both powerfully realistic and capable of detailed effects as well as larger gestures.

The ability of plays and players to create strong emotions in audiences was one of the reasons why anti-theatricalists feared the stage. Despite their denunciations of its morally and socially destructive nature, the theatre itself was not an iconoclastic institution, but a commercial one, supported by an influential elite with no investment in corrupting morals or bringing down the state. But, it has been recently argued, theatre did have the power 'to alter spectators' *relationships* to both visual and verbal representations in potentially disruptive ways', and thus to 'demystify certain privileged representations', such as those of state, and particularly of the monarchy.[68] Elizabeth's legislation in 1559 forbidding the depiction in public theatres of 'matters of religion or of the governance of the estate of the Commonwealth' recognized this, and implicitly assumed that such depictions might be subversive in their effects. *Gorboduc*, by Thomas Sackville and Thomas Norton, an Inns of Court play presented to the Queen at court, was not covered by this legislation and does directly handle such matters; Franco Moretti sees in it the start of a long process whereby the tragedy of the period was instrumental (for him, a 'decisive influence') in 'the creation of a "public" that for the first time in history assumed the right to bring a king to justice'; he continues, 'when tragedy performs the degradation of the cultural image of the sovereign, it deprives the monarchy of its central bastion'.[69] These are large claims to make for the role of the theatre, but there was clearly some contemporary anxiety about the power of stage representation to influence popular attitudes to authority. For the puritan Henry Crosse in *Vertues Common-wealth* (1603), plays subjected serious matters to mockery and encouraged the disrespect of authority: 'There is no passion wherewith the king, the soveraigne maiestie of the Realme was possesst, but is amplified, and openly sported with, and made a May-game to all the beholders.'[70] A more neutral observer, Sir Henry Wotton, writing about the fire which burnt down the Globe theatre during a performance of Shakespeare's *Henry VIII*, expressed a similar feeling about this play:

> The King's players had a new play, called *All is true*, representing some principal pieces of the reign of Henry VIII, which was set forth with many extraordinary circumstances of Pomp and Majesty, even to the matting of the stage; the Knights of the Order, with their Georges and garters, the Guards with their embroidered coats, and the like: sufficient within a while to make greatness very familiar, if not ridiculous.[71]

Wotton's emphasis on the representational accuracy and detail of the play's setting, and its unusually spectacular quality, seems to suggest that, as the play's most recent editor puts it, 'the nearer the players come to the "truth", the more dangerous their representation'.[72] The fact that the players sometimes used the cast-off garments donated by aristocratic patrons in their productions adds force to this concern about the relation of stage spectacle to the spectacle of state. The specially commissioned performance of *Richard II* on the eve of the Essex rebellion, which will be discussed in chapter 2, indicates a strong belief that theatre could not only move emotions, but also provoke people to act upon them.

That stage plays reached out to all levels of society was a further cause of anxiety. Dekker in *The Gull's Hornbook* describes theatre as a democratic institution which allows space 'as well to the farmer's son as to your Templar, that your stinkard has the selfsame liberty to be there in his tobacco fumes which your sweet courtier hath, and that your carman and tinker claim as strong a voice in their suffrage, and to sit in judgment on the play's life and death as well as the proudest Momus among the tribe of Critic'.[73] His concern for the undiscriminating spectator's ability to express his opinion may be primarily aesthetic – like Fletcher's audience for *The Faithful Shepherdess*, such people may not understand or appreciate what the playwright has to offer them – but laughter and derision are not necessarily ineffective or impotent responses. The social space of the early modern theatre, in which performer and audience were in a direct relation to one another, not separated by footlights or differential lighting for stage and auditorium, is another significant factor here. Although farmers' sons and knights increasingly found themselves in different playhouses in the course of this period, it is true that, as Robert Weimann in his important study of the social dimension of theatre says, 'the customs of the traditional popular theater presupposed a collaboration between dramatist and audience in the creation and visualization of dramatic setting'.[74] The material and conceptual flexibility of a stage space which had developed, at least in part, from the booth or innyard allowed for the interplay between different dramatic modes and a variable relationship between players and audience. Weimann's theory of a stage which could accommodate two separately functioning areas, the 'neutral, undifferentiated "place"' or downstage *platea*, and the place for 'more illusionistic, localized action' upstage, the *locus*, has been widely influential.[75] Though this idea has been subject to modification, and Weimann himself allows for the progressive loss of differentiation between the two areas, it does illuminate something of the relationship between the design of contemporary plays and the kinds of response they sought to produce. We need, of course, to remember that plays were designed to be easily adaptable to different auditoria. As Gurr says, 'Throughout the Shakespearean period companies retained the ability at the end of an afternoon's playing to take their repertory off to a private house or to court and play again there with no more aids to performance than the playing area itself and what they could carry.'[76] After 1609 the

3 A sketch of the interior of the Swan Theatre, 1596. A copy made by Arend van Buchell of the original by Johannes de Witt. Ms 842.

King's Men transferred their plays between the Globe and the Blackfriars. And in times of plague, when the London theatres closed, the companies sustained themselves by touring, playing in inns, town halls, noblemen's houses and whatever other spaces they might be offered. The chief variable, however, was not the design of the stage area but rather that of the auditorium.[77] The actor–audience dynamic was not essentially different.

The vibrant energies of the early professional theatre in the Tudor period may have been rechannelled in various ways by the 1630s, but there was much continuity. The connections between theatre and spectacle remained strong. This was a society which acknowledged the power of spectacle in both public and private contexts, as the continuing importance of civic pageantry in London and the attention and expense devoted to the court masque testify. Martin Butler calls it 'perhaps the single most under-rated fact in the history of English theatre' that plays continued to be per-formed at the public theatres, the open- air playhouses (the Fortune and the Red Bull, as well as the Globe in the summer) throughout this decade, 'with self-evident success'.[78] The plays were mainly revivals, and newly written ones were old-fashioned in style, but together they constituted an 'alternative tradition of theatre in Caroline London, running concurrently with the private court stage and the elite professional theatres' for which there existed a strong demand.[79] The plays presented at the Fortune and the Red Bull, even if the latter suffered from much contemporary derision, still constituted 'a vigorous and far from mindlessly traditional citizen repertory'.[80] Butler speculates that the espousal of conservative and neo-Elizabethan social values of social inclusivity in this popular repertoire may have helped to shape the political consciousness of those who gathered in crowds to demonstrate against Laud and the bishops in the 1640s.[81] The drama of this period was always in touch with the deepest concerns of the society which produced it, not only reflecting but also moulding them; it was peculiarly alive to the social energies in circulation, in ways to be explored in subsequent chapters.

2

Monarchy and the Stage

The theatre's power to 'demystify certain privileged representations', such as those of institutions of state power, and particularly the monarchy, has already been mentioned.[1] Sir Henry Wotton, commenting on how a performance of *Henry VIII* was done with such realistic detail that it seemed 'to make greatness very familiar, if not ridiculous' had observed such power in operation.[2] But the truth about the relationship between stage and state in this period was more complex. It is not irrelevant that the performance Wotton had attended was given by 'the King's players'. Stephen Orgel has characterized the relationship between the Renaissance stage and the crown as 'a complex mixture of intimacy and danger', and it might be said that both Queen Elizabeth and King James certainly, and perhaps also King Charles, were conscious of this.[3] As a way of exploring the role of theatre in the period, this chapter examines aspects of its political dimension, in terms both of royal reaction to the stage and of the stage's reaction to the monarch. What can we learn from instances of royal approval or disapproval, and of censorship? How far did monarchs themselves figure in the drama? What role did the court play in shaping what was put on in the public theatre?

At the outset of Elizabeth's reign the official relationship between the state and the stage was bi-fold. In elite educational institutions drama was a socially approved instrument for the inculcation of morals and the teaching of conduct befitting a gentleman. Roger Ascham, one of the greatest humanists and well connected at court, thought tragedy 'more profitable than Homer, Pindar, Vergill, and Horace: yea comparable in myne opinion, with the doctrine of Aristotle, Plato, and Xenophon' and suited to the use of 'either a learned preacher or a Civill Ientleman'.[4] One of the first Elizabethan comedies that students nowadays are apt to encounter, *Ralph Roister Doister* (?1566/7), was written by the headmaster of Eton, Nicholas Udall, for performance by the boys. A similarly familiar play, *Gammer Gurton's Needle* (?1563), was produced at Christ's College, Cambridge. In the later years of the sixteenth century the direction of commercial theatre in London was largely dictated by playwrights educated at the universities, such as Peele, Lyly, Greene and Marlowe. But the whole situation of Elizabethan theatre, the nature of its development and social influence, is complicated by the fact that actors as an occupational group were accorded a lowly and unstable social status, to which Elizabethan social legislation, especially the poor laws, markedly contributed. In the Act for the Punishement of Vagabonds (1572) common players were classed with minstrels, jugglers, peddlers, tinkers and petty chapmen as potential vagrants who, if not licensed by two justices of the peace, could be subjected to the punishments allotted to rogues and vagabonds, and might for a third offence be condemned to death.

Without the support of the Queen and court the players who made their living in the commercial theatres, and the writers who supplied them with material, would have found their lives much harder and the hostility of the City authorities more difficult to combat. But the relationship between monarchy and stage had always to be carefully negotiated. The earliest legislation of Elizabeth's reign makes it clear that limits had to be set to the activities of the players, which by implication had the potential to disrupt the stability of the still-fragile Protestant settlement; the history of the regulation of the stage, and of its censorship from this time up to the closure of the theatres, continues to be a hotly debated subject. The wording of Elizabeth's proclamation of 1559[5] forbidding plays dealing with religion and politics except in carefully prescribed circumstances might lead one to expect that public theatre would necessarily be rendered non-controversial, and that it would be impossible for political plays to be staged, except in very privileged contexts. But even without recourse to the interpretive tools and practices developed in the wake of poststructuralist theory it is clear from the stage history of plays such as *Richard II* and Middleton's *A Game at Chess*, to take obvious examples, not only that playwrights and performers were prepared to take risks, but also that they could often get away with them. It was probably Shakespeare's *Richard II* that the followers of the Earl of Essex had specially performed by the Lord Chamberlain's Men in 1601 on the eve of the earl's attempted uprising against the Queen. Many critics have believed that the performance was commissioned as an incitement to revolution, given that the play concerns the deposition of a monarch with whom Elizabeth was known to have identified herself, and that the scene of Richard's deposition was never printed in Elizabeth's lifetime.[6] But it is not only the accomplishment of Bolingbroke's takeover that might have appeared suitably subversive in Shakespeare's *Richard II*; it is also the scrutiny to which the play subjects the doctrine of divine right, and its implicit identification of kingship with performance. As Alexander Leggatt says, 'The image of the actor, here used overtly, suggests that kingship is a role that can be transferred from one man to another.'[7] But it does not seem as if the actors worried about the play's meanings; rather, they were unwilling to perform a play which they thought 'so old and so long out of use'[8] that no one would come to see it, but, offered a good sum of money, they agreed. Subsequently Augustine Phillips, one of the players, was officially interrogated about his part in the event, but neither he nor any other member of the company was punished. Some scholars have expressed doubts as to how far a performance of *Richard II* would have been regarded as dangerous propaganda,[9] but it is certainly undeniable that *A Game at Chess* (1624) was an excitingly risky business all round, and was received as such. Middleton wrote it specially as a satirical comment on England's foreign relations with Spain in the aftermath of the collapse of the marriage negotiations between Prince Charles and the Spanish Infanta. He worked fast, using some recently published tracts; the play's political allegory was easy enough to decipher in broad terms; and, although the representation of living foreign royalty and dignitaries was forbidden, one of the main characters was based on the hated Count Gondomar, until two years previously the Spanish ambassador to England, and the actor was made up to look like him. The players drew mocking attention to his well-known fistula, and even managed to obtain his 'chair of ease' and his litter, so that as one member of the audience commented, 'they counterfeited his person to the life'.[10] Yet the play was officially licensed by the Master of the Revels (though the text he saw was not necessarily identical with the version performed by the actors) and ran for an unprecedented nine days before being suppressed by the Privy Council. The King's Men were temporarily forbidden to perform, and Middleton went into hiding and perhaps briefly to prison, but the Lord Chamberlain interceded on the company's behalf with the King, and it all blew over.[11]

Tudor drama designed for court performance, as opposed to the public theatre, had long been involved with politics, often taking a position in accord with the policies of the current regime, like the anti-Protestant *Respublica*, a 'Christmas devise' acted at the court of Queen Mary by boys to celebrate England's return to the Catholic faith after five years of Protestant oppression,[12] but also ready to offer criticism and warning, like John Bale's Protestant morality plays published in 1538 or John Skelton's *Magnificence* (1515). Early English history furnished stories which could be so presented as to comment on current events. *Gorboduc*, written by Thomas

Sackville and Thomas Norton, who were young lawyers at the Inns of Court and also members of Elizabeth's first parliament, was performed in her presence at Whitehall in 1562. It represented the chaos ensuing in Britain when King Gorboduc, a legendary British king descended from the Trojan Brute, great grandson of Aeneas, divides his realm between two unworthy sons. Its message, that the Queen should lose no time in establishing a successor, was direct, and not particularly controversial. Politically the play was ultra-orthodox, especially in the strong statement of the subject's duty to the monarch, given to Eubulus, the King's wise counsellor:

> That no cause serves whereby the subject may
> Call to account the doings of his prince,
> Much less in blood by sword to work revenge,
> No more than may the hand cut off the head;
> In act, nor speech, no, not in secret thought
> The subject may rebel against his lord
> Or judge of him that sits in Caesar's seat.
>
> (5.1.42–8)[13]

These lines appeared in the first unauthorized quarto of the play in 1565, but were cut from the 1570 quarto, prepared for the press by Norton, because, it has been suggested, they conflicted with his radical Protestant views. *The Misfortunes of Arthur* (1588), another advice play, written by a group including the young Francis Bacon and performed before the Queen at Greenwich, was bolder in its choice of historical analogy, implying similarities between the relationship of King Arthur to his murderously unfaithful wife Guinevere and that of Elizabeth to the soon to be executed Mary Queen of Scots. In the character of the usurper Mordred, Arthur's illegitimate son and lover to Guinevere, the play presented the threat to the stability of Elizabeth's state incorporated in ambitious and unscrupulous courtiers and Catholic sympathizers. In this connection, it is interesting to think also of *King Lear* (1604/5), another play – though for the public theatre – written near the beginning of a new regime, which draws on the chronicle history of ancient Britain in the same tradition, and stages the threat to the stability of the realm in its fragmentation and the ensuing civil war.

In view of the distinct line of politically motivated court drama, it is not surprising to find evidence that Elizabeth's government (although not those of James or Charles) 'actively promoted Protestant propaganda in the theatre', even if against the spirit of the 1559 proclamation.[14] Censorship never in fact operated to stifle political debate in the theatre, and scholars are now generally inclined to regard it as much less repressive than had once been thought to be the case. The Master of the Revels was a court appointee, and, although his regulation of the drama sometimes appears random and arbitrary in effect, the fact that he acted in the interests of the monarch and the court as opposed to those of the city authorities allowed the drama much greater freedom of expression than it might otherwise have enjoyed, particularly in the crucial decades after 1576. Both Elizabeth and James, in different ways, were conscious of the uses to which theatre might be put to serve their own interests, though this did not deprive the drama of the ability to express criticism of and even opposition to royal practice and policies. Of existing plays from Elizabeth's reign which can be read as political in this way the anonymous *Thomas of Woodstock* (1594?), a likely source for Shakespeare's *Richard II*, is perhaps the most subversive. The extant manuscript bears the lightest of censorship, probably from after 1603, when a new censor, Sir George Buc, took over; the play, though from the evidence of the manuscript popular in its time, was not printed.[15] In this account of the reign of Richard II the hero is the King's uncle, Thomas of Woodstock, Earl of Gloucester, 'Plain Thomas', who stands for traditional English virtues, and one of the villains is the King himself, along with his malevolent and irresponsible favourites. Richard is a mock king, a lord of misrule, ultimately responsible for his uncle's murder.[16] Through his depiction as far more degenerate and wasteful than Shakespeare's king, the playwright attacks specific targets, such as unjust taxation, particularly topical in the 1590s, and the evils of favouritism at court. Elizabeth famously identified herself with Richard in an interview recorded by William Lambarde in 1601 in the aftermath of the Essex uprising: 'I am Richard II: know ye not that?' Similarities between the two monarchs in their reliance on favourites had been noticed much earlier. But there is a more pointed allusion to Elizabeth as an agent of misgovernment, in a short but astonishingly audacious masque scene. Here, Cynthia, the moon goddess, presiding over the masque, appears as a huntress in pursuit of 'a cruel tuskèd boar' who is threatening Richard, 'a faithful prince and peer'.[17] But Richard in the body of this play is a completely different sort of king, and in fact Cynthia appears to function here as a figure of misrule, a supporter of the disorderly government of Richard and persecutor of the innocent Woodstock. This subversive representation draws on the negative aspect of lunar symbolism, in which the moon signifies darkness, inconstancy and feminine changeability. The scene culminates in Woodstock's arrest by Richard's corrupt favourites. Given the prevalent identification of Elizabeth with Cynthia in plays and poems, this inversion of the accepted iconography constitutes a bold, if fleeting, comment on her rule.

Thomas of Woodstock has no contemporary history, and was not printed until the nineteenth century; nothing can be known of any reaction to its bitter portrait of misrule. But another play close in time, *The Isle of Dogs* (1597) by Nashe and Jonson, caused such outrage both to the Privy Council and to the City authorities that both playwrights and actors were ordered to prison, and all performances within three miles of the City were banned for three months. The City authorities seized this chance to petition for the 'present staie & final suppressinge of the saide Stage playes, aswell at the Theatre, Curten, and banckside, as in all other places in and abowt the Citie'.[18] Needless to say, this did not happen, even though the Privy Council was sufficiently disturbed by this 'lewd plaie . . . contanynge very seditious and sclanderous matter' to endorse the call for the playhouses to be pulled down. In the event, Jonson and two of the actors went to prison (Nashe escaped) and the owner of the Swan theatre where the play was put on never recovered his fortunes afterwards; the play itself completely disappeared. Richard Dutton observes that this episode 'initiated the most intensive phase of the Privy Council's scrutiny and control of the drama, which lasted slightly more than a decade, and occasioned a high proportion of the most notable "flash-points" of dramatic controversy in the whole period'.[19]

There were several examples in the early Jacobean years of plays containing unspecified seditious matter which offended the monarch and subsequently disappeared. James took offence at a play about the Scottish mines, and at another depicting him with his favourites, witnessed by the French ambassador at court in 1608,[20] but the surprising thing is that the players ever had the temerity to represent the monarch to his own face in the first place. Letters by diplomats and courtiers refer to the audacity with which the players satirized their new king: '[they] do not forbear to represent upon their stage the whole course of this present time, not sparing either King, state, or religion, in so great absurdity, and with such liberty that any would be afraid to hear them', wrote Samuel Calvert to Ralph Winwood in 1605;[21] but, sadly, it appears that no such plays have survived. During a period of eighteen months, while Queen Anne, who evidently enjoyed a joke against her husband, replaced the King's censor with her own nominee, the writer Samuel Daniel, a group of plays were performed by the Children of the Queen's Revels, which offered free and open criticism of the new regime, poking fun at the King's Scottish accent, his liberality in selling knighthoods and the laxity of his court. These plays included Marston's *The Fawn, Eastward Ho* by Jonson, Chapman and Marston, the anonymous *Nobody and Somebody*, John Day's *The Isle of Gulls*, and Daniel's own *Philotas*. The offence caused by *Eastward Ho* and *The Isle of Gulls* brought about the temporary imprisonment of some of those involved, although Marston, apparently responsible for the worst of *Eastward Ho* and an evident risk-taker, escaped punishment, and the other plays passed without official censure. The Queen did withdraw her patronage (and her name) from the Children of the Queen's Revels, but they continued to perform at the Blackfriars theatre until 1608, when they aroused the King's fury yet again, and it was reported that he 'vowed they should never play more, but should first begg their bread'.[22] But his bark was as ever worse than his bite, and they were back in action a year later in a new venue. Shakespeare's *Measure for Measure* was also a product of this period and, like *The Fawn*, features a ruler who absents himself from government during a time of social disorder; though nominally set in Vienna, in this context it may well have implied unfavourable comment on aspects of James's rule.

The tally of plays critical to various degrees of James I and his regime is considerable, and although several of those listed attracted no official attention, there were still what Dutton calls 'flashpoints' of dramatic controversy. But for the most part playwrights and performers suffered no real damage. Censorship of the press could be applied elsewhere in punitive and vindictive ways. John Stubbes had his right hand cut off for writing against Queen Elizabeth's proposed marriage to the Duke of Alençon in the directly entitled pamphlet, *The Discoverie of a Gaping Gulf whereinto England is likely to be Swallowed by another French marriage* (1570); William Prynne was mutilated and imprisoned for appearing to have libelled Queen Henrietta Maria in *Histriomastix*, and John Hayward went to prison for three years for writing of Richard II in terms believed by Elizabeth to have referred to herself in *The First Part of the Life and Raigne of King Henrie IIII*. Perhaps, as E. K. Chambers speculates, the apparent ability of the monarch to tolerate a measure of criticism in stage plays 'speak[s] well for the good sense of the government [and] may also justify the inference that by the seventeenth century the theatre had so far established itself as an integral part of London life that a vindictive measure of suppression had become impracticable'.[23] It may also suggest that printed texts were thought to be more dangerous to the state than staged plays. But it was not only the internal interests and reputation of the English crown that required protection; diplomatic relations with friendly continental powers might be damaged by satirical plays appealing to a xenophobic London audience.

Two plays by George Chapman which depicted near-contemporary events at the French court of Henri IV, *The Conspiracy and Tragedy of Charles Duke of Biron* (1608) so angered the French ambassador that for some time all performances were banned within the City of London, and, probably, all presentation of 'modern Christian Kings' explicitly forbidden.[24]

Foreign affairs seem to have been avoided as a subject for plays for some time; a lost play called *Marquis d'Ancre*, probably about the recent murder of a French noble, is recorded in 1617 when the minutes of the Privy Council ask for it to be suppressed before it ever reached the stage. In 1619 Fletcher and Massinger's play, *The Tragedy of Sir John van Olden Barnavelt*, depicting events in the Netherlands and the execution, only three months earlier, of a popular figure who stood up for republicanism and opposed the Prince of Orange, then an ally of James, reached the stage despite the attempts of the Bishop of London to prevent it. This play, which has been described as 'an ideologically charged work with distinct republican and anti-authoritarian connotations',[25] has survived in a contemporary, heavily censored manuscript; it was not printed until 1803. Unlike the great majority of plays referred to earlier, it was performed not by a boys' company but by the King's Men, who also performed in *A Game at Chess* six years later. Given the uproar over this play, it seems extraordinary now that it was licensed at all, and that no one suffered any real penalty on its account. Support in high places has been hypothesized as a factor here, since Sir Henry Herbert, the new Master of the Revels, cousin to the powerful William Herbert, who was third Earl of Pembroke, Lord Chamberlain and a member of the Privy Council, was a puritan and not well disposed to any Anglo-Spanish alliance.[26] The actual performances took place while the King was out of London, perhaps a careful arrangement by some influential figure; and the King died the following year, after which Anglo-Spanish hostilities resumed and the play was able to be printed.[27]

Censorship in the new regime took essentially the same direction. Charles, like Elizabeth and to some extent James, enjoyed theatre and encouraged the performance of plays at court. Henry Herbert, who continued as Master of the Revels till the closure of the theatres, was an active censor, regularly intervening to require local corrections to protect the interests of monarch and church, but rarely acting so as to suppress completely the staging of contentious material. In one instance, where the King himself censored the text, Massinger's intriguingly titled *The King and Subject* (1638), the play itself has disappeared, yet it was apparently performed, again by the King's Men, after suitable excisions had been made. Ironically, the six lines to which the King took exception have in fact survived, recorded by Herbert himself in his Office book. They come from a speech in which Don Pedro, King of Spain, asserts his determination to raise money from taxation which had not received parliamentary approval (a method also favoured by Charles):

> Monys? Wee'le rayse supplies what ways we please,
> And force you to subscribe to blanks, in which
> We'le mulct you as wee shall thinke fitt. The Caesars
> In Rome were wise, acknowledginge no lawes
> But what their swords did ratifye, the wives
> And daughters of the senators bowinge to
> Their wills, as deities, &c.

Herbert also recorded his master's comment on the lines: 'This is too insolent, and to bee changed'. He noted cryptically, 'This is a peece taken out of Philip Messinger's play, called *The King and the Subject*, and entered here for ever to bee remembered by my son and those that cast their eyes on it, in honour of Kinge Charles, my master.'[28] Massinger, who took a critical attitude to absolutist rule, sailed close to the wind on more than one occasion, but there is only one other recorded instance of his work being censored. *Believe as Ye List* (1631), another intriguingly titled Massinger play, was initially refused a licence by Herbert because, as he put it, 'itt did contain dangerous matter, as the deposing of Sebastian King of Portugal, by Philip the (Second), and ther being a peace sworen twixte the Kings of England and Spayne'.[29] But the play was revised, the action transposed to classical antiquity, licensed, and then performed. It was clearly the same play, but, as Richard Dutton says, 'The coding had been adjusted in such a way that the topicality, while undoubtedly still present, was not offensively obvious in quarters that mattered'.[30] Massinger's sceptical treatment of kingship and royal identity in Antiochus, a mysterious 'pretender' figure, a king without a kingdom (like Ford's *Perkin Warbeck*, a play of the same period, to be discussed later), raised no alarm. The play may also have contained other 'dangerous matter', in the shape of allusions to the fate of the Elector Palatine, Frederick of Bohemia, husband to Elizabeth, Charles I's sister, who had been deposed from his throne in 1620 and spent subsequent years wandering Europe in perpetual exile. This Protestant couple had strong support in England, and the failures of both James and Charles to come to their aid did not go unnoticed.[31] Neither Massinger nor contemporaries such as Shirley or Brome was deterred from critical comment on unwise government and the excesses of absolutism. The old view of Caroline theatre as escapist and politically conformist has been largely overthrown in recent years; the period from 1632 to the closure of the theatres has emerged as one in which politically sensitive material was staged with increasing frequency.[32] In 1640 one company, Beeston's Boys, boldly put

on Brome's *The Court Beggar*, a play satirizing specific and identifiable courtiers, attacking court corruption and profiteering, Charles's personal rule
and the Scottish war; they staged the play without a licence, and continued
performing in defiance of a royal order to stop. Sir Henry Herbert, Master
of the Revels, recorded that 'The play I cald for, and, forbiddinge the play-
inge of it, keepe the booke, because it had relation to the passages of the
K.s journey into the Northe, and was complaynd of by his M.tye to mee,
with commande to punishe the offenders.'[33] The company was punished
by imprisonment and their manager William Beeston dismissed.[34]

The engagement of the stage with the monarchy took other forms than
those mediated by the office of the Master of the Revels. Direct representations of living monarchs could not be risked, but playwrights created other
kinds of images of royalty which were capable of being read to refer in
various ways to the current monarch; and soon after the death of Elizabeth
plays about the English past appeared which depicted both her and her
Tudor forebears. Elizabeth herself had been extremely conscious of the
uses to which literary forms could be put in the promotion of her own
personal cult and style of rule, and by no means discouraged representations of herself through mythological figures such as Cynthia, Diana or
Astraea. These are more common in non-dramatic verse or in private
courtly entertainments, but some playwrights saw the possibilities of
mythological representation to position themselves in relation to the
Queen. John Lyly, a courtier who wrote comedies for the boys' companies
to perform at court, participated most fully in her cult, and he hoped by
this means to obtain royal support in furthering his personal ambitions,
possibly expecting to obtain the influential and well-rewarded position of
Master of the Revels; in this he was unsuccessful. But his plays are always
ambivalent in their attitude to courtly politics, and sometimes his eulogis-
tic treatment of his queen-figures is compromised. The queen's status as
an unmarried female sovereign made for some complexity in the representation of her as a figure who combined power with chastity, especially in
a period when the strong reaction against the pre-Reformation monastic
ideal was accompanied by a rise in the prestige of the institution of marriage.[35] Lyly, in *Euphues*, had acknowledged the relationship of Elizabeth's
success as a ruler to her ability both to confront and transform aspects of
patriarchal power:

> What greater mervaile hath happened since the beginning of the world,
> then for a young and tender maiden, to govern strong and valiaunt menne,
> then for a virgin to make the whole worlde, if not to stand in awe of hir,
> yet to honour hir, yea and to live in spight of all those that spight hir, with

her sword in the shethe, with hir armour in the Tower, with hir souldiers in their gownes.[36]

But in his plays he depicts Elizabeth as ruler powerful in her chastity, not in the image of a martial maid, a conventionally accepted icon of female power, as celebrated by Spenser in the figure of Belphoebe in *The Faerie Queene*, but as a desired though unobtainable goddess, and thus not obliged to challenge earthly patriarchy. The best-known is probably *Endimion* (performed in 1586, 'before the Queenes Maiestie at Greenewich on Candlemas day at night, by the Chyldren of Paules', as the title page tells us), Lyly's most elegant compliment to the Queen, written at a time when it had become clear that the Queen would never marry and her cult focused on her perpetual chastity. In Lyly's version of the myth Endimion's adoration for Cynthia is regarded by his friend Eumenides as idolatrous and blasphemous, but he will not accept this. Tellus (the earth), who loves Endimion without requital, through her jealousy causes the witch Dipsas to put a spell on him by which he is condemned to premature aging and eternal sleep. Only Cynthia's kiss can break the spell, but when it does so he has become an old man. He now acknowledges the hopelessness of his passion as a social or erotic possibility. Cynthia's kiss is a token of the gracious favour of a quasi-divine being, not an erotic sign, but Endimion is happy to pledge his life to the service of his mistress in chastity with a wholehearted selflessness that Elizabeth would not have rejected from her court favourites. Physical desire is eliminated – in the characters of the bitterly yearning Tellus and the grotesquely ugly Dipsas female sexuality is demonized. Endimion speaks rapturously of his purified feeling for Cynthia:

> From this sweet contemplation if I be not driven, I shall live of al men the most content, taking more pleasure in mine aged thoughts, then ever I did in my youthful actions. (5.3.175–8)

Cynthia then rewards his fidelity by the restoration of his youth. The play includes more gestures to compliment the Queen on her power and gracious generosity. The philosopher Pythagoras and the Egyptian soothsayer Gyptes, who have been summoned to help restore Endimion, affirm that Cynthia has cured them of 'ridiculous opinions' they formerly held, and desire only to stay at her side forever. As Pythagoras asserts fervently, 'I had rather in *Cynthia's* Court spende tenne yeeres, then in Greece one hour' (5.3.290–1). Cynthia will have no lover, but she is not indisposed towards the marriage of lesser mortals, even finding a partner for Tellus. Her chastity is figured as a mystical quality, a kind of unchanging constancy that exists outside the appearances of the natural world.

Yet Lyly's play sets alongside this mystical Cynthia a more historically specific depiction of the Queen; when Endimion is first wakened from his sleep he relates to Cynthia a vision of her endangered in a hostile and rapacious court:

> I behelde many wolves barking at thee, *Cynthia*, who having ground their teeth to bite, did with striving bleed themselves to death. There might I see Ingratitude with an hundred eyes gazing for benefits, and with a thousand teeth gnawing on the bowels wherein she was bred. Trecherie stoode all cloathed in white, with a smyling countenance, but both her handes bathed in blood. Envye with a pale and megar face . . . stood shooting at starrres, whose dartes fell down againe on her owne face. There might I beholde Drones or Beetles . . . creeping under the winges of a princely Eagle, who, being carried into her neast, sought there to sucke that veine, that would have killed the Eagle. (5.1.120–32)

He concludes with a tactfully phrased warning against favourites: 'Bees surfette sometimes with honnie, and the Gods are glutted with harmony, and your highnesse may be dulled with delight', to which Cynthia replies, in the attractively dry manner that characterizes her in this play, 'I am content to bee dieted' (5.1.139). Lyly may have had specific targets here, perhaps referring, through the drones and beetles, to the plots against her life in the years before the Spanish Armada. In a previous play, *Sapho and Phao* (performed 1584), Sapho, the Queen-figure, has a dream similar to Endimion's vision, in which she sees a cedar tree, an emblem of royalty, despoiled by ants and caterpillars, conventional images for favourites found also in *Richard II* and *Woodstock*. Lyly's allegorizing of the Queen holds both general and specific applications in a kind of tension. On the one hand, the Queen-figures compliment Elizabeth in the most flattering of terms, in *Endimion* even imaging her, it has been suggested, as a kind of world soul;[37] but on the other hand, the evident (though much disputed) topical allegory, which in each play is local and occasional rather than consistent and integral, suggests that her court and even her relationships with her intimates are vitiated by faction, favouritism and deception.

Some years later, Jonson provides a similarly double-sided vision in his early play *Cynthia's Revels: or, The Fountain of Self-Love* (1600/1), which was strongly influenced by Lyly. Like *Endymion*, it had its first performance in the presence of the Queen. The court itself, apart from the Queen, is bitterly satirized, along with some contemporary playwrights, all of whom become addicted to the waters of the magical fountain in which Narcissus saw himself; the very pointed topical references, some of which were removed from the censored quarto text published in 1601, were not filtered like Lyly's through the veil of allegory, and seem likely to have been deeply offensive to the aging queen in the last years of her reign. For instance, Asotus, an aspiring courtier of modest birth, in the longer Folio text regrets that he has no chance to attract Cynthia's attention with his dancing:

> What lucke is this, that our revels are dasht? Now I was beginning to glister, i'the very high way of preferment. And CYNTHIA had but seene me dance a straine, or doe but one trick, I had been kept in court, I should never have needed to looke towards my friends againe. (4.5.76–81)[38]

The handsome Sir Christopher Hatton had come to Elizabeth's notice in just this way, and eventually rose to the rank of Lord Chancellor. The several references to Actaeon, 'torn by Cynthia's wrath' (1.2.82–3), seem to point to the disgrace of the Earl of Essex; in her long speech of judgement in Act 5, Cynthia justifies her punishment of Actaeon on account of his presumption:

> Seemes it no crime, to enter sacred bowers
> And hallowed places, with impure aspect,
> Most lewdly to pollute? Seemes it no crime
> To brave a deitie?
>
> (5.11.19–22)

This probably refers to Essex's uninvited entry to Elizabeth's apartment after his angry return from Ireland in 1599; if included in the court performance of 1601, a reference to his rebellion and execution would have been a step too far, even for the audacious Jonson. Cynthia herself is kept apart from the satire, by being absent from the court until the last act, when she returns as a dea ex machina to restore order. The moment when the stage goddess sees her counterpart in the audience and compliments her fulsomely –

> O front! O face! O all caelestiall sure
> And more then mortall! ARETE, behold
> Another CYNTHIA, and another Queene,
> Whose glorie, like a lasting *plenilune*
> Seemes ignorant of what it is to wane!
>
> (5.8.8–12)

evidently did not compensate for the play's other failures of tact, and it was reputedly not liked at court.[39] This is less surprising than the fact that Jonson wrote the play at all, although like Lyly's plays it was written for boy actors to perform in a private theatre. By contrast, Dekker's *Old Fortunatus* (1599), close in time, was a public theatre play given a court performance over the 1599/1600 season; Dekker made special additions to his text for this performance, in which Elizabeth's long reign is mentioned and her presence alluded to in the Prologue by two old men:

> 2: See how gloriously the Moone shines upon us.
> 1: Peace, foole: tremble, and kneele: The Moone saist thou? Our eyes are dazzled by Eliza's beames. [*both kneele*].

The compliments in this play are outside the dramatic framework and not offset by any satire; this is eulogy uncompromised, unlike the more complex use of lunar imagery in *A Midsummer Night's Dream*, where the Queen's virginity is glancingly referred to in Oberon's speech about the 'fair vestal throned by the west' untouched by Cupid's bolt (2.1.158). The wish in Dekker's Epilogue that the Queen's forty-two-year reign may be indefinitely extended would have provided a satisfyingly orthodox closure to the spectacle.

The death of the Queen in 1603 liberated dramatists in different ways in their handling of the Queen's image and of the English monarchy more broadly. For example, Chapman's *Bussy d'Ambois*, printed in 1607 though quite possibly written a few years earlier, is a historical play set in France in the 1570s, in which the French courtiers are given the opportunity to discuss the court of Elizabeth. In 1.2 King Henry of France speaks lines of conventional adulation, putting forward the Queen and her court as models for the French to emulate, but the Duke of Guise, a Machiavellian character, expresses another opinion entirely:

> I like not their Court fashion; it is too crestfall'n
> In all observance, making demigods
> Of their great nobles: and of their old queen,
> An ever young and most immortal goddess.
>
> (1.2.9–12)

Elizabeth would not in fact have been an old queen in the period when the play was set, exactly the time when a marriage with the Duke of Alençon, Henry's brother, was mooted, so that the deliberately anachronistic reference, impossible in a play before 1603, momentarily disrupts the play's historical timeframe, and alerts the audience to the possibility of further topical allusions, though they are not to Elizabeth's reign. This slur on the dead queen, which must have made Chapman's audience sit up and take notice, is by no means typical of Jacobean representations of Elizabeth. As has been said, a major effect of the queen's death was to revive interest in her early life, and resulted in a hagiographical treatment of her as a kind of Protestant saint.[40] In Samuel Rowley's *When You See Me, You Know Me* (1604) and Dekker and Webster's *Sir Thomas Wyatt* (printed 1607 but written earlier, and discussed in chapter 5) Elizabeth is not physically present, but the view of her created in John Foxe's *Actes and Monuments of the English Martyrs* (1563), the seminal text of Elizabethan Anglicanism, as a quasi-martyr figure, is adumbrated. In *When You See Me*, Elizabeth's pious letter to her brother Prince Edward, urging him to 'shun Idolatrie' inspires him in his championing of the Protestant faith. Heywood's two-part play, *If You Know Not Me, You Know Nobody* (1605, 1606), echoes Rowley's title, and testifies strongly to the nostalgia for her reign that was to set in so soon after James's accession. In the first part Heywood depicts the young Elizabeth as a Protestant heroine in full Foxeian style, triumphantly surviving the machinations of Catholic enemies, including her sister Mary Tudor, to the extent that she wins the admiration even of Philip of Spain. Persecuted on her sickbed by her sister's supporters Elizabeth conducts herself stoically:

> If I miscarry, in this enterprise, and aske you why
> A Virgine and a Martyr both I dy.
>
> (341–2)[41]

In one scene she is shown as literally protected while she sleeps by angels, who place an English Bible in her hands. In the last speech of the play she draws attention to the new availability of the Bible under the Protestant regime:

> This book, that hath so long conceald it selfe,
> So long shut up, so long hid; now Lords see,
> We here unclaspe, for ever it is free.
>
> (1585–6)

In *If You Know Not Me*, part 2, Elizabeth, now crowned, appears among the people of London, opening the Royal Exchange and, at the play's end, addressing her troops at Tilbury, transformed, as has been suggested, into 'the stuff of patriotic legend'.[42]

The iconic warrior queen appears again in Dekker's allegorical play, *The Whore of Babylon* (printed 1607), which concludes its representation of Elizabeth as a Protestant champion triumphant against the machinations of the powers of Catholic Europe with another depiction of her at Tilbury, here represented as Titania, the Fairy Queen. She watches unseen while the Empress of Babylon and the Kings of France, Spain and the Holy Roman Empire bewail the miraculous defeat of the Armada: the Third King laments:

> In one day fell five hundred, Galleons fifteen
> Drownd at the same time, or which was worser taken;
> Yet not a cherrystone of theirs was sunke,
> Not a man slaine nor tane, nor drownd.
>
> (5.6.102–6)

Dekker's depiction of the Queen has been called 'a subtle misrepresenta-tion',[43] so designed to create an image of the style of militantly Protestant, anti-Spanish foreign policy many hoped James would pursue at this time. But James saw himself rather as peacemaker, *rex pacificus*, and Jacobean history plays show themselves concerned far more with celebrating the early glorious days of Elizabeth's reign than with the reign of her successor. Shakespeare and Fletcher's *Henry VIII* (1613) was written at a crucial time for the political situation of English Protestantism after the sudden death of Prince Henry, who had become a beacon of hope for English Protes-tants, and the marriage of Princess Elizabeth, James's daughter, to the Protestant Elector Palatine.[44] Its subject matter, the beginnings of the Ref-ormation in England and the birth of the future Queen Elizabeth, would have been particularly appropriate at this historical moment. The play culminates in the christening of the baby, with a prospective eulogy of Elizabeth as a 'pattern to all princes living with her', delivered by Archbishop Cranmer. He prophetically foresees not only her glorious reign but also how it will end:

> She shall be, to the happiness of England,
> An aged princess. Many days shall see her,
> And yet no day without a deed to crown it.
> Would I had known no more. But she must die:
> She must, the saints must have her. Yet a virgin,
> A most unspotted lily, shall she pass to th'ground,
> And all the world shall mourn her.
>
> (5.4.62)

Cranmer's speech is carefully shaped so as to ensure that the compli-ment to the late queen does not cast any aspersions on the current reign; he praises her successor as one who 'from the sacred ashes of her honour/ Shall star-like rise as great in fame as she was', mentioning not only the 'branches' to be spread by his cedar-like majesty (no doubt bearing in mind Princess Elizabeth's marriage and James's interests in forging dynas-tic alliances for his children) but also the 'new nations' James created, in the context probably meaning the colony in Virginia. The reign of James is celebrated as one of peace. But except in masques written specifically for performance in court or in noble households where the King was present, James and his achievements were not celebrated in such terms during his reign. In fact it took no time at all after his accession before there ensued a small flood of plays in which 'familiar critiques, particularly those excoriating the sudden rise of favourites, the dissolute ruler and the decline of courtly decorum, are encoded in foreign settings'.[45] The contrast with the spate of representations of Elizabeth in the Tudor history plays of these same years could not be more marked. One playwright in particular stands out here: John Marston, whose relish for theatrical controversy had already brought him into conflict with Jonson. Written in close succession, his plays *The Malcontent* (1603), *The Fawn* (1604) and *Eastward Ho* (1605, with Jonson and Chapman) satirized various aspects of the new regime. In *The Malcontent* and *Eastward Ho* the comments, though often sharply barbed and audacious, are mostly only local in application. This need not, of course, dilute their pungency, perhaps the reverse, and the responses of theatre audiences can be specifically directed to particular moments and effects in a stage production. The representation of court corruption in *The Malcontent*, a play which almost certainly underwent censorship, is on the whole general enough to avoid charges of specific application to one court or monarch, though there are some flashes that a quick and satirically minded audience might have caught. The remarks of the bawd Maquerelle in 2.4 about the variety of cosmetics necessary to render 'an old lady gracious by torchlight' – 'the forging of veins, sprightening of eyes, dyeing of hair, sleeking of skins, blushing of cheeks, surphling of breasts, blanching and bleaching of teeth' – might have seemed like an irreverent comment on the dead queen.[46] And there are possible allusions to the new regime too; for instance, in 4.5 Malevole asks Bilioso, the sycophantic old marshal, 'What religion will you be of now?' He replies, 'Of the duke's religion, when I know what it is'. These lines were cut from the first printed text; they may allude not only to James's doctrinal ambiguities, but also to the willingness of courtiers such as Northampton, hitherto a Catholic, to switch allegiance when expedient. In a significant speech at the close of the play, Malevole, now recognized by all as Duke Altofront, the true Duke of Genoa, in disguise for most of the action, issues a solemn reminder to 'great ones' to understand that their power has limits:

> When they observe not heaven's imposed conditions,
> They are no kings, but forfeit their commissions.
> (5.5.143–4)

Again, these are lines which appear only in one text of the play, and in the context of the new reign and James's own beliefs in royal absolutism appear very pointed. *Eastward Ho* was performed without licence from the Revels Office and got its authors into trouble for making anti-Scottish jokes and mocking the King's accent and his over-generous creation of knights. Thus two gentlemen discuss the identity of Sir Petronel Flash, a new-made but penniless knight, whose attempt to sail on a colonizing expedition has ended in humiliating failure in a shipwreck on the Isle of Dogs:

> 1 *Gentleman*: I ken the man weel; hee's one of my thirty-pound knights.
> 2 *Gentleman*: No, no, this is he that stole his knighthood o'the grand day, for four pound, giving to a page all the money in's purse, I wot well.
>
> (4.1.167–70)[47]

Another very pointed passage which seems deliberately inserted to reflect the English dislike of what was perceived at the time as a tartan invasion also occurs in the context of the colonization of Virginia, a venture strongly supported by James. In Act 3 the wily Captain Seagull, hoping to lure the gentlemen adventurers Scapethrift and Spendall on a voyage to Virginia, extols its delights in satirical terms:

> *Scapethrift*: And is it a pleasant country withal?
> *Seagull*: As ever the sun shined on; temperate and full of all sorts of excellent viands . . . And then you shall live freely there, without sergeants, or courtiers, or lawyers, or intelligencers; only a few industrious Scots, perhaps, who are indeed dispersed over the face of the whole earth. But as for them, there are no greater friends to Englishmen and England, when they are out on't, in the world, than they are. And for my part, I would a hundred thousand of 'em were there; for we are all one countrymen now, ye know; and we should find ten times more comfort of them there than we do here.
>
> (3.3.34–45)

Perhaps it was because the satire was local (and easily excised) that the play was not banned, but it did land Jonson and Chapman in jail. Marston, who was probably responsible for the most offensive passages, escaped. The next year he had another play in print, *The Fawn*, which seems to satirize James and his court in a much more sustained manner but without such deliberately inflammatory barbs, though it was not censored and, as far as we know, made no trouble for its author. It was performed by the Children of the Queen's Revels, whose plays were specially licensed by Samuel Daniel, and bypassed the Revels office. It has been suggested that it may be Marston's Duke Gonzago to whom the French ambassador alluded in his description of how James was openly mocked on the stage to the amusement of his wife: 'Consider for pity's sake what must be the state and condition of a prince, whom the preachers publicly assail, whom the comedians of the metropolis bring upon the stage, whose wife attends these representations in order to enjoy the laugh against her husband.'[48] In the play the elderly Gonzago, Duke of Urbino, described in the cast-list as 'a weak lord of a self-admiring wisdom', is a Polonius-like buffoon, constantly drawing attention to his own wisdom; the courtier Herod calls

4 Woodcut from the title page of Heywood, *If you Know Not Me, You Know Nobody* (1605).

him 'most demonstratively learned', and this trait is represented by his sententiousness and constant use of figures of speech:

> Wise heads use but few words.
> In short breath, know the Court of Urbin holds
> Your presence and your embassage so dear
> That we want means once to express our heart

> But with our heart. Plain meaning shunneth art:
> You are most welcome – Lord Granuff, a trick,
> A figure, note – we use no rhetoric.
>
> $$(1.2.179-85)^{49}$$

One editor suggests that the last words here (like some others in the play) may have been intended to echo the King's first speech to the English parliament, which was printed in 1604. Shortly before the full extent of Gonzago's self-deception and stupidity is revealed at the end of the play, he remarks complacently, 'Of all creatures breathing, I do hate those things that struggle to seem wise, and yet are indeed very fools' (5.1.380–1). His young daughter Dulcimel, whose ability to get herself secretly married under her father's nose exposes his short-sightedness, addresses him in his own style as 'Royally wise, and wisely royal father', at which the fool Dondolo comments, 'That's sententious now, a figure call'd in art *Ironia*' (5.1.439). Such lines could well have been delivered in a comically pointed way, as could the references to drinking in the last scene. Gonzago accepts the pledge offered by Faunus, otherwise the disguised Duke Hercules, with excessive eagerness:

> Give't us full.
> When we were young we could ha' troll'd it off,
> Drunk down a Dutchman.
>
> $$(5.1.155-7)$$

Hercules then speaks a satirical commendation of drunkenness: 'A most fluent and swelling virtue, sure the most just of all virtues . . . It makes the king and the peasant equal, for if they are both drunk alike, they are both beasts alike' (5.1.159–63). This Gonzago takes at face value. James's own fondness for drink was not unknown, and his reputation for lavish and drunken court festivities contributed to his unpopularity. The celebrations at the visit of the Queen's brother from Denmark in 1606 are well documented, not least in the famous account in Sir John Harington's letters, when James got so drunk that he fell over when trying to dance.[50] But if the character of Gonzago did allude to 'the wisest fool in Christendom', Marston was careful to broaden the impact of his satire by generalizing the representation of the court, which is typically filled with parasites, gulls and flatterers, and is very similar to that in *Cynthia's Revels*, which found the same faults in the court of the previous regime.

Some plays which evidently represented James unflatteringly have not survived. A letter (partly written in code) of the French ambassador of 1608 refers to a play done by a boys' company in which the king was directly depicted in the most unflattering of terms:

Un jour ou deux devant, ilz [the boys] avoient depeche leur Roy, sa mine d'Ecosse et tous ses Favorits d'une estrange sorte: car après luy avoir fait depiter le ciel sur le vol d'un oyseau, et faict batter un gentilhomme pur avoir rompu ses chiens, ilz le depoignoient ivre pur le moins une fois par le jour. (A day or two before, they had slandered their king, his mine in Scotland and all his Favourites in a most pointed fashion; for having made him rail against heaven over the flight of a bird and have a gentleman beaten for calling off his dogs, they portrayed him as drunk at least once a day.)[51]

There was another such in 1617, known only from a lawsuit, in which the King, famous for his love of hunting, is represented as saying that he would prefer to hear a dog bark than a cannon roar. And in 1620 the Venetian ambassador saw a play performed by Prince Charles's company at court, in which, he wrote, 'a king with his two sons has one of them put to death, simply upon suspicion that he wished to deprive him of his crown, and the other son did actually deprive him of it afterwards'.[52] Except in court masques, James's public image was not capable of the deification accorded to Elizabeth either in his lifetime or subsequently, and it was in this form, rather than the public theatre, that his policies were promoted and endorsed.

The same was true for Charles I. While the King's personal image seems not to have incurred the kind of lampooning that James attracted from the start, his followers and his court were harshly criticized in plays of the 1630s, as Martin Butler has shown.[53] Characteristically, perhaps, Shirley's last tragedy, *The Cardinal* (1641) (discussed in chapter 7), focuses on the title character, evoking the hated Archbishop Laud, while the King is something of an absent presence. There is an obvious irony in the fact that the last, and most splendid, of the court masques, William Davenant's *Salmacida Spolia*, had been produced a year earlier; in this piece, which cost £1,400 to put on, the King, represented as 'the great and wise Philogenes' is unfortunate in that he must 'rule in adverse times/ When wisdom must awhile give place to crimes'. Although the masque inevitably depicts him as exorcizing the spirit of discord through the mystical harmony of his rule, the references in the songs to 'the people's folly' and the storms raging over the 'too-much-happy isle' create an uneasy undercurrent at odds with the final image of concord between England and the powers above which Davenant and his designer Inigo Jones seek to promote. It was only in court theatricals that Stuart rule could be imaged in terms of splendour and power. On the public stage the monarch had not been represented in such a way for many decades.

3

Sex, Marriage and the Family

The struggles between factional interests that could be identified with
religious positions, Anglican and Puritan, ended the reign of Charles I and
closed the theatres at about the same time. The meanings of the institution
of monarchy had become increasingly fraught during the Stuart regime,
but nonetheless it always remained a significant model for the institution
of the family. 'A familie, is a naturall and simple society of certaine persons,
having mutuall relation one to another, under the private government of
one', stated William Perkins.[1] The family/state analogy was an ancient
one, and regularly developed in marriage manuals, although it was
acknowledged that such family organization was not a naturally occurring
structure, but the product of effort. John Dod and Robert Cleaver begin
their guidebook, *A Godlie Forme of Household Government* (1612), as
follows:

> A Household is as it were a little commonwealth, by the good Government
> whereof, Gods glorie may be advaunced, the Commonwealth which stan-
> deth of severall families, benefited, and all that live in that familie receive
> much comfort and commoditie. But this government of a family is not
> very common in the world, for it is not a thing that men can stumble upon
> by chance, but *wisdome* must lead us unto it. (p. 13)

As a corollary, marriage itself was a fraught topic in early modern
England, on which a range of competing discourses was in circulation.

> Whoso attempteth marriage without advisement, running rashlie upon
> the reckes of their own ruine, and entering the cumbersome conflict of
> cares . . . must patientlie beare the brunt of their own breeding

wrote William Averell, in a strongly moralistic (and alliterative) pamphlet
called *A Dyall for Dainty Darlings* (1584).[2] 'Marriage of all the humane
actions of a mans life, is one of the greatest weight and consequence, as
thereon depending the future good, or evill, of a mans whole aftertime,
and dayes', wrote Alexander Niccholes in *A Discourse of Marriage and Wiving*
(1613).[3] While it seems to be true that marriage was an institution gaining
in prestige, especially in the wake of the Reformation revaluation of celi-

bacy as an ideal, there were conflicting views and pressures on many aspects of it, for instance about the nature and place of sexual desire within marriage, the respective roles and duties of husband and wife, the social functions of marriage to ensure the maintenance of hierarchy and the proper transmission of property through inheritance, as well as its part in channelling sexual energies in ways conducive to a Christian social order. Marriage was regarded as a hazardous enterprise, and both sexes needed guidance before undertaking it. From the mid-sixteenth century onwards, handbooks and manuals to provide this began to appear in abundance, with titles like *A Looking Glasse for Maried Folkes* (1610), by R. Snawsell, *A Bride-Bush: or, A Direction for Married Persons* (1619), by William Whately, and, among the most popular, *Of Domesticall Duties. Eight Treatises* (1622), by William Gouge. The church propounded an official line, to be found in the *Certaine Sermones or Homilies, appointed to be read in Churches, in the time of Queene Elizabeth I*, which included one, 'Of the state of holy matrimony', first printed in the second volume in 1563. It strongly advocates wifely subservience, in unambiguous terms: 'Yee wives, be ye in subjection to your owne husbandes';[4] so too did King James in *Basilikon Doron*, the book of advice prepared for his son Henry's guidance: 'ye are the heade, she is your body: It is your office to command, and hers to obey'.[5]

But alongside this rigidly hierarchical model of marriage was developing another, which has become known as companionate marriage, in which the style of relationship advocated in the Homily and in *Basilikon Doron* is modified to allow the wife an enhanced status; although the husband's supremacy was still maintained, mutual respect between the spouses became a significant consideration, and the husband was advised to acknowledge his wife's importance within the structure of the household. As Dorothy Leigh counsels in *The Mother's Blessing* (1616), 'If she bee thy wife she is always too good to be thy servant, and worthy to be thy fellow.'[6] Averell, a puritan, in his advice to men on how to choose a wife, advocates a carefully poised consideration of the wife's role: 'Seeing that she was not made of the head nor the fote, but of the ryb and side of man, which it sheweth that as she may not be a mystresse, so must she be no maide, as no soveraigne, so no servant, but an equal companion, and a freendly fellow, to participate with thee of every fortune.'[7]

The concept of the marital relationship as one of companionship was especially associated with Puritan writers, who 'set forth an ideal pattern of love and marriage based upon traditional Christian morality, vitalised for popular imagination in terms of the English bible, and adapted to the new conditions in which men were having to live'.[8] In place of the medieval Catholic view of marriage as a necessary evil, derived from St Paul's blunt statement that it was 'better to marry than to burn' (1 Corinthians, 7.9), there developed what has been called a 'sanctification of marriage – "holy matrimony"'.[9] Niccholes supports this concept with his declaration that 'the greatest authority we have in praise of Marriage, is the union of Christ with his Church compared unto it'.[10] But the companionate ideal of Puritan discourse was in competition with views of marriage deriving from its social functions in relation to what Stone calls the 'pragmatic calculation of family interest'.[11] If its primary role, at least among the elite classes, was to ensure the continuance of the family line and to safeguard the transmission of property, then on what terms could considerations of duty and obligation interact with those of personal preference in the selection of a spouse? Should parents and guardians be allowed to overrule sons and daughters? Different, and largely irreconcilable value systems come simultaneously into play. the self

In drama, conflicts between individual autonomy and social pressure are often worked out through the situation of the female protagonist in opposition to members of her family; this is realized as a tragic theme in plays like *The Duchess of Malfi*, *The Changeling*, and *Women Beware Women*. In comedy, by contrast, fantasies about freedom of choice are often explored in societies where parents and other authority figures are absent or ineffective, allowing free play to young people to realize their own desires. But sexual desire, its place both within the individual psyche and in society at large, is also a problematic issue. Even within a theatrical practice where it could not be directly represented on stage, Elizabethan plays do not underestimate its importance. Two particular questions frequently raised are the extent to which marriage can accommodate (male) sexual desire, and the role of desire within marriage. Prose pamphlets and marriage manuals recognize that young men are drawn initially by beauty and sex appeal, or, as Niccholes puts it, 'love lookes sometimes as well with the eye of the body, as with the minde',[12] but such attraction is to be rationalized; a marriage will be unhappy if the husband finds his wife repulsive, but if she is too beautiful then 'every carnall eye shall bethinke thee injury'. Excessively passionate desire within marriage is also dangerous in Niccholes's view, breeding discontent because it is insatiable: 'Lust is more spacious [than love], hath no meane, no bound . . . more deepe, more dangerous than the sea, & lesse restrained, for the Sea hath boundes, but it hath none.'[13] The fate of Othello, who believed himself to be 'one that lov'd not wisely but too well', might have been an object lesson in the fatal consequences of surrendering to passion. Torquato Tasso in *The House-*

holders Philosophie (1588), urging that the husband should control his own and his wife's expression of love, 'for the Husband commeth not with those prophane and superstitious clippings as the delicate and wanton Lover doth', claims that 'there was never greater sweet in love, then that which moderatly springs of honest Matrimony. And I could compare the embracings of the husbande and the Wife to the temperate suppers of well dieted men, wherein thay taste no lesse commodity of the meats, then the most incontinent and surfeiting cōpanion.'[14] Attitudes deriving from the traditional Christian distrust of carnal love as sinful mingle here with a certain pragmatism; marriage once embarked upon could not be dissolved, and was best undertaken with its continued maintenance in mind.

Marston's comedy, *The Dutch Courtesan* (1605), seems almost as if designed to confront many of these issues head-on. The 'Fabulae Argumentum' which prefaces the published text of the play states that 'the difference between the love of a courtesan and a wife is the full scope of the play'. The implication of this – that the play will function as a moral lesson for young men – is largely borne out, but Marston's handling of the relationship between sex, love and marriage does not result in a didactic play, unlike the near contemporary anonymous play, *How a Man may Choose a Good Wife from a Bad* (1602), perhaps a source. Rather, *The Dutch Courtesan*, in its complexity, has been said to mirror 'the attempts of conflicting and contradictory marriage discourses to reharmonise a set of incompatible pressures: a traditional Christian view of sex – all sex – as filthy and lecherous; the facts of procreation; various doctrines of sacramental marriage; typologies of Christ as bridegroom; arguments for a married clergy; the importance of marriage to social order and an orderly transmittal of property through inheritance'.[15] In the main plot Freevill, a sophisticated and worldly young gentleman, probably much like those in the audience at the Blackfriars to whom Marston was directing his play, written for performance by a children's company, has become engaged to marry the virtuous Beatrice, and must abandon the prostitute Franceschina, with whom he has been conducting a passionate affair. His more puritanical and serious-minded friend, Malheureux, though horrified by the idea of prostitution, becomes violently enamoured of Franceschina as soon as he sets eyes on her. In her jealous rage at Freevill's desertion of her, Franceschina promises to sleep with Malheureux if he will kill Freevill first. Through the development of this situation the play poses a contrast between sexual passion, depicted as uncontrollable and destructive, and the temperate rational love that should exist between married couples. 'Let me be vicious, so I may be lov'd' (2.2.110), declares the smitten Malheureux to

Franceschina, and later muses to himself, 'How easy 'tis to err/ When passion will not give us leave to think' (2.2.216).[16] For Freevill, a man's need for sexual pleasure, even for surrendering to passion, must be acknowledged and met, but then it will naturally be superseded; he prides himself on having enjoyed sex with an outstandingly desirable woman, and happily recommends it to his friend, but once ready to marry he revises his ideas both about sex and about women: 'I lov'd her with my heart until my soul showed me the imperfection of my body; and placed my affection on a lawful love, my modest Beatrice' (1.2.89–91). Male sexual energy once domesticated, lust has no place within marriage, and Beatrice specifically repudiates strength of feeling; she offers Freevill her love in terms of 'what hearty gratefulness/ unsullen silence, unaffected modesty,/ And an unignorant shamefastness can express' (1.2.15–170). When he expresses his pleasure in loving her, she tries to temper his ardour: 'Dear, my lov'd heart, be not so passionate;/ Nothing extreme lives long' (2.1.49–50). Because Freevill has sated his lower desires with Franceschina, he is able to appreciate the temperance and chastity of Beatrice; he justifies the existence of brothels, 'most necessary buildings', as a safeguard for married men: 'I would have all married men love the stews as Englishmen lov'd the Low Countries; wish war would be maintain'd there lest it should come home to their own doors' (1.1.62–5).

Something of this pragmatic attitude to prostitution is also expressed in the form of a paradox, when Freevill mockingly argues for it as the female counterpart of the labour decreed to be the lot of mankind after the fall: 'Would you have them get their living by the curse of man, the sweat of their brows? So they do. Every man must follow his trade, and every woman her occupation' (1.1.93–5). But this commodification of sex is offset by the stereotyping of Franceschina as 'woman-as-whore', contrasted with her opposite in the virginal Beatrice. Abandoned by Freevill, she gives herself up entirely to intemperate rage and hatred in her longing for revenge. 'Woman corrupted is the worst of evils', she states (1.2.197), and Freevill, too, draws on religious discourse in condemning her: 'O thou tearless woman! How monstrous is thy devil!/ The end of hell as thee!' (5.1.100–1). In calling her 'this fair devil', and 'comely damnation', 'unreprievable, beyond all/ Measure of grace damn'd immediately' (5.1.60–1), Freevill categorically affirms the traditional polarization of women as madonnas or whores, and disowns the kind of passion he once enjoyed with Franceschina as having any part in marriage, where 'the modest pleasures of a lawful bed,/ The holy union of two equal hearts' (5.1.68–9), are upheld as the ideal. In contradiction of Freevill's earlier view of prostitution as a safety valve, the whore now becomes the focus for the play's misogyny, embodying a corruption which must be purged from society to enable its continuance.

But alongside this sanctification of marriage contrived through the Freevill–Franceschina–Malheureux plot exists another construction of it without idealization, as a secular institution which serves certain social purposes without necessarily satisfying all the requirements of the parties involved. This is formulated through the figure of Beatrice's sister Crispinella, who reaches an accommodation with her suitor Tysefew, characterized in the dramatis personae as 'a blunt gallant'. Given a mocking deflationary idiom and an anti-romantic attitude to love and marriage that derives from one of the play's chief and most topical sources, Montaigne's *Essays*, Crispinella counters her sister's modest and unforthcoming manner with an outspoken wit on the subjects of men, sex and marriage. 'I give thoughts words, and words truth, and truth boldness' (3.1.37), she declares. The truths that 'marriage is often without virtue, and virtue . . . more oft without marriage' (3.1.87–8), and that it is an institution more convenient for men – 'because they may and we must' (4.1.36) – than women, are perhaps defused of some of their bitterness because Marston makes Crispinella into a type of the shrew who is tamed, though less like Shakespeare's Katherine in *The Taming of the Shrew* than Beatrice in *Much Ado About Nothing*, which must have been another of Marston's sources. Tysefew woos her in terms that, for all their patriarchal assumptions, retain an appeal:

> If you will be mine, you shall be your own. My purse, my body, my heart is yours; only be silent in my house, modest at my table, and wanton in my bed, and the Empress of Europe cannot content, and shall not be contented, better. (4.1.76–9)

That marriage can be negotiated on both sides is put more crudely by Mistress Mulligrub, wife to the rich vintner who is also the play's gull: 'a fine-fac'd wife in a wainscot carved seat is a worthy ornament to a tradesman's shop, and an attractive, I warrant' (3.3.10–12). For her, as for Tysefew, the categories of wife and whore are not as separate as Freevill and Beatrice would believe; elsewhere, in city comedies such as Middleton's *A Trick to Catch the Old One* (1606) or *A Chaste Maid in Cheapside* (1613), they are specifically conflated, but Marston never goes this far, and the idealist position on marriage remains the dominant one.

The play supports the view taken by many critics of city comedy of it as a conservative genre, typically concerned with 'the preservation of wealth and the right use of wealth – and beneath it all the stability of society'[17] to which the property-based marriage is central. Many of the issues around marriage that are explored in *The Dutch Courtesan* reappear in comedies of courtship from the Beaumont and Fletcher canon, especially the city plays *The Scornful Lady* (c.1609) and *Wit Without Money* (c.1614), and the later *The Wild-Goose Chase* (1621) and *Rule a Wife and Have a Wife* (1624), though they are less conservative in their depiction of the terms on which marriage may be agreed. Beaumont and Fletcher significantly situate their characters in a world without fathers or other figures to represent the structures and principles of patriarchy. The women in *The Scornful Lady*, *Wit Without Money* and *Rule a Wife and Have a Wife* head their own households and can make their own marital arrangements without familial constraints. When male kinsfolk do put in an appearance, as in *The Wild-Goose Chase*, their concern is not with the values of family, property or inheritance, but with ensuring that their female charges secure the husbands that society requires them to have while behaving with the utmost propriety. In *The Scornful Lady* the protagonist (who has no proper name) loves Elder Loveless and he her; but he has devalued himself as a suitor in her eyes by making his feelings for her too public, and she orders him to go abroad for a year as a punishment. The narrative of the play's main plot is directed by stratagems employed by Elder Loveless to secure her affection and also her commitment to marry him on his own terms. She counteracts his tricks with some of her own, also designed to fool him into emotional exposure, as when she tests his love by playing dead. His most successful device is to pretend to be marrying another woman (in fact, a man in disguise and her former suitor Welford), who is the exact opposite of the Scornful Lady, submissive, humble, modest and even a good housewife. The Lady is so piqued by this prospect that she agrees to marry Elder Loveless instantly, even kissing him in public; and when she discovers the spoof, she acknowledges that she has been won by trickery superior to her own. The currency at stake here is wit, which also serves to obtain marriage-partners for the other men in the play. Young Loveless, a prodigal, is eager to repair his fortunes by marrying the play's rich Widow (who again has no name), but refuses to reform or cast off his entourage of shiftless companions in order to get her; instead, he wins her on his own terms with a witty speech in which he 'proves' that 'the maintenance of / But Corne and water' in the form of ale, will be sufficient to provide his followers with all they need: 'In this short sentence Ale, is all concluded:/ Meate, Drinke, and Cloth' (4.2.61–2).[18] The Lady's cast-off suitor, Welford, who has acted as Elder Loveless's accomplice to trick her, is taken in his woman's disguise into the bed of the Lady's sister, Martha, whom he seduces, and thus obliges to marry him. So he too wins an heiress by merely taking part in a trick, and completes the play's gaily subversive account of the place of marriage in society. After her marriage the Lady is questioned by Young Loveless: 'Now my pretty Lady Sister,/ How doe you finde my brother?' She replies, 'Almost as wilde as you are'. He responds, 'A will make the better husband' (5.4.119–22).

In *Wit Without Money* the claims of wit and 'wildness' to be the currency of marriage are evaluated against those of financial stability. This time the relationship of the indigent young man, Vallentine, to the wealthy widow, Lady Heartwell, is central, but complicated in various ways. Although Vallentine is a prodigal gentleman who has squandered his own wealth, he is not interested either in restoring it or in marrying the widow. To the bafflement and despair of his uncle, creditors and tenants, he has opted for the freedom of living by his wits in the easy freemasonry of a society of city companions in preference to attempting to reclaim his hereditary status as gentleman and rural landlord. He has chosen what has been termed 'the solidarity of the male community' in preference to marriage:[19]

> Why 'tis a monstrous thing to marry at all,
> Especially as now 'tis made; me thinkes a man,
> An understanding man, is more wife to me,
> And of a nobler tie, than all these trinkets.
>
> (2.2.45–8)[20]

However, as a service to his three drinking companions, Fountaine, Bellamore and Harebrain, who do not share his loyalty to his own sex and are strongly tempted by all that Lady Heartwell has to offer, he agrees to 'try' the widow, guaranteeing not to woo her for himself, in order to see if she is worth their efforts. This central encounter takes the form of a battle of wits between Vallentine and Lady Heartwell, in the course of which the antagonists reverse their relations to one another. He attempts to goad her into displaying the vices which, as a woman and a widow, he believes she must possess, to reveal herself (and her sex) as arrogant, vain, hypocritical, and obsessed with pleasure and display. She counters by exposing the hidden assumptions that support misogyny, eloquently denouncing the sexual double standards constructed by a male-dominated society to secure its own interests:

> Are not we gaily blest then,
> And much beholding to you for your substance?
> You may doe what you list, we what beseemes us,
> And narrowly doe that too, and precisely,
> Our names are served in else at Ordinaries
> And belcht a broad in Tavernes.
>
> (3.2.129–34)

Each leaves the scene surprised, impressed and prepared to change, Lady Heartwell acknowledging the success of Vallentine's clever stratagems: 'how prettily he fooled me into vices/ To stirre my jealousie and finde my nature' (3.2.197–8). Vallentine not only re-evaluates his ideas of women and marriage but also reassesses his relationship with the free camaraderie of unmarried men, throwing his three fortune-hunting friends out of Lady Heartwell's house. Lady Heartwell, who has hitherto guarded her wealth over-protectively, learns how to use it for the benefit of others, and disburses charity to her younger sister. Although it takes a witty stratagem on the part of Vallentine's uncle Master Lovegood and his friend, the Merchant, to ensure Vallentine's compliance, the couple eventually marry. Despite Vallentine's compromise over his original espousal of 'wit without money', the play still sets a high valuation on wit; it is the means by which he not only wins the widow's heart but also proves himself worthy of her. But this play belongs less in the wish-fulfilment world where wit is king than does *The Scornful Lady*; and concomitantly it has more to say about the right use of money. Vallentine has to abandon his vision of a life where wit can take the place of money and 'all gentlemen/ That love society love me; all purses/ That wit and pleasure opens, are my Tennants' (1.1.158–60). After his entry into Lady Heartwell's world he sees the life of tavern camaraderie as a fantasy, substituting for a reality of humiliating indigence, of existing on others' leavings.

> Til Tavernes
> Allow you but a Towell roome to tipple in,
> Wine that the Bell hath gone for twice, and glasses
> That looke like broken promises, tied up
> With wicker protestations, English Tobacco
> With halfe pipes, nor in halfe a yeare once burnt, and Bisket
> That Bawdes have rubb'd their gummes upon.
>
> (4.5.67–71)

Marriage constitutes an acceptance of the material basis of society, although, of course, this is still the society of a young man's fantasy, where the finance to support a comfortable household is supplied by a wife who is desirable as well as rich.

The Beaumont and Fletcher comedies speculate about the consequences for a man without money if he has to find a rich woman to marry, thus reversing the usual assumptions about the balance of power in a marriage, but, despite the autonomy apparently accorded to an independently wealthy woman, they do not overturn these assumptions. The Scornful

Lady exercises her power over potential suitors by taunting and humiliating them, but she recognizes this as a perversity of her sex:

> What fine foolery is this in a woman
> To use those men most forwardly they love most?
> (4.1.370–1)

Her behaviour reflects the stereotype of the curst, forwardly woman who needs a man to govern her deviant appetites (Katherine in *The Taming of the Shrew*), and she is given a soliloquy in which to acknowledge the unnaturalness of her behaviour and her inability to contain it:

> O what are wee!
> Men you must answer this, that dare obey
> Such thinges as wee command.
> (5.2.19–21)

The restoration of normal social relations requires the imposition of male control.

The same point is made in more bluntly farcical style, as the play's title suggests, in *Rule a Wife and Have a Wife*. Here Donna Margarita, another figure of masculine fantasy, 'faire, and young, and wealthy,/ Infinite wealthy', seeks a husband who will be tame and tractable so that she may pursue affairs with other men under the cover of marriage. (In Fletcher's source, *El Sagaz Estacio Marido Examinado*, the Margarita figure is in fact a prostitute.)[21] The humble soldier whom she chooses appears to fit the bill, being shy, slow-witted, sexually inexperienced, servile and compliant, a token husband, 'the mere sign of a man', but once married he reveals the true meaning of this sign. When the Duke, who expects to become Margarita's lover, arrogantly draws his sword to claim possession of her, Leon draws in turn to assert his rights as husband:

> He that dare strike against the husbands freedome
> The husbands curse stick to him, a tam'd cuckold,
> My wife be faire and young, but most dishonest,
> Most impudent, and have no feeling of it,
> No conscience to reclaim her from a Monster.
> (3.5.132–6)[22]

Leon's role is, as he says, reclamatory. Margarita's disordered appetites need curing, but she is reluctant to abandon her bid for dominance and sexual freedom without a struggle. When the Duke persists in his attempts to collude with her in undermining Leon's marital authority the soldier threatens a quasi-medical appropriation of his wife's body and mind:

Ile have thee let blood in all the veines about thee,
Ile have thy thoughts found too, and have them open'd,
Thy spirits purg'd, for those are they that fire ye.
(5.3.78–80)

Margarita's monstrosity is eliminated, and she submits to Leon as a convert to the true faith: 'I have lost myself, sir,/ And all that was my base self, disobedience' (5.3.85–6). Leon, though of low social rank, has justified his claim to share in Margarita's wealth and status by his qualities as a husband and by his normative masculinity.

Although the Beaumont and Fletcher plays ultimately modify or even deflate the wealthy woman's claims to power and autonomy in marriage, they nonetheless tend to focus their exploration of the mechanisms of sexual desire on the female characters, in the sadomasochistic power games played by the Scornful Lady, for instance, or Margarita's acceptance of, and eventual collusion in, Leon's strategies for curative taming. In *The Wild-Goose Chase*, however, the female characters win their elusive male partners through various forms of role-play. The sexual dynamic of the play derives from the assumptions that all young women desire marriage and all young men freedom. The sexy, assertive sisters, Rosalura and Lillia-Bianca, are determined to marry their suitors Pinac and Bellure, newly returned from foreign travel, as expeditiously as possible, if necessary reshaping the unpromising husband material into something acceptable. Thus Rosalura describes her plans for Bellure to Lillia-Bianca:

Peace: he's modest:
A bashfulness, which is the point of grace, Wench:
But when these fellows come to moulding, Sister,
To heat, and handling: as I live, I like him;
And methinks I could form him.
(3.1.131–5)[23]

The two women mock and baffle the men, enacting a 'range of behaviours . . . subtle and new' taught them by their tutor Lugier; Lillia-Bianca, for example, deceives Pinac by presenting herself so convincingly as repentant of her youthful follies and desirous only to become a submissive wife, 'yoak't, and govern'd' (4.1.80), that he is almost speechless when she reveals that this was only play-acting. Rosalura similarly allows the timid Bellure to believe that she has been humbled and brought to the verge of tears by his assertion of manly authority; at the point when he is prepared to judge the extent of her submission by the quality of her ability to shed tears – 'Cry now instantly;/ Cry monstrously, that all the Town may hear thee;/ Cry seriously, as if thou hadst lost thy monkey' (4.2.67–9) – she calls in a band of women who jeer at him and demolish his masculinity as a pose:

Come hither to fright Maids, with thy Bul-faces?
To threaten Gentlewomen? Thou a man? A May-pole,
A great dry Pudding.

                                    (4.2.81–3)

Just as the women play at womanliness, so, the play suggests, manliness itself may be an appearance, a cover for sexual inadequacy. Lugier instructs the sisters in their parts, and the process of courtship is revealed as the operation of the codes which define sexual behaviour. The 'wild-goose' of the title, Mirabel, a confirmed libertine, whose addiction to foreign travel is made a metaphor for his propensity for sexual exploration, is eventually ensnared by the ability of Oriana, the woman out to capture him, to present herself in a sexual role that is particularly appealing to him, that of the exotic stranger. She has taken on various guises with him earlier, including simulating madness, but he sees through each of them. However, when Oriana is introduced as a mysterious Italian, wealthy, foreign and unknown, Mirabel cannot resist her. She pretends to retreat from his advances: 'How can you like me, without I have Testimony,/ A stranger to ye', but he responds without hesitation, 'I'll marry ye immediately./ A fair State, I dare promise ye' (5.6.71–4). When she reveals her true identity, asserting triumphantly, 'I have out Travell'd ye', Mirabel capitulates, claiming to have been pleased by the deceit, and (in imitation of Falstaff at Gadshill) to have recognized Oriana anyway: 'I'll burn my book [of sexual conquests] and turn a new leaf over' (5.6.87). That the women get their men in the end, and that marriage is necessary mainly to regulate female desire, are not the most interesting points the play has to make. The recognition of the diverse forms taken by sexual desire and the relation of role-play both to the construction of gender and to the arousal of desire are more striking, and, for the period, more innovative, perceptions.

Sophisticated comedies of contemporary mores such as these, whereby sex is a commodity and marriage arrived at by bargaining and negotiation, situate marriage as an institution in what has been termed a world of 'competitive individualism' by contrast with the 'humanised patriarchy' of Shakespeare's comedies.[24] Even if, ultimately, their sexual politics rests on traditional assumptions about gender and power which can be translated in terms of 'the triumph of romantic over libertine values',[25] their underlying ethos is that of the marketplace, which is perhaps partly why they had such appeal in the theatre of the Restoration period.

The ways in which marriage, and the commodification of female sexuality, serve the interest of a male-dominated, property-based society are also explored in tragedies of the period, particularly those by Webster and Middleton, where they come into conflict with interests of a different kind.

The role of the family is more prominent in this genre, typically depicted in a negative light, where the tragic dilemma is created around the marital or sexual situation of a woman. Fathers and brothers pursue their own agendas at the expense of daughters and sisters; mothers and aunts, although rarer figures, are no less exploitative – Cornelia in The White Devil, Livia in Women Beware Women, for instance. In these plays the tragic theme of conflict between the individual and authority is worked through at the family level, with particular focus on the situation of the sexually available woman. Vermandero, father to Beatrice-Joanna in The Changeling, promotes first Alonso de Piraquo, then Alsemero as suitors to his daughter, in order to satisfy his own sense of social propriety and, as importantly, of authority. 'He shall be bound to me,/ As fast as this tie can hold him; I'll want/ My will else' (1.1.219–20), he says of one potential son-in-law. Brothers, too, may adopt excessively proprietorial attitudes towards their sisters' sexual liaisons; the prototype is Lorenzo in The Spanish Tragedy (discussed in chapter 7). The brothers of Vittoria in The White Devil and of the Duchess of Malfi have complex motives for their involvement in their sisters' affairs. Flamineo encourages Vittoria's adulterous liaison with the powerful Bracchiano, head of the Orsini dynasty, because it constitutes 'a path so open and so free/ To my preferment' (1.2.339–40) that he cannot afford to let the considerations of 'shame and blushing' urged by his mother to stand in his way. The voyeuristic interest this brother takes in the development of his sister's love affair is transformed, in The Duchess of Malfi, into something darker by the strong implications of incestuous feeling that animate Ferdinand's concern to control his sister's sexuality. Although Catherine Belsey says that this play 'celebrates the family, identifying it as a private realm of warmth and fruitfulness separate from the turbulent world of politics',[26] in fact it explores the family as a site of conflict more fully than any other tragedy of the period in its depiction of the multiple and conflicting obligations and commitments of the Duchess. As the third member of a ruling house she is of what the Cardinal calls 'our blood,/ The royal blood of Aragon and Castile' (2.5.21–2),[27] which stands in danger of being defiled by an unsanctioned sexual liaison. She is also a dowager duchess, an independently wealthy widow, and mistress of her own household by virtue of the rank of her late husband, by whom she has a child. Already a mother, she embarks on the creation of a second family through the clandestine marriage to Antonio, her household steward, which rapidly produces more children. This family thrives at the expense of the first, until her outraged brothers discover and take steps to eradicate it. The play's uniquely tender scenes of domesticity and marital love between the

Duchess and Antonio privilege the second family, and the claims to privacy and self-fulfilment that it embodies, over the first, apparently public, dynastic union, which the Duchess places firmly in the past, together with the claims of widowhood, by telling Antonio as she woos him,

> This is flesh, and blood, sir,
> 'Tis not the figure cut in alabaster
> Kneels at my husband's tomb.
> (1.2.375–77)

Yet, preparing for death and resistant to Bosola's attempts to humiliate her, she famously asserts: 'I am Duchess of Malfi still' (4.2.147), seeming to find comfort in her former status and, *in extremis*, to prefer this identity to that of Antonio's wife. The play raises important questions about the family and especially the woman's role within it, but refuses to give easy answers to them. The issue of the Duchess's remarriage is one, and so too is the relationship between marriage and the family; for the Duchess's brothers, marriage is a homosocial arrangement, to be made for the prestige and enhancement of the dynasty, but for her and Antonio it is 'an assertion of individual fulfilment'.[28] These positions cannot be reconciled.

In *Women Beware Women* the woman's identity as wife-material is depicted in quasi-comic vein. Unlike the Duchess, neither Bianca's nor Isabella's status in the marriage market is compromised by being a widow or a mother, and each is viewed, explicitly, as a commodity, by families with unambiguously mercantile values at their heart. The young clerk Leantio, who has recently eloped with the Venetian gentlewoman Bianca, daughter of a better family than his own, expresses his infatuation with his bride in terms that define her importance for him as emotional capital; she is a 'treasure', 'the most unvaluedst purchase' and 'a most matchless jewel'; his stolen marriage to her is 'the best piece of theft that ever was committed'. As his mother understands, Bianca is an inappropriately valuable piece of merchandise for their 'plain' household to possess, and needs to be kept hidden so as not to attract covetous eyes. But although the family is well aware of the worth of their illicitly acquired property, they are without the necessary resources to hold on to it. The Mother, who is flattered to be invited by her social betters to play chess and enjoy supper while (unbeknownst to her) her precious daughter-in-law is being seduced by the Duke, shows how easily maternal protectiveness may be subverted. 'Here's an old wench would trot into a bawd now/ For some dry sucket or a colt in marchpane' (3.2.188–89), Bianca remarks cynically.[29] Fabritio, father to Isabella, is hard-headed about ensuring that he gets value for money when disposing of her. He determines to marry her off to a rich young ward, regardless of the fact that the ward is an idiot, and silences his daughter's appalled objections brusquely: 'He's rich; / The fool's hid under bushels' (1.2.84–85). The nature of marriage as a commercial transaction is exposed in a scene where the two young people are introduced to one another, in which Isabella's father and the ward's guardian each take pains to ensure that they will be getting a good bargain. 'She's a dear child to me . . . dear to my purse, I mean', Fabritio clarifies,

> 'She has the full qualities of a gentlewoman:
> I have brought her up to music, dancing, what not,
> That may commend her sex, and stir her husband.
>   (3.3.108–10)

Guardiano is briefer in his commendation: 'He's a great ward, wealthy, but simple; / His parts consist in acres'. Fabritio, proud of the valuable commodity he has on offer, urges the Ward to dance with her: 'You shall see, young heir, what y'have for your money, / Without fraud or imposture' (3.3.175–6). The Ward, though witless, is not without a crude commercial sense, and in a further scene, encouraged by his leering servant Sordido, undertakes a detailed physical examination of Isabella as if she were a horse, checking her breath and her teeth, and finally looking under her skirt in the pretence of checking her gait.

Isabella is a pawn in this game, and bitterly conscious of her own powerlessness. Middleton gives her a long angry speech after she has first seen the Ward in which to articulate her sense of marriage as a trap:

> Oh the heart-breakings
> Of miserable maids, where love's enforced!
> The best condition is but bad enough:
> When women have their choices, commonly
> They do but buy their thraldoms, and bring great portions
> To men to keep 'em in subjection –
> As if a fearful prisoner should bribe
> The keeper to be good to him, yet lies in still,
> And glad of a good usage, a good look sometimes.
> By'r Lady, no misery surmounts a woman's:
> Men buy their slaves, but women buy their masters.
>   (1.2.166–76)

But Isabella is no blameless victim; and encouraged by her manipulative aunt, the widow Livia, she finds a way to turn the repulsive marriage to her own advantage by using it as a cloak for an affair. 'This marriage shall go forward', she tells her dumbfounded lover, Hippolyto, who, as he knows but not she, is also her uncle; '"Twould be ill for us else'. (2.1.206–7). The women in these plays may be used and subjected because of social structures outside their control, but sympathy is not invited for them merely on this account. Isabella's virginity and marriageability do not equate with purity or innocence, and although Beatrice-Joanna in *The Changeling* appears like Isabella to be pitiably at the mercy of an autocratic father when it comes to marriage choices, the transgressive means she employs to circumvent this constraint only intensify her entrapment and involve her in further loss of power. She hires the servant De Flores to murder the suitor her father foists upon her, believing that she can pay him off and displace onto him the responsibility for the deed. She does not understand that his eager acceptance of the commission results from his own, completely different, agenda. He spells this out when she tries to fob him off with a cash payment for the murder, which he angrily rejects:

> I place wealth after the heels of pleasure,
> And were I not resolv'd in my belief
> That thy virginity were perfect in thee,
> I should but take my recompense with grudging,
> As if I had but half my hopes I agreed for.
> (3.4.115–9)[30]

Beatrice-Joanna is naively horrified by his demand, and unable to accept the commercialized valuation of her virginity:

> Why, 'tis impossible thou canst be so wicked,
> Or shelter such a cunning cruelty,
> To make his death the murderer of my honour!
> Thy language is so bold and vicious
> I cannot see which way I can forgive it
> With any modesty.
> (3.4.120–25)

De Flores's unforgettable riposte is the first step in teaching Beatrice-Joanna that all actions have consequences:

> Push, you forget yourself!
> A woman dipp'd in blood, and talk of modesty?
> (3.4.125–6)

Affronted by such impudent language, she attempts to secure her status and preserve the distance proper to a relationship between a great lady and a servant, but De Flores points out to her that she has herself crossed this boundary:

> Fly not to your birth, but settle you
> In what the deed has made you, y'are no more now;

> You must forget your parentage to me;
> Y'are the deed's creature.
>
> (3.4.134–7)

Dollimore suggests the radical implications of De Flores's speech: 'an act of transgression and its consequences actually disclose "blood" and "birth" to be myths in the service of historical and social forms of power, divested of which Beatrice becomes no more than what "the act" has made her'.[31] But if rank and status are, in materialist terms, 'myths', it is these myths which are responsible for much of the emotional charge created in the relationship that develops between Beatrice and De Flores. Their sexual partnership reveals her growing dependency on him and appreciation of his qualities. Her loss of virginity must be concealed from Alsemero, her suitor of choice and now husband, in whose favour Alonso was eliminated; and, ever ready to exploit a servant in her own interests, she has her maid Diaphanta substitute for her on the wedding night in Alsemero's bed, but once again the plan goes wrong. De Flores is called in to help, and he devises a characteristically ruthless if efficient method to dispose of Diaphanta when she has outstayed her welcome, for which Beatrice is all admiration:

> How rare is that man's speed!
> How heartily he serves me! His face loathes one,
> But look upon his care, who would not love him?
> The east is not more beauteous than his service.
>
> (5.1.69–72)

The depth of commitment in the illicit relationship between the two not only demonstrates Beatrice-Joanna's re-evaluation of the notion of 'service', but also exposes by contrast the hollowness of her sanctioned marriage with Alsemero; and De Flores in his suicide speech confirms the meaning of this partnership forged in defiance of social custom and constraint:

> I lov'd this woman in spite of her heart;
> Her love I earn'd out of Piracquo's murder.
> . . . and her honour's prize
> Was my reward; it was so sweet to me
> That I have drunk up all, left none behind
> For any man to pledge me.
>
> (5.3.165–71)

The frisson created by this love affair exists not just because of Middleton's extraordinary exploration of sexual dependency but because of the transgressive relationship between lady and servant. De Flores is a gentleman 'thrust out to servitude' by social misfortune; and although he is not depicted as consciously radical, his social decline is accompanied by a loss of belief in the inherent significance of birth and rank. His physical disfigurement perhaps also symbolizes his loss of status, and it also seems to justify the repulsion with which the other characters regard him. In the end, the play endorses this view, as Vermandero, Alsemero, and the rest regroup in its final moments to celebrate their survival after the cataclysm, and reconstitute a society organized on traditional lines, where the distinction between 'beauty' and 'ugly whoredom' is real and there is true horror in the change 'from servant obedience/ To a master sin'. The terms 'servant', 'service', 'servitude', and 'serve' constitute a rich sub-text of interconnected discourses ranging between the Petrarchan lover's voluntary service of a courtly mistress, the idea of sexual servicing, and the retainer's paid, and socially required, duty.[32] Masters expect and can command service from their servants, by virtue of an unquestioned acceptance of the notion of social hierarchy, and women can invoke service from lovers, and lovers tender it, by virtue of the conventions of erotic rhetoric. But women, being sexually inferior, may serve men, and service in the play becomes confused and confusing. The blurring of boundaries between servant and served is a deep source of anxiety, which the play's conclusion does not resolve.

The alliance of the woman with a servant/outsider figure is a cause of scandal in other tragedies focused on the household. The prototype for this in the period is the relationship of Alice Arden and her husband's servant Mosby in *Arden of Faversham*, discussed in chapter 4. In *Women Beware Women* Livia takes as a lover Leantio, transgressing social convention because he is both a younger man and her social inferior. To her brother Hippolyto this act is more outrageous and demeaning to the family honour than his own incestuous alliance with his niece. In *The Duchess of Malfi* the Duchess's choice of her steward Antonio as her second husband arouses murderous rage in her brothers, who unite to avenge it. To the Cardinal, the typical venial and lecherous prelate of early modern tragedy, this act of his sister's is enough to justify the extremest sanctions against the couple: the seizure of his sister's lands, their banishment and the Duchess's imprisonment and eventual murder. By comparison, his own transgression of religious vows in conducting a liaison with a married mistress is a mere irregularity. In a comedy, *Twelfth Night*, the possible alliance between the Countess Olivia and her steward Malvolio is a subject for ridicule, and Malvolio is shown as deservedly tormented and persecuted for ever having entertained the idea. Antonio, also a steward, is an honest and efficient household servant, who is justifiably full of apprehension when his employer makes advances to him:

Ambition, madam, is a great mans madnes,
That is not kept in chains and close-pent rooms,
But in fair lightsome lodgings . . .
Conceive not, I am so stupid but I aim
Whereto your favours tend. But he's a fool
That, being a-cold, would thrust his hands i'th'fire
To warm them.
                                        (1.1.343–5, 348–51)

He is, however, persuaded to do just that, perhaps because he is too good
a servant, and throughout the play remains in a secondary, effeminized
position in relation to the Duchess, always apprehensive, never secure. As
he notes bitterly, when she calls him a 'lord of misrule', 'Indeed, my rule
is only in the night' (3.2.7). Whereas in *The Changeling* it is the clever and
opportunistic servant who, in alliance with Beatrice-Joanna, undermines
the family from within; in *The Duchess of Malfi* the threat to the family
structure is more diffuse, and the notion of family enlarged and complicated by that of dynasty. The family as the essential unit within society is
at risk of attack from within as well as from outside. Ferdinand's incestuous
desires in *The Duchess of Malfi*, which mean that because he cannot marry
his sister himself he cannot tolerate any other partner for her, are not as
directly destructive as De Flores's desire to possess Beatrice, but they represent a self-destructive force at the heart of this family. The perverted
possessiveness of Flamineo towards Vittoria, by which he constitutes
himself her pimp, is similar to the feelings of Livia for her brother
Hippolyto, which motivate her to encourage his incest with Isabella. Such
'sexual distortions', as Richard McCabe calls them,[33] indicate the propensity for rottenness within the structures of the family.

Marriage as an institution is open to question in all these plays, which
participate actively in the contemporary debate occasioned by the coexis-
tence of contradictory views on the subject. Both comedy and tragedy can
demonstrate the cost of the accommodations which need to be made in
order to support it, and disasters which can result when compromise is not
available. Fears and fantasies about women and their sexuality underlie
these plays, and it is they which illuminate the tensions between the private
and individual meanings of marriage and the family on the one hand, and
the public and communal on the other. There is a consciousness in these
plays that traditional patriarchy is at odds with emerging notions of companionate marriage and the wife's role within it, and that the fissures
between the notions of marriage as a spiritual ideal and as a social contract
are widening.

4

Journalistic Plays

The aim of this chapter is to look at a kind of drama which, in terms of its content, has a more direct relationship with the society that produced it than any other, at plays that dramatized recent events, referred to long ago as 'dramatic journalism'.[1] I have chosen not to use the term 'domestic tragedy' for two reasons: partly because not all such plays were in fact tragic, but mainly because 'domestic tragedy' can include plays without a factual basis (Heywood's *A Woman Killed with Kindness* is an obvious example), and my emphasis here is on the relation of this drama to real events quite possibly known to its original audiences. Also, the term 'domestic tragedy' is sometimes applied to plays about high-born and noble characters, such as *Othello*; but the journalistic plays discussed here all centre on the lives of the non-elite, not a typical focus for early modern tragedy, and on the ways in which ordinary people find themselves involved in extraordinary events.

The plays treat this subject matter rather like modern news reporting, presenting the event from a specific angle and implying, with varying degrees of explicitness, a comment on it. Alison Findlay's observation about witchcraft writing applies equally well to other sorts of materials dramatized here: 'Like the sensational stories of today's media, witchcraft was a kind of news which drew attention to the news-making process: something with credibility which invited sharp critical evaluation.'[2] In almost all cases that I discuss, the events were also written up in the other news media of the day – ballads and pamphlets – so that audiences might well have been familiar with the stories that they saw dramatized, and the playwrights were able to draw on that familiarity in their shaping of the narrative for the stage. The best-known of these now are the anonymous *Arden of Faversham* (printed 1592), and *The Witch of Edmonton* (1621) by Dekker, Ford, Rowley and Webster; not many of those known to have been written have actually survived. For instance, while five journalistic plays, all of them tragedies, printed between 1590 and 1610 are in existence, there are records of more than three times that number which are not extant.[3] As Sir Sidney Lee, one of the first critics to take an interest in plays about news, wrote, 'That domestic tragedy was a popular form of drama is unfortunately proved, not by the number of extant plays, but from the lost plays accessible to us in such places as Henslowe's Diary or the Stationers' Register.'[4] While *Arden of Faversham* is often treated as if it were the first such play, others almost certainly preceded it, such as two plays known to have been produced at court in 1578 and 1579, *Murderous Michael* (possibly also on the subject of the Arden murder) and *The Cruelty of a Stepmother*, evidence of which is found only in court records, and perhaps the play *The History of Friar Francis*, which Thomas Heywood describes in *An Apology for Actors* as provoking a startling response from a member of the audience. Robert Yarrington's *Two Lamentable Tragedies* (printed 1601) depicts a murder which took place in 1594; payments for another play on the same subject, *The Tragedy of Merry*, are recorded in Henslowe's *Diary* for 1599, but it has not survived. In the same year Henslowe recorded the unusually high payments of £6 for the 'book', and £10 for women's costumes for another domestic murder play, *Page of Plymouth*, by Jonson and Dekker, but this too is lost.[5] This is a particular misfortune for the history of early modern English drama, partly because, as we know from several ballads and other accounts, the murder of Master Page at the hands of his wife and her lover excited huge interest comparable to that of the murder of Thomas Arden; but also, such a play would have represented a considerable novelty in the oeuvre of Ben Jonson, whose early theatrical career remains somewhat mysterious, especially where the question of collaborative writing is concerned.

It is impossible to know now why the survival rate among so many plays of this type is so low, but it may be that the topicality which made these plays attractive may also have made them dangerous, in an age of strict, if not necessarily systematic, censorship. There is evidence that plays relating to topical political news, such as *The Isle of Dogs* (1597) by Nashe and Jonson and *Gowrie* (performed in 1606) were suppressed because of causing offence in high places; although this was less likely to be the case with domestic news, nonetheless a comic play by Dekker and others, *Keep the Widow Waking* (1624), about a recent scandal, which resulted in Dekker making an appearance before the Court of Star Chamber accused of libel, has also disappeared.[6] It is also likely that topical plays, while of great interest at the time, quickly lost their appeal and were not considered worth printing. But even here one can make caveats. Topicality in the modern sense was not always an issue; several of these plays were neither written nor staged until some time after the original event, and *Arden of*

Faversham, the most notorious example, dramatizes a murder which took place in 1551, while the play seems to have been written nearly forty years later. *A Warning for Fair Women* depicts events of 1573, but the play was not printed till 1599. However, by contrast, *The Witch of Edmonton* (1621) was on stage only a few months after the witch's execution, and Brome and Heywood's *The Late Lancashire Witches* (1634) was seen in London (and an eyewitness account exists) while some of the witches were in prison awaiting their fate.

In most cases the events dramatized had already reached print in some form; clearly the playwrights, or theatrical entrepreneurs such as Henslowe, had already seen the stage and commercial potential of the narratives. The exception is *The Late Lancashire Witches*, and although the story of the trial and the witches' confessions circulated in many forms, nothing had reached print before the play was performed in mid-August 1634. It has been conjectured that the playwrights and the company (the King's Men) may have been accorded privileged access to official depositions by the Privy Council, which wanted the women convicted.[7] A comparison between the prose pamphlets on which *Arden of Faversham*, *A Warning for Fair Women*, *A Yorkshire Tragedy* and *The Witch of Edmonton* were based and the plays themselves is instructive in suggesting how theatrical representation could operate to complicate and add nuance to narratives of crime and punishment, told didactically, as the pamphlets tended to be, so as to point up a clear Christian message and a socially orthodox moral. The source for *A Warning for Fair Women* was a pamphlet called *A Briefe Discourse of the Late Murther*, published anonymously in 1573 by 'A. G.', actually the Puritan writer and translator Arthur Golding. Golding, who had translated the works of Calvin, deliberately sets out to show 'the secret working of Gods terrible wrath in a guiltie and bluddie conscience',[8] with its emphasis on the hearty remorse and penitence of all concerned so that readers will take a lesson for themselves of God's judgement of sinners. But the play, with its twofold style of dramaturgy, alternately realistic and allegorical, is far more complex in its exploration of human motivation.

It was at one time assumed that domestic plays served the same purpose as moral exempla in sermons, following a basic pattern of 'sin, discovery, repentance, punishment, and expectation of divine mercy',[9] and were designed to illuminate God's providential control over human life. This view, set out in Henry Hitch Adams's book, *English Domestic or Homiletic Tragedy, 1575 to 1642*, has been profoundly influential, and does of course draw attention to the place occupied by such plays in the development of a secular drama out of the religious drama of the pre-professional theatre. 'The morality play in its severest form, as a fable of guilt and responsibility followed by retribution'[10] which was on stage in the 1550s and 1560s, is clearly a precursor. But towards the 1990s many critics, particularly those of a feminist persuasion, have found Adams's providentialist readings of the meaning of crime in these plays less than satisfying, and the homiletic formula inadequate as an account of what the plays actually achieve. A secular, historicist reading of this drama in relation to its social and political context in the culture of early modern England can suggest how the plays expose problems and contradictions not only within a providentialist view of human life but also within the patriarchal ideology governing domestic relations. In doing so, they also incidentally reveal how 'the most profound and significant explorations of social and ethical issues are often focussed on a female character',[11] and thus reinforce emphases apparent in other kinds of play, such as the tragedies discussed in chapter 3.

Unlike the tragedies of Webster and Middleton, domestic plays explore the lives of the non-elite social classes. In this way they constituted a new kind of drama in the late sixteenth century, when images in any form of such lives were a novelty, and playwrights were self-conscious about their social, and generic, experimentation. In the epilogue to *Arden of Faversham* Franklin addresses the audience:

> Gentlemen, we hope you'll pardon this naked tragedy
> Wherein no filed points are foisted in
> To make it gracious to the ear or eye;
> For simple truth is gracious enough
> And needs no other points of glozing stuff.
>
> (14–18)[12]

This is not a tragedy in the kind of Senecan high style that the audience might have been expecting, a point made in other plays. In the Induction to *A Warning for Fair Women* Tragedy discusses the claims of Comedy and History to the stage, asserting that it is her turn to 'raigne as Queene' for the day; and although Comedy mockingly characterizes Tragedy as a pretentiously high mode in terms of a 'filthie whining ghost' who 'cries Vindicta, revenge', perhaps reminding the audience of *The Spanish Tragedy* or even the pre-Shakespearean *Hamlet*, Tragedy herself assures them that her style is different, and nearer to home:

> My Sceane is London, native and your owne,
> I sigh to thinke, my subject too well knowne,
> I am not faind.
>
> (95–7)

At the end of the play she reappears to reaffirm the connection between the tragedy of local events and truth, excusing the absence of high drama ('Perhaps it may seeme strange unto you al, / That one hath not revenged anothers death, / After the observation of such course'), and referring to the play as 'this true and home-borne Tragedie'. In similar vein, the Induction to *Two Lamentable Tragedies* introduces Truth, who stresses the fact that one of the play's two crimes was 'done in famous London late', and that 'most here present know this to be true'. These plays are dramatic novelties, distanced from the fashionable forms of stage tragedy, but authenticated by the peculiar contact they have with the lived experience of their audiences, a claim never made for what we now regard as the more conventional kinds of Elizabethan tragedy. One critic has referred to this play as a 'social experiment'[13] in that it takes for its subject a murder committed by a tavern-keeper on a chandler; perhaps Yarrington, a writer about whom no one has been able to discover anything, thought it too risky an undertaking to devote a whole play to the interaction between socially insignificant Londoners, and his other 'lamentable tragedy', thematically related to the Beech murders through motives of avarice and envy, is more conventionally set in Italy and concerns the destruction of a high-born and wealthy family.

Generically, many of these plays are mixed and anomalous. Like *Two Lamentable Tragedies*, *A Warning for Fair Women* falls into two parts, though here because a single narrative is handled in two contrasting modes, the realistic and the symbolic. Both plays intersperse the action with passages of dialogue spoken by the sort of characters who originate in medieval morality plays. *Arden of Faversham* is called a tragedy, but, as has been noticed by one of its editors, the structure is 'closer to that of comedy or tragicomedy than to even the "mixed" tragedy of that period'.[14] *The Witch of Edmonton* has three plot-lines, of which two end tragically in executions, but one has a happy resolution. The action of *The Miseries of Enforced Marriage* appears to be on the verge of tragedy in scene 11, but in the concluding scene 12 the sudden production of an unexpected legacy changes everything. Such dramatic structures are obtrusive, at least to us, and seem to work against any sense that these are narratives following the course of 'real' lives.

Yet the appeal of these plays undoubtedly lay in the fact that they dramatized not only events and localities known to their first audiences, but also a variety of current English social types and professions, from the minor gentry (Alice Arden and her husband in *Arden of Faversham*, the landowning classes such as the Wife and Husband in *A Yorkshire Tragedy* and Sir Arthur Clarington in *The Witch of Edmonton*), merchants and farmers, through tavern-keepers, goldsmiths, painters, household servants of many kinds, down to the socially marginalized like the cutthroats Black Will and Shakebag in *Arden of Faversham* or Mother Sawyer in *The Witch of Edmonton*.

The plays are rooted in the material world of early modern England, and the action is often represented in what has been termed 'grim journalistic detail' reminiscent of the police courts;[15] the low-life careers of Black Will and Shakebag, the courtroom re-enactment in *A Warning for Fair Women*, the hideous onstage murders and even executions in *Two Lamentable Tragedies* exemplify this attention to materiality. Take the following exchange from scene 2 of *Arden of Faversham*. Bradshaw, a goldsmith, but formerly a soldier at Boulogne with Black Will, wants to find out the identity of the man who framed him by bringing stolen plate to sell in his shop: he describes this man to Black Will in graphic language:

> A lean-faced, writhen knave,
> Hawk-nosed and very hollow-eyed,
> With mighty furrows in his stormy brows,
> Long hair down his shoulders curled,
> His chin was bare, but on his upper lip
> A mutchado, which he wound about his ear.
>
> (2.47–52)

Black Will then asks what this distinctive individual was wearing, and the observant Bradshaw replies:

> A watchet satin doublet all to-torn
> (The inner side did bear the greater show),
> A pair of threadbare velvet hose, seam rent,
> A worsted stocking rent above the shoe,
> A livery cloak, but all the lace was off;
> 'Twas bad, but yet it served to hide the plate.
>
> (2.54–9)

Black Will has one further question: 'Sirrah Shakebag, canst thou remember when we trolled the bowl at Sittingburgh where I broke the tapster's head of the Lion with a cudgel-stick?' After which he announces triumphantly, 'Why, it was with the money that plate was sold for', and identifies the culprit as one Jack Fitten, 'now in Newgate for stealing a horse'. Thus, in an economically written scene, the playwright (who has often been identified as Thomas Kyd) conjures up in Dickensian detail the image of the grotesque Jack Fitten with his ruined clothes and ravaged face, still able to outrage respectability with an extravagant moustache, a world of casual crime and violence, and also a social transaction between two old servicemen, one of whom can do the other a favour and demonstrate his own superior knowledge of life at the same time.

Although this may have represented to its first audiences a faithful depiction of the material reality of contemporary low-life, there is nothing documentary about the writing, which is that of a playwright with a truly dramatic imagination and sense of stage characterization. This, with other vignettes of everyday life, such as the little incident with the bookseller's prentice in scene 3, and the conversation-making of the ferryman in scene 11 'buttress the feeling of everyday reality in the play',[16] but also construct a self-consistent stage world. By contrast, the courtroom scenes in *A Warning for Fair Women* savour of official reportage; the clerk's recital of the indictments, the law lords' interrogations, the delivery of the verdicts are all rendered with few dramatic flourishes. This is a kind of documentary drama, like that which at the present day is presented both on television and on the stage: reconstructions of recent events based on court reports, witness statements, contemporary journalism and so on, such as *The Colour of Justice. The Stephen Lawrence Enquiry* (1999), and *Justifying War. Scenes from the Hutton Enquiry* (2003), both first staged at the Tricycle Theatre, London, and described as 'edited' (rather than written) by a journalist, Richard Norton-Taylor. Like the domestic murder plays, these works cater to the desire of the public to understand how the institutions of society operate, and perhaps to question the ideologies which inform these operations. Detail which creates the effect of the minutiae of everyday life is all-important. The detail that George Browne, who has pleaded guilty to murder in *A Warning for Fair Women* and therefore, according to procedures of the time, needed no trial by jury, has a brother also in prison, is handled in a perfunctory way that carries immediate conviction. The Lord Chief Justice simply remarks, 'Wel, two bad brothers, God forgive ye both', to which the chastened Browne duly replies, 'Amen my Lord, and you, and al the world'. His stated wish to be spared the additional humiliation of having his corpse hanged in chains after his death would probably remind the audience that, as all the prose accounts tell us, this wish was not observed. Realistic social detail, of a balder kind, is provided in the stage directions for *Two Lamentable Tragedies*. The brutality of Merry's murder of the harmless chandler Beech is graphically indicated: '*Then being in the upper Rome Merry strickes him in the head fifteene times*', followed by '*Merry wiped his face from blood*' (sig. B4).[17] Subsequently Merry dismembers the body and packs up the parts in separate sacks, one of which is discovered by the Thames watermen, who initially identify it as 'the hang-mans

Budget', carelessly cast aside after execution, but then realize that this can't be the case because 'Bull always strips all quartered traitors quite', and this severed leg still has a hose and shoe. The macabre detail about the hangman's professional habits (Bull was a hangman and executioner operating at the end of the century) has the effect of providing the audience with a bit of insider knowledge. All this happens onstage. Yarrington's appetite for the staging of assaults on the body seems unlimited; at the end of the play Merry and his sister Rachel in turn ascend the scaffold and are hanged in full view of the audience. One is reminded of the fact that public executions took place in London on a large scale at this time, and that they were staged in such a way as to create what has been termed 'a theatre of punishment'.[18] The hangman then orders,

> Cut downe their bodies, give hers funeral,
> But let his body be conveyed hence,
> To Mile-end greene, and there be hang'd in chaines.
>
> (sig. K2v)

Despite the horrific aspect of all this violence, there is a certain lack of sensationalism about the manner of its dramatization. Yarrington is simply presenting a series of recent events which contemporaries found particularly newsworthy, to judge from the fact that a pamphlet, five ballads and at least one other play (all lost) were also written about them; he is catering to a desire for news, and perhaps also to the tastes of those who would turn up to witness such executions. These were distinctive features of cultural life in the period. Domestic murder plays, like public executions, might function to reinforce in the minds of witnesses to the spectacle both Christian ideology and also the distinction between the legitimate violence exercised by the state and the illegitimate violence of the criminal.

Beneath this high level of realistically depicted contemporary life in its more exceptional aspects, a range of broad social issues is explored. These domestic plays deal with the everyday problems raised for early modern English people by class, rank and status, marriage and domestic life, gender relationships, money and its management, threats to stability in the form of the criminal underclass, vagrants, malcontents and social outcasts of many kinds, as well as the disruption of established institutions and hierarchies by social mobility. The plays are rooted in everyday life through their insistence on the local. Two of them, *A Warning for Fair Women* and *Two Lamentable Tragedies*, are plays of London life, and the writers draw audiences into the narrative with references to familiar street names and areas that relate the action to the audience's understanding of the geography of their own lives. In *A Warning for Fair Women* George Browne questions Anne Drury for information about her neighbour Anne Sanders, with whom he has fallen in love:

> *Browne*: But where's her house?
> *Drury*: Against *Saint Dunstones* church.
> *Browne*: *Saint Dunstones* in Fleetstreete?
> *Drury*: No, neere Billingsgate,
>   *Saint Dunstones* in the East, thats in the West.
>
>   (302–5)

At several points the action is carefully localized, as when Drury's servant Roger describes how he has stalked George Sanders, following his movements from his house to the Cornhill, then on to the Burse (the Royal Exchange), and after lunch to Lion Quay and by boat down river to Greenwich, so that Browne can be waiting at Lion Quay for Sanders's return in order to murder him there. In the Induction to *Two Lamentable Tragedies*, Truth promises to tell of the crime 'done in famous London late,/ Within that streete whose side the river Thames/ Doth strive to wash from all impuritie' (sig. A3). The Thames-side location becomes significant later on, when Merry has dismembered Beech's corpse and intends to take parts of it by boat to Paris-Garden, on the south bank, and throw it into the ditch there; he plans for the rest to be disposed of 'in some dark place nere to Barnardes castle'. But in both cases the body parts are retrieved, and traced back to Merry's house. The factuality that is intrinsic to the appeal of much present-day crime fiction is evident here. *Arden of Faversham* and *The Witch of Edmonton* are full of references to their rural settings; the place names help to establish the plays in the contemporary material world, as well as serving other dramatic functions, such as the creation of atmosphere, the evocation of certain aspects of rural life and, in the case of *Arden of Faversham*, developing the play's pervasive irony, since much is made of the fact that Arden's corpse is deposited behind the Abbey of Faversham, on land to which his rights of ownership were disputed. Franklin's recital in the Epilogue of the fates of those involved in the crime achieves its journalistic effect partly through the use of place names:

> Thus have you seen the truth of Arden's death.
> As for the ruffians, Shakebag and Black Will,
> The one took sanctuary and being sent for out

5 Woodcut from the title page of the 1633 edition of *Arden of Faversham*.

Was murdered in Southwark as he passed
To Greenwich where the Lord Protector lay.
Black Will was burnt in Flushing on a stage.
Greene was hanged at Osbridge in Kent.

(1–70)

The newsworthiness of these plays is an evident aspect of their appeal, especially in a period when the non-elite had little access to images of their own lives. Although the focus of the action is on a crime or other exceptional events, the depiction of contemporary English society was essentially one in which such audiences might see themselves mirrored.

Lena Cowen Orlin calls domestic plays 'chief witnesses to the struggle of early modern men and women to fix their relationships with family members and household fellows and to impose a logic on their immediate environment'.[19] Of the social interactions explored in them, marriage, the family and the life of the household are central, and relationships were certainly the site of many kinds of struggle. Many historians have characterized the period as one of 'special ferment' in gender relationships, extending even to a kind of crisis of order, which some feminist critics have identified particularly in domestic tragedy.[20] Alice Arden's iconoclastic attitude to her marriage vows – 'Love is a god, and marriage is but words' – is not typical of the broader representation of marriage, but marriage is commonly a fraught subject. In *A Warning for Fair Women* Anne Sanders's dilemma when she discovers herself without sufficient cash to pay the tradesmen typifies the problem of situating the wife's role within the structure of the early modern Protestant family. Marriage was commonly regarded as hierarchical, with the husband as the head and the wife as the body, or the husband as ruler and the wife and family as his commonwealth; but, according to the Puritan-influenced domestic conduct books then current, it was, or ought to be, a partnership. How this contradiction might compromise a woman's authority within the household is illustrated in scene 4, when Anne needs ready money to pay the draper and milliner who have brought goods to her house, and finds that her husband has temporarily commandeered all the household cash to meet his own commercial transactions. Sanders has no doubt that his needs take precedence, although, as his servants point out, Anne has already requested the cash.

> *Man*: What shall I say unto my mistres, sir?
>   She bad me tell out thirtie pounds even now,
>   She meant to have bestowed on linen cloath.
> *Sanders*: She must deferre her market till tomorrow,
>   I know no other shift: my great affaires
>   Must not be hindred by such trifling wares.
>   (574–9)

When the servant denies Anne the money she asks for in the presence of the tradesman, she is humiliated:

> I am a woman, and in that respect,
> Am well content my husband shal controule me,
> But that my man should over-awe me too,
> And in the sight of strangers, mistris *Drurie*,
> I tell you true, do's grieve me to the heart.
>   (655–9)

The moment of resentment is not developed into domestic rebellion, but it does provide an opportunity for the wily Anne Drury, acting as George Browne's agent, to exploit the fissure in the smooth surface of the Sanders' marriage revealed by the incident, and it also discloses the contradictions inherent in the contemporary ideology of marriage.

How family bonds and obligations impinge especially on women is explored in *Two Lamentable Tragedies*, when Rachel Merry is drawn in as an accomplice to her brother's murderous activities and eventually pays the ultimate price for her loyalty to him. Although Rachel is horrified by the discovery of her brother's crimes, in the perpetration of which she plays no part at all, she never contemplates betraying him. As an unmarried woman her only home is his house, and she owes him loyalty both as kinswoman and (through her sex) as his social inferior, and her sense of duty overcomes her moral dismay:

> I am your sister, though a silly Maide
> Ile be your true and faithfull comforter.
>
> (sig. D2v)

So she helps clean up the house after the murders, and dispose of the bodies; later she restates this moral stance in stronger terms:

> Let others open what I doe conceale,
> Lo he is my brother, I will cover it,
> And rather dye then have it spoken rife,
> Lo where she goes, betrai'd her brothers life.
>
> (sig. F4)

When she goes to the scaffold as an accessory at the end of the play, the unfairness of her punishment is implicitly stressed; not only does Merry himself reiterate her innocence but Truth points out how Rachel is penalized by the fact of her gender. Williams, Merry's manservant, is convicted along with Rachel, but as a man is allowed to claim benefit of clergy, whereby, for a correct recital of his 'neck-verse', he can be punished by branding rather than execution. But, as Truth points out,

> . . . wretched Rachels sexe denies that grace,
> And therefore dooth receive a doome of death
> To dye with him, whose sinnes she did conceale.
>
> (sig. I2v)

In her scaffold speech Rachel gives the play's message, that loyalty to masters or brothers should not outweigh one's duty to God and the truth, but the play's dramatization of the dilemma created by conflicting loyalties acknowledges the tragic potential of the situation, rather than acceding to simple didacticism.

The constrictions of the family as an institution impact on men as well as women, though the ways in which they are explored are very different. Enforced marriage is explicitly a theme in George Wilkins's play, *The Miseries of Enforced Marriage*, and *The Witch of Edmonton*, and perhaps underlies the situation in *A Yorkshire Tragedy*. In each case, individual autonomy is at odds with social pressure, and the opposition is irreconcilable. In *The Witch of Edmonton* a complex situation of social dependency and exploitation is the setting for a tragic outcome. In one of the play's two fictional strands, Frank Thorney, son of an impoverished gentleman, agrees under pressure from his father to marry Susan Carter, the daughter of a wealthy yeoman; the Thorneys' lack of money is offset in Old Carter's eyes by their superior social status, while Carter's money will help the status-conscious Thorneys regain the title to their land and also provide Frank with an inheritance. Frank, however, has already secretly married Winifred, with the inducement of a portion of two hundred pounds from their joint employer, Sir Arthur Clarington, who, unbeknownst to Frank, has made Winifred pregnant and needs to be rid of her. Having then also married Susan the feckless Frank plans to desert her, using her dowry to abscond with Winifred; but the devil, in the shape of the Dog whose major role in the play is that of the Witch of Edmonton's familiar, tempts him to take what seems an easy way out, and he puts an end to his bigamous condition by murdering Susan. The strength of social pressure on Frank Thorney is implicitly acknowledged when he is driven to the desperate recourse of murder to dispose of his unwanted wife. 'The poisoned leeches twist about my heart' (2.2.117), as he puts it. At the end, as he goes to his execution, he simplifies the situation, blaming his fate on greed:

> O that my example
> Might teach the world hereafter what a curse
> Hangs on their heads who rather choose to marry
> A goodly portion, than a dower of virtues!
> (5.3.107–10)

But this formulaic didacticism occludes the complications that have arisen from Frank's emotional attachment to Winifred, his first wife, and the play's exploration of how social and financial inequalities impact on individual freedom is more nuanced than Frank's scaffold speech suggests. His choice was much less straightforward; Winifred was not the conventional poor but honest woman implied in 'a dower of virtues', but a woman already pregnant with another man's child; Frank's marriage to Susan was undertaken because of his father's moral blackmail rather than his own desire for her money, and facilitated by a self-serving lie about Winifred from Sir Arthur Clarington. The play fully recognizes the complexity of the network of duties and obligations from which society is constructed.

Family bonds are also the tragic subject of *The Miseries of Enforced Marriage* (1607) by George Wilkins, a curious play which originates from the same real-life events as *A Yorkshire Tragedy* but uses them to completely different effect, by deliberately fictionalizing, and generically reorganizing, the story. The horrific events that took place in Yorkshire in 1605, when Walter Calverley, a young but debt-ridden gentleman of good family, killed his wife and two of his children and also attempted suicide in an apparently inexplicable frenzy of rage, became the subject of two pamphlets and a ballad, though only one pamphlet, *Two Most Unnatural and Bloodie Murthers* (1605), survives. The anonymous play, *A Yorkshire Tragedy*, performed by the King's Men and ascribed on its title page to Shakespeare, was printed in 1608, but almost certainly written soon after the murders took place (and not by Shakespeare), before the outcome of Walter Calverley's trial was known. Even here, the main characters are not given proper names, but this apparent attempt at severing the play from its real-life origins (perhaps because of feared objections from the influential families involved) is countered by the insistence on the title page that it is 'Not so New as Lamentable and true'. In *The Miseries of Enforced Marriage* Wilkins renames the main characters and invents new characters and new incidents, so that what was in the earlier play and the pamphlet a tragic narrative of a wild husband and the destruction of a family becomes a tragicomic fantasy about a prodigal who is saved from disaster at the last minute by an unexpected legacy. As in *The Witch of Edmonton*, a somewhat irresponsible young man, Young Scarborow, commits himself to one woman, Clare Harcop, and is then pressurized into marrying another. But the social milieu of the characters is much removed from that of *The Witch of Edmonton*, more gentrified, more urban and specified in much less detail. This is, in a sense, a journalistic play but at one remove. Scarborow, is, as his friend Sir Francis Ilford calls him, 'a little Villaine of fifteene hundred a yeare' (51),[21] but he is also under age and therefore bound to do as his guardian, Lord Falconbridge, requires. The system of wardship in this period was notoriously open to abuse; young fatherless heirs and heiresses who were made wards of court commonly had their marriages arranged for them by their guardians, who had purchased the wardships from the crown, with an eye to financial advantage rather than the feelings of the young people concerned, the practice satirized by Middleton in *Women Beware Women*.[22] Falconbridge, ostensibly to keep Scarborow on the straight and narrow when he goes to live in London, but obviously in the interest of his own family's fortunes and with the connivance of Scarborow's uncle, marries him off to his niece Katherine. When Scarborow tries to back out on the grounds of a pre-contract to Clare, Falconbridge threatens to despoil his lands in Yorkshire, withhold his rightful monies and even marry him to a chambermaid. The tragic consequences of the enforced marriage rebound initially on the abandoned Clare. Believing herself socially and morally compromised, and as Scarborow's 'Troth-plight wife' not free to marry anyone else, she commits suicide. As with Rachel Merry, the problematic situation of the unmarried dependent woman in a society organized for the benefit of men is briefly glanced at. When he learns of Clare's suicide Scarborow is filled with despair, rejects Katherine and the children born to her and returns to London to live as a prodigal, squandering the fortune he has come into through his marriage: 'All ryot now, since that my soules so blacke'.

Like Frank Thorney, Scarborow believes himself damned and behaves accordingly, and the grimness of the account of the consequences of forced marriage is hardly mitigated by the clapped-up ending whereby Falconbridge dies and leaves his fortune to Scarborow in penitence for the havoc he has caused. In *A Yorkshire Tragedy*, the anonymous playwright depicts the prodigal career of an unnamed Yorkshire gentleman, who squanders his inheritance, rejects his wife, and kills her and two of his children, intent on wiping out his whole family rather than live in beggary. The pamphlet source provides some material motivation for this grotesque behaviour, in that Calverley was apparently obliged (like Scarborow) to marry his guardian's niece despite being betrothed elsewhere. But the enforced marriage is suppressed in the play, and the Husband's violent and bloodthirsty conduct, incomprehensible to all around him, is ascribed, for lack of much other explanation, to demonic possession. In the last scene, the Husband, as suddenly penitent as he became violent, observes, 'Now glides the devil from me,/ Departs at every joint, heaves up my nails' (7.18–19), a remark which a Jacobean audience would probably have taken literally. When the Husband sees the bodies of his children, one a baby, that he has killed, he exclaims, 'O 'twas the enemy my eyes so bleared!' (8.47). But the Husband's tumultuous and uncontrollable feelings have some social and material basis too, although the play is so short (it seems not to have been intended as a full-length tragedy) and its exploration of situation and motivation so schematic and perfunctory that this is barely sketched in. His horror at the thought of the poverty and social disgrace to which his prodigal spending has reduced his family is partly conditioned by aristocratic pride:

> Now must my eldest son be a knave or nothing; he cannot live upo'the fool [live as a prodigal], for he will have no land to maintain him. That mortgage sits like a snaffle upon mine inheritance and makes me chew upon iron. My second son must be a promoter, and my third a thief, or an underputter, a slave pander. (2.46–50)[23]

He cannot contemplate a life without the gentlemanly style and status conferred by inherited wealth: 'Shall it be said in all societies/ That I broke custom, that I flagg'd in [borrowed] money?' In broad terms, his attitudes reflect the gentry ethos which Stone analyses in *The Crisis of the Aristocracy*,

6 Woodcut from the title page of the 1658 edition of *The Witch of Edmonton*, by Dekker, Rowley and Ford.

and the higher values attached to financial independence acquired through land ownership and inheritance rather than any kind of employment. In fact, Walter Calverley, although from a very old landed family, had married well above himself, to Phillipa Brooke, an heiress and aristocrat related to the Cecils, and there were probably tensions within the marriage arising from the wife's independently wealthy status which contributed to Walter Calverley's violent response to the prospect of his own financial disgrace. Although the Brooke/Cecil connection is completely expunged from both pamphlet and play, public knowledge of it may have increased the play's sensational appeal.

Issues of class and status are prominent in other domestic plays, although not treated at such a high social level. In *The Witch of Edmonton* and *The Miseries of Enforced Marriage* they are intrinsic to the financial basis on which the marriages are arranged. In *Arden of Faversham*, too, class and status interact unfortunately with marriage, although the situation here is very different. The social tensions which are suppressed in *A Yorkshire Tragedy* are foregrounded in this play. Alice Arden is a woman of higher rank than her husband (in reality, a step-daughter of Lord North, who was a member of parliament and of the Privy Council), a fact known to all in the play, which not only puts Arden in a position of dependency to her but allows her to present herself as undervalued by an ungrateful husband. Greene, a man wronged by Arden who has procured abbey lands that Greene regards as his own entitlement, is all too ready to see Alice in this light:

> Why, Mistress Arden, can the crabbed churl
> Use you unkindly? Respects he not your birth,
> Your honourable friends, nor what you brought?
> Why, all Kent knows your parentage and what you are.
> (1.488–91)

On the other hand, Alice's lover Mosby is a low-born man, a tailor, or, as Arden and his friend Franklin call him, a 'botcher', who has risen in the world and now presents himself with the accoutrements of a status to which the jealous Arden feels he has no right, wearing a silken gown and carrying a sword, which was only permitted by Sumptuary Law to men of a certain rank. Arden accuses Mosby of social climbing, and taunts him with his mean origins:

> Why, what art thou but a velvet drudge,
> A cheating steward, and base-minded peasant?
> (1.322–3)

He takes away Mosby's sword and mockingly tells him instead to 'use your bodkin,/ Your Spanish needle, and your pressing iron' (1.312–13), a taunt which Mosby recalls when he has dealt Arden the first of many death blows: 'There's for the pressing iron you told me of' (14.241). That the cuckolded and sexually insecure husband should try to downgrade his rival socially is only to be expected; but the triangular situation is given extra piquancy by the fact that Alice too uses Mosby's low-class background against him in their lovers' quarrels. In a manner typical of her capricious and power-seeking behaviour, she accuses Mosby of stealing her good name and substituting his own for it:

> Even in my forehead is thy name engraven,
> A mean artificer, that low-born name.
> (8.76–7)

But a moment later, she is trying to win him round by praising his intelligence and social manners. He responds bitterly:

O no, I am a base artificer,
My wings are feather'd for a lowly flight.
Mosby? Fie, no! not for a thousand pound.
Make love to you? Why, 'tis unpardonable;
We beggars must not breathe where gentles are.

                              (8.135–9)

This pervasive class-consciousness in *Arden of Faversham* specifically illuminates the scandal of Alice's behaviour, and helps to explain the almost totemic stature she was to acquire as a husband-murderer,[24] but also thickens the social texture of the play. Only *The Witch of Edmonton* matches it in this respect.

The two plays also have in common that what they are centrally concerned to represent is the nature of certain threats posed to stability and community in contemporary society. Alice's behaviour is one such threat, and so too is Mosby's behaviour as an upstart, trespassing on the prerogatives of the better-born. Arden, keen to present himself as 'by birth a gentleman of blood', has enemies, several of whom, such as Greene and Richard Reede, believe themselves wronged by his greed for land. Franklin states in the Epilogue that

> Arden lay murder'd in that plot of ground
> Which he by force and violence held from Reede.
>
>   (10–11)

Such property disputes would have had considerable resonance in the minds of an audience to whom the consequences of the dissolution of the monasteries and the rapid rise to power of unscrupulous men who gained possession of monastery lands were no distant memory. And Arden's greed seems to sanction the disrespect for law exhibited by people at many different social levels in the play, from Greene, ready to hire 'some cutter' to do away with Arden, to Black Will, who will kill anyone, anywhere, for twenty angels: 'Give me the money, and I'll stab him as he stands pissing against a wall, but I'll kill him' (2.97–8). Nearer home, even Arden's servants, Michael and Susan, feel no loyalty towards their master, and collude in the plot against him to serve their own interests.

In *The Witch of Edmonton* the idea of community and how society works is more fully fleshed out, in positive as well as negative terms. Community, neighbourliness and reputation are all interwoven within the kinds of society depicted in these plays; and the plays show how the bonds, ties, duties and obligations from which the social fabric is created are dangerously subject to fracture. The playwrights' source material for *The Witch of Edmonton*, a pamphlet by Henry Goodcole, *The Wonderfull discoverie of Elizabeth Sawyer, a Witch* (1621), which appeared less than a month after Elizabeth Sawyer was hanged, is integrated into a three-plot play, with fictional action concerning the forced marriage already discussed. Unlike *Arden of Faversham*, this play attempts a definitive closure, whereby the bonds of society, damaged by anti-social acts such as vow-breaking and deception as well as by supernatural intervention, are reinforced, by the execution of the miscreants, Frank Thorney and Mother Sawyer (as she is called here), the disempowerment of the diabolic Dog, and also by acts of social restitution. Winifred, repentant over her misconduct, is accepted as a daughter by Frank Thorney's father, and forgiven by Susan Carter's father, while the dissolute Sir Arthur Clarington pays 1,000 marks to Winifred for wronging her. Her response that it is 'too great a sum to be employed/ Upon my funeral' perhaps implies that class privilege may substantiate social reparation, but will not atone for moral wrong.

The play does not polarize community against the isolated individual in terms of the good and socially acceptable and its reverse, and community is not without its negative aspects; in the Frank Thorney plot the enforced marriage comes into being largely to satisfy social requirements, duty to the father and the preservation of family and status. In the Mother Sawyer plot her first speech, a highly dramatic soliloquy, openly recognizes the formative role of society in the construction of witchcraft:

> And why on me? Why should the envious world
> Throw all their scandalous malice upon me?
> 'Cause I am poor, deform'd, and ignorant,
> And like a bow buckled and bent together
> By some more strong in mischief than myself?
> Must I for that be made a common sink
> For all the filth and rubbish of men's tongues
> To fall and run into? Some call me witch,
> And being ignorant of myself, they go
> About to teach me how to be one.
> (2.1.1–10)[25]

The immediate appearance of her chief adversary, Old Banks, a superstitious and curmudgeonly local farmer, chasing her off his land with the words, 'Out, out upon thee, witch', confirms all that she has been saying, and it is not surprising that she is soon seeking means to transform herself into the alarming creature Banks assumes her to be. Banks foments local hysteria against Mother Sawyer, blaming her for all manner of problems and accidents in the community, and encouraging the country people to set fire to her thatch to flush her out. A Justice of the Peace intervenes to protect her from mob violence and to point out the absurdity of the thatch-burning practice:

> Come, come; firing her thatch? Ridiculous:
> Take heed sirs what you do.
> Unless your proofs come better arm'd
> Instead of turning her into a witch,
> You'll prove yourselves stark fools.
>
> (4.1.40–4)

But although the play suggests that it is social and cultural practices which turn Mother Sawyer into a witch, and thus empower her in ways otherwise denied to her by her poverty and low status in the community, it does not support the idea that witchcraft itself is a cultural fabrication. The sinister figure of the Dog, who first appears when Mother Sawyer is cursing and makes a pact to help her be revenged against those who have harmed her, and who also induces Frank Thorney to murder Susan, is no hallucination. He appears also to Old Banks's son, Cuddy, though Cuddy is too innocent to recognize him as the devil, and he creates havoc during the morris dance, which symbolizes country solidarity. His intervention in Mother Sawyer's life shifts her witchcraft from its material basis to one in the occult, thus mystifying the play's exploration of the structures of life in this rural community.

The Late Lancashire Witches, in more comic vein, also depicts witchcraft as a threat to community values, particularly those of domestic order and patriarchal society. In the bewitched household of Old Squire Seely, the world has turned upside down; children overrule parents, and servants dominate masters. The society of rural gentlemen finds its traditional pastimes such as hunting endangered and its order destabilized by the unruly behaviour of the witches, who are of course all women. They pose a direct threat to masculinity. A newly married man, Lawrence, is rendered impotent by the witch Mall, his former lover. Another witch, Peg, admits to regular sex with the devil, who pleased her well, 'only his flesh felt cold' (2756).[26] The chief witch is Mrs Generous, the wife of Squire Generous, a gentry landowner and the most socially eminent member of the community; one of her tricks is to make three of the gentlemen believe themselves to be bastards, thus striking at the heart of the patriarchal family. More importantly, her involvement in witchcraft constitutes a betrayal of her husband, which is represented in semi-tragic terms. And although when found out she promises to repent and 'beg a generous Pardon' from heaven, she subsequently reneges on this, telling the other women that she is 'once and ever/ A Witch' (2049–50). According to the one contemporary spectator's testament that has survived, *The Late Lancashire Witches* was regarded as 'a merry and excellent new play',[27] and certainly much of the witchcraft is presented through comic spectacle; but witchcraft is also a diabolic, and criminal, practice, creating not only havoc in society but also imperilling souls. Although the final verdict on the real-life witches was evidently not known when the play was written, the assumption of the countryfolk at the end is that the witches, once arrested, wait in expectation of the gallows.

With the exception of *The Miseries of Enforced Marriage* and *The Late Lancashire Witches* all these plays are tragic, and they deal both with anti-social behaviours and also with sin. Even if they are not so simply moralistic in their accounts of crime and punishments as the pamphlet sources on which most of them are based, they still speak to us of a society with a strongly Calvinistic climate of thought, with an emphasis on human weakness and the propensity to sin. Crime and sin were not clearly differentiated; in such a world the devil was a real and active presence, and his temptations, as in *A Yorkshire Tragedy* and the witchcraft plays, destroy both social harmony and human souls. Personified sins, like Lust and Avarice, who appear in *A Warning for Fair Women* and *Two Lamentable Tragedies*, testify to the vitality of a religious view of human motivation. Thomas Merry, in *Two Lamentable Tragedies*, is recognizably a tavern-keeper of early modern London, with the sort of tradesman's worries over money and petty competitiveness with his shopkeeper neighbour that would easily be recognizable to an audience from the non-elite classes. The soliloquy in which he plans the murder of Beech traces his thought processes step by step, and convinces us as the expression of a grounded subjectivity; but at the same time it is as if the personification of Envy were speaking through him. In *A Warning for Fair Women* Anne Drury, Anne Sanders's neighbour, is richly characterized as a social type, the dangerous widow, a woman of independent financial means possessed of many talents, including 'a sweete tongue, as wil supple a stone' (259–60), a 'pretty' ability in surgery and 'matchlesse skil in palmestrie' (692); but, as the agent of Anne Sanders's moral downfall she is also 'that wicked *Drurie*, the accursed fiend,/ That thrusts her forward to destruction' (824–5). Plays like these, primarily designed to exploit items of sensational topical news, derived much of their appeal from the ways in which they staged and anatomized contemporary society in its material forms. They also demonstrate how important it was to contemporaries that through the mundane activities of early modern men and women in England, people like themselves, the operations of God's providence might be discerned.

5

History Plays

Many recent discussions of the history play in early modern England have taken off from a polarization between those written by Shakespeare and the rest, developed in an influential book on English nationhood in the period by Richard Helgerson, *Forms of Nationhood: The Elizabethan Writing of England* (1992). Helgerson's view is that Shakespeare's history plays foregrounded the interests of the king and the nobility over those of the commons to the extent of creating a royalist bias and thus giving a broadly negative account of popular concerns, particularly those resulting in rebellion against the monarchy. This has positioned Shakespeare in a way that is often seen as unattractively conservative and exclusionary. Concomitantly, the other writers of history plays, such as Peele, Chettle, Dekker and Heywood, who wrote for companies other than the Lord Chamberlain's (or King's) Men, are contrasted to Shakespeare in being more populist and socially inclusive in their representation of the English past. According to this view, Shakespeare treats history as being created by great men, to whose activities those of the common people serve as a backdrop, whereas the non-Shakespearean playwrights are more concerned to explore the 'body of England' as composed of diverse social groups with meaningful interests of their own. Is the nation to be identified with the king or with the people? It is a question to which the plays give different answers.

It cannot be denied that Shakespeare's achievements in the history play have tended to overshadow those of other dramatists, and also that in their own time they 'helped call into being' the whole category of the history play,[1] not then an established dramatic genre like comedy and tragedy. Helgerson's account of Shakespeare has been challenged and modified, but it has set the terms of a still-current debate, as to whose voices are heard and whose excluded, and where the centre of interest lies, in those plays in which early modern playwrights explored their nation's past. Not all plays on historical subjects focus on English history as such; plays such as Marlowe's *The Massacre at Paris*, the anonymous *An Alarum for London* and the French histories of George Chapman in the early seventeenth century are evidence of what has been termed 'the cosmopolitan character of early modern English drama',[2] and certainly English playwrights were interested in exploring the highly topical subject of England's relations with neighbours on mainland Europe. But since my concern here is with history plays about the history of England, although Marlowe's play is discussed in this chapter, a discussion of most of the others will appear elsewhere.

This chapter is largely devoted to non-Shakespearean history plays to which some Shakespeare histories form a counterpoint; our familiarity with them often proves a starting point or baseline from which to examine the nature of different sorts of achievement in this mode. Undoubtedly, Shakespeare's histories gave a vital impetus to the spate of plays relating to national affairs that were produced in the wake of the Armada of 1588. Nashe's comment on the joy 'brave Talbot' would have experienced to see his exploits celebrated in *Henry VI, Part 1* is well known. For him this play, of which he was probably part-author, proved the value of the stage against its detractors by demonstrating how, by preserving the memory of past English heroes, it inspired audiences to feelings of patriotism and loyalty to the crown. *Henry V*, the last of Shakespeare's 1590s histories, is one of the seminal texts of nation-building of its age. The 1590s are, properly, regarded as the most important decade for the history play, in which the whole subject of the English past became dramatically fashionable and what has been styled an 'explosion' of such plays took place,[3] but, as the lists of history plays given in critical accounts such as Irving Ribner's dated but still valuable study, *The English History Play in the Age of Shakespeare*, and Benjamin Griffin's more recent *Playing the Past. Approaches to English Historical Drama 1385–1600* will show, there were plays written on subjects from English history both before and after this decade. Those of the very end of the decade and first years of the seventeenth century, such as Heywood's two-part *Edward IV* and *If You Know Not Me, You Know Nobody*, the anonymous *Thomas Lord Cromwell*, Dekker and Webster's *Sir Thomas Wyatt* and Dekker's *The Whore of Babylon* (some of these discussed elsewhere), form a coherent group, reflecting on the Tudor regime and Elizabeth's part in it in new ways, and demonstrating emphatically that the tradition of the English chronicle play was not yet exhausted. But it is the case that, with some few important exceptions, such as Shakespeare's *Henry VIII*, and Ford's *Perkin Warbeck*, plays about English historical subjects lapsed markedly in popularity after about 1608. Some critics have felt that this was because too great a gap had opened up between historiography as the study of facts and public events and drama as 'ahistorical, private, outside time'.[4] Exceptions to this broad distinction can be made, like Chapman's French history plays or Fletcher and Massinger's *Sir John van Olden Barnavelt* (1619), which was set in the Netherlands, although it concerned events which impinged on English political interests. But the fact remains that the English history play as such was a genre which the most prolific and influential playwrights of the early Stuart era like Fletcher and Massinger did not touch.

Although the history play was not a traditional genre, and indeed many histories share strong generic affinities with either tragedy or comedy, the fact that the compilers of Shakespeare's First Folio separated 'history' as a category in its own right acknowledges the history play's existence as such, at least in the 1620s. But what constitutes a 'history' play? Even when confining one's attention to plays about the English past there is confusion. Ribner's list includes such plays as Dekker's *The Shoemakers' Holiday*, the anonymous *The Fair Maid of Bristowe* and Shakespeare's *Cymbeline*, which may sound very little like history to any modern reader of the drama of this period, as well as *King Lear* and *Macbeth*, whose titles suggest history, but which we would be more likely to categorize differently. 'History' itself was an ambiguous term, signifying both the textual record, and the past events recorded. In the absence of any clear indication (other than the First Folio) of what early modern readers and audiences would have considered to be real 'history' plays, it seems most useful here to restrict attention to plays which treat historical events as of interest and significance in their own right, and not as the background to invented subjects. It is pointless to be prescriptive about degrees of historical accuracy: although Elizabethan history plays are nearly always based on historical chronicles, such as Edward Hall's *The Union of the two Noble and Illustre Famelies of Lancastre and York* (1548) or Holinshed's *Chronicles of England, Scotland and Ireland*, which came out in a second edition in 1587, adherence to facts and to chronological sequence is invariably subordinate to other kinds of dramatic purpose, and the chronicles themselves were by no means history in any modern sense.[5] Holinshed's *Chronicles* of 1587 have been referred to as 'something of a last gasp' of the old-style chronicle history, then being superseded by 'a more sceptical antiquarianism'[6] from writers such as John Stow and also by the 'politic history'[7] of Tacitus, so significant an influence on Jonson's *Sejanus*.

For the Elizabethans plays of national history could serve a number of purposes in depicting exciting events from the past: crises such as wars, usurpations, domestic rebellions and uprisings, changes of monarchy, civil dissention and feuding, invasions and foreign threats. Such episodes were generally chosen both because they were significant in their own right, and also because they could reveal troubling implications for contemporary audiences. These plays might warn, teach lessons, celebrate victories, or demonstrate God's providential design for the English people. Equally, they might demystify such notions as the sacredness of royal power, the naturalness of hierarchy and succession or the operations of providence. They might speak for the forces of law as marshalled by, and in the interests of, the ruling classes, but many are capable of being read more subversively, as posing awkward questions about the relations of subject and monarch, and the origins of state power. Dominique Goy-Blanquet expresses the significance of historical writing in this period well by calling it 'a double-edged weapon, as dangerous as it was powerful'.[8] History plays might pose questions which would force audiences to think for themselves:

> What subject can give sentence on his King?
> And who sits here that is not Richard's subject?
> (*Richard II*, 4.1.121–2)

This is a highly charged question for audiences in the later 1590s, when the Queen's judgement was being challenged by some of her influential subjects. The play itself gives no direct answer, and the same question was rephrased in Massinger's *The Roman Actor* (1626); 'Who can sit/ A competent judge o'er Caesar?', asks the Emperor himself. His answer is, 'Caesar by Caesar's sentenc'd'.

History was valued by humanist educationalists as a teaching tool and a source of moral lessons; Sir Thomas Elyot in *The Boke Named the Governor* (1531) was typical in the terms in which he stressed its value: 'Surely if a noble man do thus seriously and diligently rede histories I dare affirm there is no study or science for him of equal commoditie and pleasure, havynge regarde to every tyme and age.'[9] The writing of history, historiography, is commonly regarded as a conservative genre, in which 'obedience, duty, and deference to social and political hierarchy' are the predominant values.[10] And scholars view the history play as aiming 'to achieve the authentic purposes of renaissance historiography'.[11] But this is not to say that this is the lesson which contemporary readers and, especially, theatre audiences, invariably drew from representations of the past. There is no doubt that such representations could also be interpreted more subversively, as a source of analogies to contemporary events and those people involved in them, and the potential dangers of this practice were widely recognized. Sir John Hayward's *Life and Reign of Henry IV* (1599), dedicated to the Earl of Essex, was ordered to be burnt and its author thrown into prison on suspicion that through his account of the usurpation of Richard II he was commenting on present times; the book was brought up as evidence at Essex's trial for treason. 'Application is now grown a trade with many', wrote Jonson in the Epistle to *Volpone* (1606), disingenuously trying to clear himself from the imputation of intending personal satire; his experience with *Sejanus*, which had landed him in front of the Privy Council, taught him at first hand the perils of interpretation (or misinterpretation).

David Bevington's view that the English history play was 'just coming into being'[12] after the Armada victory is justified, and many, though not all, of the history plays of the 1590s respond to this critical moment in the life of the nation. The assertion of English sovereignty in the near-triumphalist words of the Bastard Falconbridge at the end of Shakespeare's *King John* (?1596) represents one such response:

> This England never did, nor never shall,
> Lie at the proud foot of a conqueror
> But when it first did help to wound itself.
> . . . Naught shall make us rue
> If England to itself do rest but true.
>   (5.7.112–14, 117–18)

Falconbridge, who is the illegitimate son of Richard Coeur de Lion, and thus isolated from the 'corrupt and empty shell of monarchy'[13] represented by the weak and hypocritical King John, is allowed in this play to speak for England as the 'very spirit of Plantagenet' (1.1.167), although he can be only a 'temporary guardian of legitimate values'[14] because of his birth. The play raises important questions about legitimacy, John's claim to the throne being distinctly shaky, which would have been significant in the 1590s, when Queen Elizabeth's own claims to the throne were still debated against those of the Catholic Mary Queen of Scots, whom she had had executed less than ten years earlier. Anachronistically, the play makes both John and Falconbridge proto-Protestant champions of an English church against the church of Rome, although it is much less militant in this respect than the anonymous play, *The Troublesome Reign of John, King of England* (published 1591), which was probably its main source. The 1590s were a crucial decade for defining England's identity as a Protestant nation-state.

Marlowe's *The Massacre at Paris* (1593) also contributes to this definition, in exploiting the current of anti-Catholic fever that characterized the popular theatre at this time, and using French history to do so, though in this case without anachronism. It was in fact one of the first plays to present very recent political events on the stage.[15] Its subject is the massacre of the Huguenots by the ruling Catholic Guise family in 1572, immediately following the marriage of the Catholic princess Marguerite to the Protestant Henry of Navarre, and its aftermath. It ends with the death of King Henry III, which happened in 1589, very close to the time of the play's composition and the succession of Henry of Navarre as Henry IV. Although Marlowe never knew it, Henry was soon to abjure his Protestant faith, converting to Catholicism in 1593 with the legendary remark, 'Paris vaut bien une messe', and the evident instability in the condition of the monarchy in a country never regarded as a reliable ally of England sits well with Marlowe's disenchanted view of power in the play. Although *The Massacre at Paris* has come down to us in a corrupted form, probably about half the intended length, a strong and cynical vision of the destructive forces of religious hatred comes across clearly enough in the simplified, almost caricature-like depiction of internecine strife among the ruling classes of France. The characterization of the Machiavellian Duke of Guise and the cunningly plotting she-devil Queen Catherine de Medici, the long series of sadistic onstage killings in interestingly varied ways – poisoning, stabbing, strangling – may appear as aspects of the play's enjoyment of violence and cruelty; but they also testify, at least in this pared-down version that we have, to the existence of a propagandistic agenda. Like other plays of the 1590s, such as George Peele's chauvinistic *Edward I* (?1590), with its absurdly xenophobic representation of the proud Spanish Queen Eleanor, and George Gascoigne's *An Alarum for London* (1599), it is a piece of unashamed Protestant polemic, trading on the insecurity of the English nation which found an outlet in xenophobic depictions of foreigners, especially the French, Spanish and Italians, and simplistic nationalism. But Elizabethan xenophobia was not restricted to Catholic nations, especially when the foreigners in question were close to home; it is relevant that in 1593 and again in 1595 there were riots against the Huguenots who had fled from France after the St Bartholomew's Day Massacre and settled in London, because of fears that they were taking up housing and employment needed by the English. These riots are implicitly referred to, again utilizing the device of anachronism, in *Sir Thomas More* (?1593).

Although *The Massacre at Paris* is concerned with events in France, Marlowe draws on the ever-present threat of Catholic Spain, strongly felt in England throughout the 1590s:

> *Spaine* is the counsell chamber of the pope,
> *Spaine* is the place where he makes peace and warre
>
> (sc. 16.12–13)[16]

asserts Henry of Navarre, who was at the time of the play's first performance Elizabeth's ally. He hopes to 'with the Queene of England joyne
my force,/ To beat the papall Monarck from our lands' (sc. 18.15–16). The
play's prominent references to the Queen suggest that it is designed to
function as a warning to her: when Henry III is dying, murdered by an
agent of Duke Dumaine in revenge for Henry's own killings of the Duke
of Guise and the Cardinal of Lorraine, he sends a message of support to
Elizabeth, promising, should he survive, to destroy the Pope and his 'anti-
christian kingdom':

> These bloudy hands shall teare his triple Crowne,
> And fire accursed Rome about his eares.
> Ile fire his crased buildings and incense
> The papal towers to kisse the holy earth.
>
> (sc. 24.61–4)

In context, this speech of Henry's might well have been received as
hysterical boasting, given that he has only minutes to live, and, accordingly, the ending of the play as ambiguous: it depicts a situation of such
instability in France that England can take no comfort from it, although
there is no ambiguity about its political stance as such. Strangely similar
lines to these occurred in *Edward II*, where Edward in soliloquy upholds
the insults that he and his favourite Gaveston have earlier heaped on the
Bishop of Coventry by claiming that the Bishop is a minion of Rome and
should have no authority over the King of England:

> Why should a king be subject to a priest?
> Proud *Rome*, that hatchest such imperial groomes,
> For these thy superstitious taperlights,
> Wherewith thy antichristian churches blaze,
> Ile fire thy crased buildings and enforce
> The papall towers, to kisse the lowlie ground.
>
> (sc. 4.97–101)

The similarity may be a result of textual corruption in *The Massacre at
Paris*, and the lines are more interestingly ambiguous in the earlier play.
But in *Edward II* this is a curiously opaque moment, at least for a modern
reader of the play; on the one hand, the anti-popish sentiments would
undoubtedly appeal to a large segment of Marlowe's audience in 1592, but
on the other, put into the mouth of a weak and vacillating king to justify
high-handed, even tyrannical behaviour, they might come across as bom-
bastic fantasizing. One cannot easily estimate how far some members of a
socially mixed audience might have sympathized with such popular, even
populist, sentiments, even if in context they are subjected to criticism. This

is a richer and more complex play than *The Massacre at Paris*, set this time in English history of the fourteenth century. Edward II, son of the warlike and successful king Edward I, the 'hammer of the Scots', has just succeeded his father at the beginning of the play, and at the end is succeeded by his own son, who was to become another strong king and a formidable presence behind the monarchs whom Shakespeare depicted in his second tetralogy. For an audience familiar with the image of the powerful Edward III, legendary father to seven sons, celebrated in *Richard II* and in the anonymous *Thomas of Woodstock* (?1596), this conclusion in which the child king is already capable of kingly action, unhesitatingly disposing of Mortimer, his father's murderer, and even sending his own guilty mother, Queen Isabella, to prison in the Tower, would have supported the idea that a strong monarchy is the true source of national unity and stability.

Like *Richard II*, written only a few years later, this play depicts the dilemma created by the reign of a king who is temperamentally at odds with the requirements of his title, and is opposed by strong forces among the aristocracy. For although Edward is by no means an Aristotelian tragic hero, the play traces his downfall from high estate, and, particularly in the scenes showing the king imprisoned and humiliated in the last act, the depiction of his suffering has an immensely tragic quality. The focus on Edward as an individual is stronger in this part of the play than anywhere else; and the detailed process of his degradation, fed in a dungeon on bread and water, washed in filthy water, shaved of his beard by brutal jailors, kept from sleep by continual noise, culminating in the intensely sadistic scene of his onstage murder, creates a strong sense of tragic pity. He begs Lightborn, his torturer,

> Tell *Isabell* the Queene, I lookt not thus,
> When for her sake I ran at tilt in *Fraunce*.
>
> (sc. 22.67–8)

Although Marlowe, unlike Shakespeare in *Richard II*, makes no allusion to the doctrine of the divine right of kings, the handling of Edward's torture and death at the hands of Mortimer's henchmen does implicitly show kingship as a sacred object subjected to pollution, which is intensified by the particular manner of his murder. Mortimer, the instigator of the crime, does not escape; and he ascribes his fate to a kind of metaphysical necessity:

> Base fortune, now I see, that in thy wheele
> There is a point, to which when men aspire,
> They tumble hedlong downe, that point I touchte

And seeing there was no place to mount up higher,
Why should I greeve at my declining fall?

(sc. 23.59–63)

But the earlier part of *Edward II* takes a more secular and political line on Edward's downfall, ascribing it rather to clashing notions of power and authority, in a class struggle between the monarch and the aristocracy. Edward's view, that because he is the king he is entitled to prioritize his desires over those of his subjects, and over the good of his country, is harshly criticized. Initially the object of his desires is the foreign-born upstart, Gaveston, 'that slie inveigling Frenchman', as Mortimer calls him, represented as an aspirant to power who will without hesitation use the king's favour to obtain it. In Holinshed's *Chronicles*, one of Marlowe's sources, Gaveston is an aristocrat, but Marlowe has socially downgraded him and also Spenser, the other favourite, to stress both the King's assertion of his prerogative and the social origins of the barons' enmity towards his promotion. Edward showers Gaveston with honours, and is prepared to sacrifice anything, including his marriage, for the continuance of their pleasure together. When the barons, who are too powerful for Edward, have Gaveston murdered, Edward, flamboyantly autocratic, responds by adopting as a new favourite, the even more transparently aspiring Spenser. A contemporary audience might have seen here an allusion to the young King James, well-known for his love of male favourites. Holinshed had commented on how his 'roiall qualities' had been 'obscured by the craft & subtilitie of some lewd and wicked persons of no desert or woorthinesse, and for the most part of base linage'.[17] James's passionate devotion to his aristocratic French cousin Esmé Stuart, Sieur d'Aubigny, to whom he gave titles and honours, aroused much disquiet among the Scottish nobility and ministers of the kirk. It was felt that d'Aubigny, who was made Earl of Lennox, exercised an unhealthy influence over the then teenage James, and eventually he was ordered to return to France, and died en route.[18] Although in *Edward II* the barons are not represented with any particular sympathy, their dislike of foreign influences on the King would have appealed to a contemporary audience, who no doubt recalled Queen Elizabeth's flirtation with the possibility of marriage to a Frenchman, and they are alert to the threats to England's security posed by potential rebellion, especially from the Scots and the Irish. They fight for national security in a way that Edward has no interest in doing, and as a group, they stand for more than their own private or class interests. They complicate the question of who speaks for England. But Mortimer, who emerges as their leader, is a compromised figure, whose ruthless ambition illuminates the danger to the country from a weak ruler who can neither control the aristocracy nor retain its support. Where Shakespeare in *Richard II* problematizes the opposition between weak king and strong usurper by his oblique portrayal of Bolingbroke's motivation, Marlowe simplifies the issue by his demonization of Mortimer's aspiration. Hence the emergence of the boy-king Edward III is the solution to the problem and the nation is saved.

The subject of rebellion against a legitimate ruler was of great topicality in this decade. Shakespeare had already treated it episodically in Jack Cade's uprising in *Henry VI, Part 2*, and *Richard II*, a full-scale exploration of the subject, appeared just a few years later, in 1595; the play was printed first in 1597, and twice more the next year, although until 1608 without the scene showing Richard's deposition. Richard's reign was also chosen by two other playwrights, neither known to us by name, to explore this subject: *The Life and Death of Jack Straw, A notable rebel in England: Who was kild in Smithfield by the Lord maier of London*, printed in 1593, and *The First Part of the reign of King Richard the Second or Thomas of Woodstock*, which remained in manuscript, unpublished, until 1870. Both concern events in Richard's early years as king, but treat different forms of rebellion against the monarch, and from very different viewpoints. *Jack Straw* depicts the Peasants' Revolt of 1381, depicting the ringleaders as irrational radicals whose lust for an extreme and crude form of social justice propels them into chaotic and indiscriminate violence against any manifestation whatsoever of social order. To do so, it suppresses the 'substantial citizen involvement' that in actuality formed part of the movement,[19] and stresses the loyalty to the crown of the people of London against an invasion from outside.

The play begins with the act that, according to chronicles, set off the Peasants' Revolt, when Jack Straw refuses to pay a tax for his daughter, declaring that she is under age and accusing the tax collector of 'unmanly' and 'beastly' behaviour in making a body search of the girl. But the search itself is not depicted, and the playwright's attitude here remains ambiguous, despite the fact that in sources which he might have consulted, such as Holinshed's *Chronicles* or Stow's *Annals*, the accounts are sympathetic to Straw, and the Tax Collector's action regarded as an assault on the girl.[20] The Collector strikes Straw, who retaliates by killing him, an overreaction, perhaps, to provocation. But once Jack Straw's supporters, led by the rabble-rousing Parson Ball, who declares 'Herein thou hast done good service to thy country' (50) and together with Wat Tyler begins to ferment rebellion, any initial possibility of sympathy for the cause of the poor vanishes. The demands of Ball and Tyler for social equality are obviously meant to be wildly misconceived, like the anti-elitist rant of Jack Cade and his followers in *Henry VI, Part 2*; Ball's assertion that 'the Rich have all, the poore live in miserie' is followed by Straw's promises to 'have all the Rich men displaste' and to make Ball Archbishop of Canterbury and Chancellor of England. The comic representative of the people, Nobs, a sort of Vice figure and chorus, is entirely without illusions about the morality of rebellion, and does not make the mistake of Straw and Bull of seeing it as the demand for justice. Nobs comments in doggerel verse at the end of the first scene,

> Heres even work towards the hangman, did you ever see such a crue,
> After so bad a beginning, whats like to insue?
> Faith even the common reward for Rebels, Swingledome, swangledome,
>   you know as well as I.

$$(149-52)^{21}$$

The King (who is never named) by contrast with the rebels is mild-mannered, rational and dignified; his extreme youth is emphasized, as is his sacred status. Sir John Morton advises him to confront the massed rebels, reckoned to be 20,000 strong,

> . . . with resolution fitting your degree,
> Your Grace must shew your selfe to be a King
> And rule like Gods vicegerent here on earth.
>   (436–9)

The King agrees to meet the rebels, but is unable at first to address them because of their unruliness; he remarks on the indignity he has been offered:

> . . . a King to be thus hardly handled,
> Of his own people and no other foes,
> But such as have bin brought up and bred in his own bosome
>   (630–2)

Nonetheless, he bravely confronts them in Smithfield with so small a train that the Lord Mayor fears for his safety, and offers them a general pardon. The Essex men disband, but Straw remains discontented: 'I came for spoile and spoile Ile have' (758). In a second confrontation between the King and the remaining rebels, Jack Straw seizes a sword from Newton and threatens him; the Lord Mayor, fearing for the King's life, stabs Straw. This is represented as a restorative act, and the Lord Mayor is praised for his 'Noble courage in the Kings behalfe' (956). At the end of the play he is knighted for his loyalty, a symbol of the loyalty of the city.

Throughout the play the key term used to designate the rebels is 'unnatural'. Their actions and desires are contrary to right order, challenging the proper authority of the King and the nobility. In the speech of pardon extended to all except Parson Ball and Wat Tyler, which in the 1594 quarto is carefully printed in black-letter type, to mark it out from the rest of the text and to imply its status as a royal proclamation, Sir John Morton describes the chief rebels as 'degenerate from your naturall obedience, and nature of your country' (1089–90). Their conduct is not only self-assertive, in denial of the obligations and duties owed by all members of society to one another, of which taxation, defended in the play by the Archbishop of Canterbury, is an essential part. It is also treacherous and unpatriotic, and they are deemed 'unnaturall Englishmen' (1144). The play's strong condemnation of rebellion and its glorification of the young Richard II has been seen as a message to rural malcontents of the later sixteenth century who took part in uprisings against the enclosure movement, and an endorsement of the taxation policies of Elizabeth, overlooking the unpopularity of the means by which taxes were collected, thus urging trust in a divinely appointed monarch.[22] The orthodoxy of this lesson emerges with clarity when the play is compared with the near-contemporary *Thomas of Woodstock*, set in the same historical period.

This is a more sophisticated play in terms of dramatic technique, and also one with a more complex account of the problems created when a number of the king's subjects become justifiably discontented with his rule. Historical fact is treated with extraordinary freedom in order to produce this account, particularly in creating the central figure of Woodstock, the loyal, straight-talking English patriot, who bears no resemblance at all to his treacherous plotting counterpart in Holinshed, but much more to the 'good Duke Humphrey' of Shakespeare's *Henry VI, Part 2*.[23] Richard is no longer a boy king, although still immature at the start of the play; he is presented by his uncle Thomas of Woodstock to Anne a Beame (Anne of Bohemia), whom he married at the age of 15 in 1383, as 'a very wag i'faith . . . a blossom' (1.3.29–30).[24] Nor is he the dignified and merciful paragon of *Jack Straw*, but rather a much less sympathetic version of Shakespeare's character, headstrong and wilful, easily led by corrupt favourites, ready to exploit his subjects and his realm to fund his personal extravagances and even, ultimately, to condone the murder of one of his own uncles, Woodstock himself, who stands in his way. The opposition to Richard is led, not as in *Jack Straw* by malcontented peasants, but by men of royal blood, descended like him from the noble line of Edward III and his son the Black Prince (Richard's own father). In Act 5 the ghosts of Edward and the Black

Prince appear to Woodstock as he lies asleep in prison in Calais, where Richard has had him conveyed in order to kill him. The Black Prince recalls his patriotic feats of arms in the battle of Crécy where he took prisoner the French King John and his sons; Edward II also recalls his glorious past, and contrasts his own sons with Richard 'my accursèd grand child', rehearsing the King's crimes against the state, and urging Woodstock to escape prison and join with his brothers, the dukes of York and Lancaster, against the king. His speech implies that his true successor would have been one of the seven sons, and that in fact Richard is responsible for usurping the place that was Woodstock's due:

> . . . My princely son,
> Behold me here, sometimes fair England's lord:
> Seven warlike sons I left, yet being gone
> No one succeeded to my kingly throne;
> Richard of Bordeaux, my accursèd grandchild,
> Cut off your titles to the kingly state
> And now your lives and all would ruinate.
>
> (5.1.82–87)

Not surprisingly, Richard's status as legitimate king and descendant of a noble dynasty is never mystified as divine (as it is in *Richard II*), and his reference to himself as 'the highest God's anointed deputy' is positioned as clear self-interest, though the idea of the royal bloodline of England is not in itself without meaning. The towering figure of Edward III looms over the play, and the strength of the English nation is rooted in the military victories won by him and the Black Prince against France. Englishness is betrayed by Richard, here constructed as the impostor king of mongrel blood. The question of Englishness is complicated when even Richard's foreign-born wife Anne shows greater patriotism, rejoicing at her first appearance to be 'in England's faire Elysium' (1.3), and claiming her right to be accepted as native:

> . . . having left the earth where I was bred,
> And English made, let me be Englishèd.
> They best shall please me, shall me English call.
>
> (1.3.47–49)

Englishness becomes not a matter of birth but of moral character. Richard's lack of identification with his country is pointed up by his love of extravagant foreign fashions; Cheney describes in detail how the King and his followers dress themselves in 'French hose, Italian cloaks and Spanish hats,/ Polonian shoes with peaks a handful long,/ Tied to their knees' (2.3), whereas Woodstock himself is known as 'plain Thomas' and is famous for his simple tastes. Richard plans to 'alter/ The vulgar fashions of our homespun kingdom' (3.1) with an ostentatious display of wealth. The condition of the country under the rule of Richard and his favourites is imaged as a pasture ravaged by wolves while the shepherd stands by, and, as in *Richard II*, as a garden overrun by 'rancorous weeds' (5.6). Rebellion here is equated with reclamation. The play is uncompromising in its disapproval of the King, and his moments of remorse towards the end – 'we have too much provoked the powers divine' (4.3) – emerge as perfunctory and empty of feeling. The influence of the favourites, especially the Machiavellian Tressilian, is a major factor in the play's implicit justification of rebellion. Tressilian is positioned antithetically to Woodstock and his two brothers, the dukes of York and Lancaster, on either side of the King in a dramatic structure derived from the model of the morality play. While Bushy, Bagot and Greene encourage the malleable Richard in extravagance and frivolity, Tressilian, like the social upstart Gaveston in *Edward II* takes a more aggressively political role in the creation of misrule. He is particularly responsible for measures such as the production of blank charters that alienate the people from the King and ferment a national mood of rebelliousness with which the nobility led by Woodstock can only sympathize: 'Th'oppression of the poor, to Heaven doth call' (2.2). Tressilian, expecting to be appointed Chief Justice by Richard, looks forward to 'frighting the Lowsye Rascalls' once in power, and promises Bagot and Greene that he will

> . . . screw and wind the stubborn law
> To any fashion that shall like you best.
> It shall be law what I shall say is law,
> And what's most suitable to all your pleasures.
> (1.2.45–48)

The exercise of this power is depicted in a scene where Tresilian's blank charters are distributed by Master Ignorance, the Bailey of Dunstable, who can nether read nor write; Tressilian's own men are on the prowl to find evidence of dissension among the common people, and the Schoolmaster's servant remarks bitterly on the ubiquity of spies: '' 'Sfoot, the country's so full of intelligencers that two men can scarce walk together but they're attached for whisperers' (3.3.169–71). In fact the Schoolmaster himself is arrested for writing a libel against Tressilian, and so too is a cowherd, for 'whistling treason'. The people are not represented as ignorant or foolish or credulous in this play, but well aware of what is going on and of their inability to change it. The scene depicts a version of the police state. The true nobility side with them – the Queen is shown taking steps to alleviate the sufferings of the poor – but oppression does stem from above, from a degenerate monarch and corrupt favourites.

The play exists only in manuscript, in an incomplete but apparently well-used condition, which suggests that it may have been performed at some point. It has been read as a reproof to Queen Elizabeth (who famously identified herself with Richard II) and her taxation policies, and may also glance at her dependence on favourites.[25] It certainly reflects broader anxieties about social disorder, but its peculiar interest lies in its unorthodox handling of the problem of the tyrannous ruler, which is in line, not with the Tudor Homily Against Rebellion, advocating passive obedience, but rather with the tract Vindiciae Contra Tyrannos (1579), which permitted rebellion against an evil king if carried out in the interest of the people. Until recently, critics and editors of Shakespeare's Richard II, in which responsibility for Woodstock's murder is made a vexed question in the opening scenes, assumed that Woodstock was one of its sources, and that, by implication, Shakespeare was providing a more ameliorative account of the king. But now the view has been put that in fact this play postdates Richard II, and the relationship between the two is therefore reversed.[26] Whatever the truth, the significance of a group of plays close in time all dealing with the problem of rebellion against the monarchy cannot be denied.

Another such play is The Famous History of Sir Thomas Wyatt, by Dekker and Webster, written in the early years of the seventeenth century and printed in 1607. The playwrights may have been working on it even before the death of Elizabeth, since Henslowe records in his diary for 1602 payments to Dekker, Webster and others for 'the playe of ladye Jane'.[27] It deals, daringly, with more recent events than any English history play so far, the uprising by Sir Thomas Wyatt against Mary Tudor in 1554, which constituted a huge crisis in the history of the Tudor regime and came close to unseating the monarch.[28] Once again, the issue of justifying rebellion is problematized. Mary is a legitimate ruler, 'the true immediate heires of our dread Father' (1.3.30), whose claim to the throne is upheld in the play against that of her rival Lady Jane Grey. Lady Jane, and her husband Guildford Dudley, have been forced by their ambitious fathers, the dukes of Suffolk and Northumberland, into claiming succession to Henry VIII against their own desires; and although the play takes the view of them as given in Foxe's Acts and Monuments as martyrs for the Protestant faith when Mary's supporters have them executed, the rightfulness of Mary's claim is not in question. Mary, of course, is a Catholic who fully intends to reinstate the old religion and even rebuild the monasteries her father destroyed, but these are not in fact the most important considerations for Wyatt when he instigates rebellion against her. He is depicted as a man of conscience, both arguing against Lady Jane's succession even though he shares her faith, but also pleading with Mary to acknowledge Jane's kinship and not put her on trial for rebellion. He is not an eager rebel. It is when Mary announces her intention to entertain Philip of Spain's courtship that Wyatt's loyalty is tested to breaking point. The servility of Mary's other courtiers towards Philip's embassy arouses Wyatt's anger, which in the context both of the play itself and of the popular hispanophobia that persisted throughout the 1590s and into the 1600s, despite King James's efforts to make peace, emerges as justified. The Bishop of Winchester, always a vilified figure in Protestant-slanted plays dealing with mid-sixteenth-century politics, embodying, as Bevington puts it, 'the institutional power of the episcopacy',[29] is obsequiously delighted to hear of the King's approaches; Wyatt interrupts him in a rage:

> *Winchester*: . . . we have cause to thanke our God,
>   That such a mightie prince as *Phillip* is,
>   Sonne to the Emperor, heire to wealthy *Spaine*,
>   And many spacious Kingdomes, will vouchsafe –
> *Wyat*: Vouchsafe! My Lord of *Winchester*, pra'y what?
> *Winchester*: To grace our mightie Sovereigne with his honourable
>   Title.
> *Wyat*: To marrie with our Queene: mean you not so?
> *Winchester*: I doe, what then?
> *Wyat*: O God!
>   Is she a beggar, a forsaken maide,
>   That she hath neede of grace from forraigne princes?
>   (3.1.71–82)[30]

At the end of this scene Wyatt decides in soliloquy that he can no longer support Mary, who has shown no gratitude for his efforts in helping her to the throne: 'Ile into *Kent*, there muster up my friends,/ To save this Countrie, and this Realme defend.'

There can be no doubt that Wyatt's motivations for rebellion, patriotism and anti-Spanish feeling, would have drawn on strong popular sentiment from the audience at the time of the play's first performances, whether in 1602 or a few years later. The translation of this sentiment into crude xenophobia in the comic scenes between Bret, Wyatt's unstable follower who deserts him, and the Clown, does not reflect adversely on Wyatt's principled stance, and would no doubt have commanded support among some factions in the audience. Not only is the fall of the play's hero lent something of a tragic quality by its juxtaposition with the falls of Jane and Dudley, but his rebellion against a Spanish takeover is justified. His injunctions to his supporters, in places recalling the phrasing of Henry V, are couched in terms of topical patriotism:

> You free your Countrie from base spanish thrall,
> From ignominious slaverie, Who can disgest a Spaniard, that's a true Englishman?

> (4.1.19–21)

So sympathetic a presentation of an uprising against a queen would have been a risky undertaking in the early seventeenth century, when the rebellion of the Earl of Essex, executed for treason in 1601, was a very sensitive subject. Essex was strongly anti-Spanish, and his faction accused their enemy Cecil of preparing the way for a Spanish landing on English shores.[31] Other current plays which were felt to sympathize with or allude to Essex, such as Samuel Daniel's *Philotas* (1605) and George Chapman's *The Conspiracy and Tragedy of Byron* (1608), fell foul of the censor.[32] Essex, like Wyatt, had been concerned with the question of succession to the throne, and had desired to secure a Protestant successor to Elizabeth, who had aroused her subjects' anxieties by refusing to name anyone. Most recent commentators on the play consider that Wyatt would have been regarded as an Essex figure at the time;[33] but there is no evidence that the play caused any trouble, perhaps because, as McLuskie suggests, its political position is (conveniently) equivocal: 'The overall political impact of the play does not oppose the stoic individual to the corrupt and repressive monarch, for this is a politics of negotiation among contradictory alternatives, aware of the realpolitik of competing hierarchies and the establishment of legitimate authority.'[34]

One of the reasons for the failure of Wyatt's uprising is that he cannot command the support of the people of London, despite promising them 'freedome, from a forraigne Prince', and when the citizens refuse him entry his followers desert him. The relations between monarch and people, especially the people of London, are the particular focus of other history plays written around or soon after the turn of the century, especially Heywood's two-part plays, *Edward IV* (printed 1600), and *If You Know Not Me, You Know Nobody* (1604, 1605, discussed in chapter 2). Like *Wyatt*, *Edward IV*, part 1 also deals with an uprising against the monarch which fails because it receives no support from the people of London. Falconbridge's followers are men from the southern counties (Sussex, Kent and

Essex) who want to take over London, where they expect to find rich pickings. He is boastful, a proud rebel, and his force is characterized as 'desperate, idle, swaggering mates/ That haunt the suburbs in the time of peace'(sc.5.37–8).[35] As in *Wyatt*, the rebels are outsiders, and have no power base inside the city; conspicuously, even the apprentices, in the real-life London of the 1590s notably prone to outbursts of rebellion against city law and order, despise them. The Lord Mayor of London recalls the Peasants' Revolt, and the loyalty then shown by the city and its people to the crown. But, despite Heywood's reputation as a playwright whose appeal is derived from a straightforward dramatic style, the play by no means simplifies the many problem areas with which it deals. Falcon-bridge's actions are also concerned with the question of legitimate succession – he aims to reinstate 'the true and ancient lawful right/ Of the redoubted house of Lancaster' (sc. 2.33–4) against the Yorkist Edward – and he remains true to this allegiance even at execution, where he poses the troubling question asked in *Richard II*,

> O God, thou pouredst the balm upon his head:
> Can that pure unction be wiped off again?
> (sc. 15.70–1)

The theme of royal legitimacy invades the play's comic scenes also; when Edward in disguise susses out popular opinion by questioning Hobs the tanner on the subject of the monarchy, Hobs hedges his bets: 'If it be Harry, I can say "well fare Lancaster"; if it be Edward, I can sing "York, York, for my money"' (sc. 13.46–7). Though he will not agree with the proposition that Edward is a usurper, he recognizes that an element of political correctness is necessary in answering.

As its latest editor says, the play 'tenaciously addresses tensions which had threatened to tear 1590s London apart',[36] such as class antagonisms, food shortages, taxation and, especially, relations between the monarch and the people. The highly tricky theme of a monarch's invasion of the rights of his subjects is explored through the King's seduction of Jane Shore, virtuous wife to a loyal citizen, which Heywood carefully contrives to dramatize without ever directly questioning royal authority. Edward is made a more attractive character than in Holinshed's *Chronicles*, more like the figure in Hall, which Shakespeare also used for *Richard III*; his scenes in disguise among his subjects, to which the play's subtitle draws attention as 'his merry pastime with the Tanner of Tamworth', display him as a good-humoured populist who moves easily among his subjects (when unknown). In the first half of *Edward IV*, part 1, when he is pitted against

Falconbridge, the loyalty of the Lord Mayor and his followers, with Matthew Shore, Jane's husband, at their head, encourages a positive view of the King. There is a strong and orthodox anti-rebellion discourse, reminiscent of *Henry VI, Part 2*; the Lord Mayor remarks to his followers, 'See how rebellion can exalt itself/ Pruning the feathers of sick discipline' (26–7). But at the same time Matthew Shore, in Heywood's sources a man 'crookt, old, and cold',[37] is made a young, attractive and sympathetic character, loyal to the King, modest in refusing honours, whose deep love for his wife is returned.

Once the amorous King has seen, and been smitten by, Jane Shore, the play negotiates interestingly between competing positions. On the one hand Sir Humfrey Bower, a justice of the peace, calls upon the people of London to make voluntary contributions in support of the King's wars in France, stressing Edward's forbearance in not imposing a tax, and exposing the meanness and hypocrisy of those who refuse to pay up. At this point the play emphasizes the King's need of the support of his subjects, and their reciprocal obligations to him. But the dilemmas that arise when Edward persists in his wooing of Jane Shore are neither side-stepped nor reduced to the status of a private marriage breakdown. Jane's spiritual misery is revealed in a scene where she seeks advice from her equivocal confidante, the significantly named Mistress Blage (or Blague), who acts rather like False Counsel from a Morality play in suggesting that the King's favour is in some way above and outside morality.

> So we do say, dishonour is no shame,
> When slander does not touch th'offender's name.
>
> (sc. 19.41–2)

The King then appears on the scene to close the deal; he is not deterred by Jane's appeal – 'How if the Host of Heaven at this abuse/ Repine? Who can the prodigy excuse?' (sc. 19.98–9) – and makes it clear that she has no choice. After Jane has departed, 'sent for to the King, in a close coach', the Shore family laments, and Matthew resolves to leave England rather than accept any favours from the King. In their farewell scene, he recognizes the special nature of his dilemma: 'Oh, what have subjects that is not their king's?/ I'll not examine his prerogative' (sc. 22.112–13).

Implicitly, criticism of the King's assumption of his 'droit du seigneur'[38] emerges from Matthew Shore's dignified stance in both parts of *Edward IV*, and is especially focused in the shaping of the melodramatic scene in part 2, a complete invention of Heywood's, where Jane is brought before Queen Elizabeth, also, of course, a betrayed woman. The Queen's initial anger at her rival turns to pity and even forgiveness at the sight of Jane's humility; each woman then goes on her knees to Edward to beg his love for the other, the monarch positioned between them as debtor to both. Heywood's extended depiction of Jane's reduction to beggary after Edward's death, and her victimization at the hands of his successor, Richard III, further underscores the very different emphasis of this sort of play from the Shakespearean model, where, predominantly, the interests of the monarch are elevated over those of his subjects. In Heywood there is considerable evidence of the 'emotional costs of loyalty to the king',[39] and perhaps even, in its relationship to *Richard III* and to *Richard II*, a challenge to 'the assumption of the "history play" as defined by Shakespeare's practice'.[40] Rowland, who treats *Edward IV*, parts 1 and 2 very much as plays of London life, states that 'the rich evocation of the spectators' quotidian existence contextualises, critiques, and sometimes effaces, the antics of not one but two kings'.[41] While there is some truth in this, and the plays do foreground what is often relegated to background in the chronicles, it is hardly the case that the Jane Shore plot depicts 'quotidian' existence, and the issues raised in the plays about kings in relation to their subjects, despite Heywood's uneasy negotiations, extend beyond comic antics and 'merry pastime[s]'.

In the Prologue to *Perkin Warbeck* Ford observes self-consciously:

> Studies have of this nature been of late
> So out of fashion, so unfollow'd, that
> It is become more justice to revive
> The antic follies of the times than strive
> To countenance wise industry.
>
> (1–5)

In what is usually regarded as the last significant history play of this period, *Perkin Warbeck* (acted 1633, printed 1634, though possibly written earlier), the playwright takes for his subject events in the reign of a monarch, Henry VII, which only became available for the stage after the end of the Tudor regime. Indeed, Henry's claim to the throne 'constituted the very basis of the providential view of history as propounded by Tudor and Stuart governments',[42] and as such required delicate handling. In its account of the pretender, Perkin Warbeck, who claimed to be Richard, Duke of York, son of Edward IV and the younger of the two princes in the Tower, and thus the true king of England, the play, like *Edward IV*, achieves significant effects by complicating the relationship between domestic and political loyalty. *Edward IV* raises the question of true succession through Falconbridge and his support for the Lancastrian cause, but here the Wars of the

Roses and their outcome are treated as a 'given' background. On the other hand, *Perkin Warbeck*, returning to a focus on the history made by 'great men' rather than the commons, handles the predicament of its protagonist in such a way as to arouse an 'unsettling'[43] degree of sympathy for the man who challenges King Henry's right to the throne of England. For not only is Warbeck a courageous and eloquent figure, always completely assured of his own royal identity and for much of the play championed by King James IV of Scotland, ancestor to King James VI and I of England, but he is also further ennobled by the unswerving love and fidelity of his wife, the Scottish aristocrat, Lady Katherine Gordon, a blood relation to James I of Scotland. In short, Warbeck appears to have all the virtues of a king; 'How like a king a' looks . . . Plantagenet undoubted' (2.3.73, 76), comments King James, who believes, at least initially, that he has identified Warbeck's royal blood through 'instinct of sovereignty' (2.3.42).[44] But, as in other plays about rebellion against a king, Warbeck's position is compromised by the quality of his foolish and self-interested followers, although he is defeated in the end by what appears to be historical necessity, when James abandons his support in favour of 'a league of amity with England' (4.3.1–2), including all the major countries of Europe, plus the promise of marriage to Henry's daughter Margaret (whose great-grandson was to become King James VI and I). But to the end Warbeck proclaims himself royal, asserting as he goes to the scaffold that 'the glorious race / Of fourteen kings Plantagenets determines / In this last issue male' (5.3.193–5), and Ford changed his sources so as to leave open the validity of Warbeck's claims.[45]

This late 'chronicle history', as the play is called in one of the dedicatory poems published with it, consciously draws on Shakespeare in its recollecting of *Richard II*, and the dilemma about what constitutes kingship. It seems nostalgic also in that it harks back, during the later years of the Stuart regime in England when disenchantment with the rule of King Charles I was growing, to a greater past and a 'charismatic figure of lost royalty'.[46] By having Warbeck as his Richard II, the man best equipped to 'play the king' and concomitantly as Henry Bolingbroke, the pragmatist without imagination who wins out through strategy, Ford complicates the whole question of royal legitimacy; and he also allows the recalling of the events that brought about Richard III's demise and Henry's succession (by Dawbeney in 1.1 and Warbeck in 5.2) to suggest that Henry's claim to the throne was in part a matter of fortune and bold opportunism combined, rather than true right.

Perkin Warbeck has been seen in relation to another contemporary play about a pretender, *Believe as You List* (1631), by Philip Massinger as a play which 'resurrect[s] the myth of the hero who returns from the dead' in such a way as to imply that its 'real subject is England under the reign of Charles I',[47] and to comment on 'what seemed at the time to be the dangerous innovation and autocracy of Charles's rule'.[48] The fact that in 1633 Charles's Scottish coronation 'provoked a collective soul-searching on the subject of national identities'[49] would have made the 1634 publication of *Perkin Warbeck* particularly topical. As with the history plays of the post-Armada period, *Perkin Warbeck* may be read as a response to a crisis in the life of the nation; but the writing of English history plays had become so unfashionable during the reign of James VI and I, after the flurry of the 1590s and early 1600s, that it was an isolated example in this mode, although nostalgia for a greater past was expressed in other literary forms. It nonetheless relates in many important ways to the earlier history plays in its concerns with issues of legitimacy and rebellion against the monarchy, and with relationships between the crown and the people. Who speaks for England? If Ford's answer seems to be the Tudor and Stuart kings, it is given with some unease.

6

Tragedies of Tyrants

'I stampe! I stare! . . . I rent! I rave! And now run I wode [mad]!'. This is
the exclamation of the archetypal tyrant, King Herod, in the Coventry
Pageant of the Shearman and Taylors (779–83). Hamlet seems to recall it
when he urges the visiting players to perform their parts temperately and
not 'tear a passion to tatters' so that it 'out-Herods Herod' (3.12.10–14). In
sixteenth-century and earlier drama the tyrant was characterized as a boastful, ranting figure who loses control of himself and runs mad. In the
Coventry pageant the stage direction states that 'Erode ragis in the pagond
and in the street also'. This figure retained an imaginative appeal after the
plays in which he had first appeared ceased to be performed, and estab-
lishes a theatrical style for the staging of tyranny well into the later sixteenth century.[1] In a period when kingship, authority and good government
were such key subjects of discourse, many plays which deal with the abuses
of government depict the figure of the tyrant. Although Elizabeth's long
reign brought stability of a kind to her people, the origins of the Tudor
dynasty and its earlier history took place in times of violence when regime
change was a not infrequent occurrence, and these times were constantly
recalled, as in the plays discussed in chapter 5. Amongst English monarchs
of the preceding two hundred years, two in particular, Richard III and Mary
Tudor, were regarded in Protestant England as bad rulers. The former, in
the words of Francis Bacon, was seen as 'King in fact onely, but Tyrant
both in title and regiment';[2] Mary, according to the *Homily Against Disobedience and Wilful Rebellion* (1571) was given by God to chastise the people of
England, after 'he took away our good Josias, King Edward in his young
and good years for our wickedness'.[3]

From other perspectives, however, Elizabeth's rule could be seen as
tyrannical. John Knox, in *The First Blaste of the Trumpet against the Monstrous
Regiment of Women*, published in 1558 just before her accession to the
throne, wrote that women were inherently incapable of good rule 'because
in the nature of all women, there lurketh such vices, as in good governors
are not tolerable',[4] and hence they became like tyrants because they could

not control their passions. For Pope Pius V, who excommunicated Elizabeth in a Bull of 1570, *Regnans in Excelsis*, and supported the cause of Mary Stuart, Elizabeth was not only a heretic but an evil ruler 'exercysinge an absolute Tyrannie' who deserved to be deposed and even eradicated. Questions of good and bad government and how to deal with a bad ruler concerned many countries in Europe during this period of increasingly centralized power. The moral and political responsibilities of princes and the problems which resulted from their non-observance were debated in a range of texts, many of a humanist persuasion, such as Sir Thomas Elyot, *The Boke Named the Governor* (1531), Pierre de la Primaudaye, *The French Academie* (first printed in English in 1589) and Erasmus, *The Education of a Christian Prince* (1516). Some works constructed a specific antithesis between the king and the tyrant; La Primaudaye expresses it as follows:

> And as a good king conformeth himselfe to the lawes of God and nature, so a tyrant treadeth them underfoot . . . the one taketh revenge of publike injuries, and pardoneth his owne, the other cruelly revengeth injuries due to himselfe, and forgiveth those that are offered to others . . . the one maketh great account of the love of his people, the other of their feare: the one is never in feare but for his subjects, the other standeth in awe of none more than of them.[5]

This schematic view has a long history in European writing, going back to Plato's *Republic*, and was influential not only on the literature of statecraft, but also on the depiction of good and bad rulers in many plays, including sixteenth-century interludes such as Thomas Preston's *Cambises* (1569/70) or Richard Edwardes's *Damon and Pythias* (printed 1571).

This is not, however, to say that the tyrant plays of early modern England directly reflect the rhetoric of statecraft, or offer audiences a straightforward didactic spectacle of contrasted styles of rule. This was not the case even with the earliest example, and still less in the seventeenth century. There are a number of factors which bring complexity to the exploration of tyranny on stage. Admittedly, the exposure of tyranny was cited as a factor in defences of theatre against its opponents. Sidney praised 'high and excellent tragedy, that openeth the greatest woundes, and sheweth forth the ulcers that are covered with tissue, that maketh kings fear to be tyrants, and tyrants manifest their tyrannical humours',[6] and also claimed that two Greek poets were more effective than the philosophy of Plato in converting a tyrant into a just king. Heywood in *An Apologie for Actors* recalls this passage from Sidney and applies it to a particular performance of the tragedy of *Richard III* at St John's College, Cambridge, acted 'so essentially, that had the tyrant *Phaleris* beheld his bloody proceedings it had mollified his heart, and made him relent at the sight of his inhumane massacres'.[7] But such arguments, not without self-interest in Heywood's case, were evidently flawed. Sidney admitted that the tyrant Alexander Pheraeus, although moved to tears by a tragedy in the theatre, did not necessarily desist from violent acts in real life. In Massinger's play, *The Roman Actor* (1626), the actor Paris mounts a long and eloquent defence of his profession, based largely on the morally transformative power of theatre, which is strongly applauded by his fellows onstage and sometimes regarded as a set piece; but the plays performed by Paris for the tyrant Domitian have no didactic effects whatsoever, and it is indeed Paris's skill as an actor which is instrumental in bringing about his own death at Domitian's hands. It is also the case that the part of the tyrant – Richard III, Macbeth, Jonson's Sejanus and Tiberius, and Massinger's Domitian – is the focus of each play's theatricality and at the heart of its dramatic success. Rebecca Bushnell has spoken of the 'horror and admiration' that tyranny evoked in classical Greek culture,[8] and the same terms are appropriate to most depictions of tyrants in early modern plays; it may be that, as she says of *The Roman Actor*, the plays 'raise the question of how far the theater itself was implicated in fashioning the tyrant's image and power'.[9]

The spectacle of tyranny, then, may be more exciting onstage than the image of good kingship. Perhaps Shakespeare did not need to create the figure of Richmond, the future King Henry VII, in any sort of complex or intriguing way for an audience of the 1590s who had never known life under any other dynasty, even if for audiences of the present day he is a disappointingly shadowy antagonist for the outrageously vital and dynamic Richard III. But was it always the case that the true king and the tyrant could be so easily differentiated? And by what criteria could the true king be known? Shakespeare's Richard II, the last Plantagenet king, is in no doubt that a king is 'God's deputy, elected by the Lord' and can never be mistaken for anyone else; Richard's strongest supporter, the Bishop of Carlisle, endorses this view, calling the king 'the figure of God's majesty,/ His captain, steward, deputy elect,/ Anointed, crowned, planted many years' (4.1.125–7). According to sixteenth-century orthodoxy, kings were God's chosen representatives on earth, and this divine authority was passed down the line, from father to son, or, in the case of Mary and Elizabeth Tudor of England, to daughter, or, in the case of James VI and I, to the designated successor. This concept of kingship was supported by European monarchs wishing to bolster their autocratic regimes against discontented subjects, and one consequence of the considerable ideological weight it acquired was the promotion of the doctrine of passive obedience. Should the legitimate king rule badly, or at any rate not to the satisfaction of many of his subjects, what was to be done? As the *Homily against Disobedience and Wilful Rebellion* allowed, citing the example of Mary Tudor, such a situation was not impossible; but in the view promulgated in this document, which was of course an instrument of the Protestant Elizabethan settlement for the promotion of dynastic nationalism, active resistance was prohibited. It was firmly stated that 'kynges and princes, as well the evyl and the good, do raigne by Gods ordinaunce, and that subjectes are bounden to obey them'.[10] According to the religious, or, as we might see it, mystificatory, conception of royal power, the fate of a people was in the hands of God and controlled by his providence, in which no human intervention was permitted. King James gave expression to this doctrine in his published writings, putting forth an uncompromisingly absolutist view of the royal prerogative in *The Trew Law of Free Monarchies* (1598) and *Basilikon Doron* (1599), both reprinted in the year he succeeded to the English throne. He accepted that the antithesis between the true prince and the evil tyrant might break down, and that the former might behave in a manner characteristic of the latter, but he allowed for no redress to the ruler's subjects. 'A wicked king is sent by god for a curse to his people, and a plague for their sinnes', he stated, and even more unequivocally: 'the wickednesse . . . of the King can never make them that are ordained to be judged by him, to become his judges'.[11] Martin Butler writes of a Europe 'destabilized by civil and religious conflicts and in which the nation state firmly established under the rule of the absolute and autocratic monarch was coming to be the order of the day'.[12] England under Charles I was certainly a country to which such conditions pertained.

There were, however, European theories of monarchy in which the problems created by the misuse of sovereign authority were differently conceptualized. An important text, referred to by J. W. Lever as a 'classic of political radicalism',[13] the anonymous *Vindiciae Contra Tyrannos* (1579), published initially in Latin as an intervention in the French wars of religion, openly discusses the destructive effects of tyranny and presents tyrannicide as an honourable tradition. The author, probably Phillipe du Plessis-Mornay, styles himself 'Junius Brutus', recalling both Brutus the assassin of Julius Caesar, and his legendary ancestor, Lucius Junius Brutus, who founded the Roman republic. This text acknowledges that tyrants may be of two kinds, those who gain sovereign power by illicit means, and those who are 'invested . . . by lawful election or succession', and nonetheless misuse their power. If the former rules justly, then he is preferable as a monarch to the latter:

> It may well so come to pass, that he who possesses himself of a kingdom by force, and he on whom it descends by lawful title, to rule unjustly. But for so much as a kingdom is rather a right than an inheritance, and an office than a possession, he seems rather worthy the name of a tyrant, who unworthily acquits himself of his charge, than he who entered into his place by a wrong door.[14]

Just as this author challenges the notions of absolute monarchy and the divine right of legitimate kings, so too he asserts that both civil law and the law of nature permit active opposition to tyranny; tyrannicides such as Brutus and Cassius are to be seen as heroic liberators of their country. He noted among the 'viperous brood' of tyrants who came to power through popular support which they then exploited, not only Julius Caesar, but also 'divers princes of Italy',[15] which makes him sound remarkably like Machiavelli.

It is clear, then, that playwrights wishing to explore tyranny as a dramatic subject were working within a cultural context which made it relevant to current conditions, but also very complex. In early modern England the shift from the Tudor dynasty, ending with the death of Elizabeth in 1603, to the first period of Stuart rule, comprising the reigns of James and his son Charles, and culminating, importantly for the purposes of this chapter, in what many regarded as an act of tyrannicide in 1649, is in itself significant. As Matthew Wikander says, 'the most volatile component of the dramatic experience is a play's relation to the politics of its time',[16] and the growth of Stuart despotism, once James had become established on the English throne, is a key factor which illuminates the changing preoccupations of tyrant plays in the seventeenth century. Shakespeare engages with the issue arising from the presence of a tyrant in the seat of power in three plays, two on Anglo-Scottish history, *Richard III* and *Macbeth*, and one, *Julius Caesar*, on a classical subject. The first of these is the most conservative in its ideology, and also in many ways typical of sixteenth-century representations of the tyrant and his power. Its political orientation is predictably conditioned by its relation to the Tudor dynasty. Together with the *Henry VI* plays *Richard III* forms the final part of what has come to be regarded as a tetralogy, and, from *Henry VI, Part 3* at least, it is clear that Shakespeare planned the rise and fall of the monstrous Richard to demonstrate how the quasi-miraculous inauguration of the Tudor regime under Richmond/Henry VII put an end to a long era of civil war and ushered in a time of 'smiling peace and fair prosperous days' (*Richard III*, 5.8.34).

Shakespeare inherited from his historical sources, particularly Sir Thomas More's *History of Richard III* and *Historiae Angliae* by Polydore

Vergil, Henry VII's apologist, a tradition of demonizing Richard which he could hardly have challenged or modified if he had wanted to. But his depiction of Richard is enriched and complicated by a variety of other influences. It has been convincingly suggested that the Herod of medieval drama is one of them, not so much in his histrionic ranting mode, perhaps, as in Herod the epitome of the two-faced hypocritical tyrant, also the murderer of children, and, especially, the false potentate whose fall is inevitable when the destined virtuous rival appears. Richmond, whom Richard thinks of scornfully as 'a little peevish boy' (4.2.96), comes, like the saviour foretold to Herod by the Magi and the prophets of the Bible, to end his reign of horror and usher in a new era. He announces his other dramatic ancestor himself, in claiming to play 'the formal Vice, Iniquity' who will 'moralise two meanings in one word' (3.1.82–3), showing one meaning to the characters within the dramatic narrative, a different one to the theatre audience for whom he plays his part. He has another role as Machiavel, claimed in the self-defining soliloquy in *Henry VI, Part 3*:

> Why, I can smile, and murder whiles I smile,
> And cry "content" to that which grieves my heart,
> And wet my cheeks with artificial tears,
> And frame my face to all occasions.
> I'll drown more sailors than the mermaid shall;
> I'll slay more gazers than the basilisk;
> I'll play the orator as well as Nestor,
> Deceive more slyly than Ulysses could,
> And, like a Sinon, take another Troy.
> I can add colours to the chameleon,
> Change shapes with Proteus for advantages,
> And set the murderous machiavel to school.
> (3.2.182–93)

These claims are realized in *Richard III*, especially in the scene where Shakespeare lays bare the stratagems by which, in collusion with his supporter Buckingham, Richard hoodwinks the mayor and aldermen of London into endorsing his claim to the crown. Between scenes 3.5, in which Richard and Buckingham, 'in rotten armour, marvellous ill-favoured' as the stage direction has it, form their plan to defame Edward IV and his children with accusations of bastardy, and 3.7, where Richard 'aloft, between two bishops' presents himself as reluctant but dutiful claimant to the throne, Shakespeare inserts the Scrivener's brief soliloquy, in which he demonstrates that Richard's Machiavellian practices are more transparent than he believes:

Here's a good world the while! Who is so gross
That cannot see this palpable device?
Yet who so bold but says he sees it not?
(3.6.11–13)

The tyrant rises through manipulation and through terror. The play is open in its account of how power can be achieved.

At the same time, it offers a more comfortable reading of power and authority through its strongly providentialist shaping. The plethora of bestial and diabolic images that surrounds Richard – hog, toad, spider, dog, 'slave of nature and the son of hell' (1.3.227), and so forth – the schematically enunciated and fulfilled prophecies of Margaret, and of course the ghostly interventions in Act 5, all testify to a religious conception of human history in which, while God may chastise his people from time to time with a usurping tyrant, he will always ensure the ultimate triumph of legitimacy and good government.

The ideology underpinning *Richard III* is unquestionably orthodox; but in the theatre it can be subverted by the theatricalism of the stage tyrant. This is not just a matter of Richard's being the longest and most fully realized role in the play, but that the role itself is conceived of in terms of performance. Richard will 'seem a saint when most I play the devil' (1.3.336), and his scheming can take a wide variety of guises, from ardent lover, concerned brother and uncle, bluff truth-teller and even a 'holy man', which successfully deceive wherever they are intended to. At the same time as the play's moral aesthetic condemns Richard, its success depends on the theatrical exploitation of his evil. To a lesser extent, this also holds good in *Macbeth*, but the representation of tyranny in this play is complicated by other means too. The two plays have in common the fact that they explore the process of becoming a tyrant as much as the consequences for the realm that ensue. Like Richard, Macbeth is propelled by ambition, but he has before him the model of a good king, as he acknowledges, and this fills him with moral horror as he contemplates the act of regicide:

... this Duncan
Hath borne his faculties so meek, hath been
So clear in his great office, that his virtues
Will plead like angels, trumpet-tongued against
The deep damnation of his taking off.
(1.7.17–21)

However, once installed on the throne, it seems as if he had no choice but to rule as a tyrant, and the term is regularly applied to him from Act 3 onwards. He ruthlessly attempts to dispose of threatening rivals (Banquo, Macduff), he operates by means of spies and hired assassins, and he imposes a reign of terror on his countrymen. The horror of tyranny is amplified by the play's religious and mystical framework; Macbeth's actions bring about disruption in the cosmos and the natural world. The traditional bond between king and country is inverted in Macbeth's relation to Scotland, and by contrast reinforced in the account of Edward the Confessor in England, curing his subjects' illnesses with the 'healing benediction' of his holy touch. Yet black as the image of tyranny is painted in 'devilish Macbeth', usurper and regicide, the play also suggests that the antithesis of true king and evil tyrant is capable of being deconstructed. Appropriate to its atmosphere of ambiguity and equivocation, where 'fair is foul and foul is fair', and the witches do speak truth, is the action of the strange and disturbing scene where Malcolm, true heir to Scotland, tests Macduff by pretending himself to be a potential tyrant. He claims that in his own nature exist 'all the particulars of vice so grafted/ That when they shall be opened black Macbeth/ Will seem as pure as snow' (4.3.52–4), especially limitless avarice and sexual intemperance. Macduff attempts to exonerate Malcolm where he can, even advocating strategies of concealment: 'You may/ Convey your pleasures in a specious plenty/ And yet seem cold. The time you may so hoodwink' (4.3.71–3). Much extenuation can be allowed to the failings of a king: 'All these are portable,/ With other graces weighed' (4.3.91–2). It is only when Malcolm asserts that he has no 'king-becoming graces' at all to offset his vices that Macduff is forced to admit that such a person is fit neither to govern nor to live. That Malcolm then owns that none of this is true does not detract from the fact that even in this play, which dramatizes the killing of a monarch who is both virtuous and legitimate and which represents the moral and spiritual chaos ensuing from the rise of a tyrant, there is no final distinction to be made between the moral character of the king and of the tyrant.

The depiction and interpretation of tyranny in *Richard III* and *Macbeth* is constrained by their closeness, in different ways, to the current regimes. As playwrights recognized, more freedom to explore issues arising from tyranny could be gained by drawing on classical rather than native history, and a number of seventeenth-century plays used the lives of the Roman emperors in this way. Although the stratagem was widely understood, it was still safer to engage with current political concerns, and sometimes contentious matters of authority and government, by means of stories set in other times and cultures. Shakespeare's *Julius Caesar*, the first of his political plays and one of the earliest in the public theatre to be set in the

ancient world, is not perhaps an obvious example of this, and as Robert
Miola says, 'the hints and half-guesses of tyranny in this play look slight
and insubstantial next to the lurid obscenities of Shakespeare's other
tyrants, of Richard III and Macbeth'.[17] But it does enter the current debate
on the problem of tyrannicide, and through its ambiguous and multi-
faceted representation of both tyrant-figure and tyrannicides it returns no
simple answers.

Julius Caesar has potentially tyrannical characteristics, and sees himself
in grandiosely absolutist terms:

> . . . Danger knows full well
> That Caesar is more dangerous than he.
> We are two lions littered in one day,
> And I the elder and more terrible.
>
> (2.2.44–7)

he tells Calphurnia, as she begs him to stay away from the Senate House
on account of evil omens. But he is, as the conspirators know, susceptible
to flattery, and readily changes his mind. Moments before the assassination
he proclaims himself 'constant as the Northern Star/ Of whose true fixed
and resting quality/ There is no fellow in the firmament' (3.1.60–2). He is
capricious and wilful, regarding himself as a superior being not answerable
to 'ordinary men' for his decisions. 'The cause is in my will; I will not come'
(2.2.71), he tells Decius when asked to explain his absence from the Senate
House. But although fearful of plots he is also a warm friend to those he
trusts, such as Brutus and Antony, and his act of bequeathing his private
lands to the people of Rome in perpetuity contrasts with the tyrant's traditionally grasping and avaricious nature. The tyrannicide Brutus does not
share Cassius's scorn and jealousy of Caesar, and he is unable to find sufficient justification in Caesar's behaviour for an assassination:

> . . . for my part
> I know no personal cause to spurn at him,
> But for the general. He would be crowned.
> How that might change his nature, there's the question.
> . . .
> Th'abuse of greatness is when it disjoins
> Remorse from power. And to speak truth of Caesar,
> I have not known when his affections swayed
> More than his reason.
>
> (2.1.10–13, 18–21)

Brutus finds that he must 'fashion' a cause on which to proceed, and
buoys himself up with the recollection that it was his ancestor Lucius

Junius Brutus who drove the tyrannical Tarquinius Superbus from Rome and established the republic. He encourages the other conspirators to mask any doubts and anxieties they may have, and 'bear it as our Roman actors do' (2.1.225). The theatricality of the assassination excites the conspirators; Cassius imagines the 'lofty scene' being constantly re-enacted in times to come, and Brutus follows this up with the macabre speculation: 'How many times shall Caesar bleed in sport'. Their own emotional volatility is reflected in the changeability of the mob, ready at one moment to receive Brutus as a hero, and soon after to burn down his house and drive him from the city. Pictured in these terms, the will of the people can never be sovereign, nor can its endorsement of any particular action be taken to have political significance. Caesar is only ever a potential tyrant, 'a serpent's egg' (2.1.32), and how Rome would have fared had he been given the crown he longs for can only be speculation; but the consequences of tyrannicide in the 'domestic fury and fierce civil strife' that Antony gleefully predicts are all too vividly realized. The Tudor horror of civil war that permeates *Richard III* is evoked here, leaving the play with a complex sense of the instability of human affairs. As Miola says, 'The images of public hero and vain self-deluder are every bit as protean as those of tyrant and just king.'[18]

Shakespeare's use of classical history in *Julius Caesar* seems to have influenced writers of the seventeenth century, particularly his contemporary Jonson. Annabel Patterson talks, with perhaps some over-emphasis, of 'a massive exploitation of Roman history as a context for interpreting contemporary events, a context that became ever more specifically applied', supplying the basis for 'a specifically political language'.[19] But unlike Shakespeare, playwrights of the seventeenth century tended to be attracted to classical subjects on which the judgements of history were unequivocal. The Roman emperors Tiberius and Domitian, whose reigns were chosen for dramatization in two major tyrant plays, Jonson's *Sejanus* (1603) and Massinger's *The Roman Actor*, were generally accepted exemplars of tyrannical excess in its worst forms. *Sejanus*, though not a success when first performed, is the greatest dramatic account of life under the rule of a tyrant and of the methods by which a tyrant maintains his power that has come down to us. It got its author into trouble with the Privy Council, and he was accused 'both of popperie and treason' on account of it.[20] The facts that Jonson had already satirized aspects of Elizabethan court life in *Cynthia's Revels* (1599), that his source for *Sejanus* was Tacitus, known for republican sympathies, along with the play's bitter representation of a world where free speech is suppressed and 'no innocence is safe/

When power contests' (4.1.40–1) may have alerted contemporaries to the likelihood that Jonson was using first-century Roman history to raise issues relevant to his own day and age. As Jonson's editors, Herford and Simpson put it, 'It was no doubt hard to believe that [Jonson] . . . had portrayed the court of Tiberius in the guileless spirit of a scholar bent only on the historical accuracy of his play'.[21] But it is in this spirit that Jonson presents himself in the address 'to the Readers' published in 1605, emphasizing particularly that the marginal notes included (an unusual feature in a quarto of this period) were 'to show my integrity in the story' and prevent misinterpretation. But the printed text of 1605 needed to atone for whatever it was that excited official displeasure when the play was first performed in 1603, and it is not surprising that Jonson took pains to make it politically inoffensive, even insisting on its orthodoxy in the pious conclusion to the Argument that prefaces the text:

> This do we advance as a mark of terror to all traitors and treasons; to show how just the heavens are in pouring and thundering down a weighty vengeance on their unnatural intents, even to the worst princes: much more to those for guard of whose piety and virtue the angels are in continual watch, and God himself miraculously working. (39–54)[22]

Sejanus, the protagonist, is the favourite of the Emperor Tiberius, and believes himself to be in a position of unstoppable political ascent; he consolidates this position by becoming the lover of Tiberius's daughter-in-law Livia, and organizing the murder of her husband Drusus. He imagines that he can manipulate Tiberius, who prefers to operate behind the scenes rather than in public, to his own ends, using the old man both to get rid of their mutual enemies, especially the virtuous family of Germanicus, Tiberius's own brother and leader of a prominent faction, and to incur the hatred that will result. He hopes to 'thrust Tiberius into tyranny' (2.391), and thus achieve sovereign power for himself. But in all this he underestimates the political cunning of Tiberius, who is prepared to support and even indulge Sejanus when it suits him to do so, but when Sejanus proposes to marry Livia and by implication 'take control of the family tree'[23] he has gone too far. As Tiberius says, 'Those are dreadful enemies we raise/ With favours, and make dangerous with praise' (3.637–8). There is never a shortage of favourites, and Tiberius now chooses a new minion, Macro, whom he employs to spy on Sejanus. Immediately after what seems like the height of Sejanus's ascent, he is bloodily overthrown; and Tiberius, not even present in the play's last act, remains fully in control.

That the play speaks to its times is not in doubt, although critics have disputed the specifics of this. It is tempting to consider the parallels between King James's style of rule and that of Tiberius, as Jonathan Goldberg does,

and to read the play in the light of the unease created by the growth of
Stuart despotism: 'Like James, at last, he rules by the pen. Nearly invisible
when seen, Tiberius remains as unseen as possible, retired even when
present.'[24] Such a view might explain the high regard in which the play
was held in the seventeenth century; and the relationship of Sejanus and
Tiberius was evidently perceived to be relevant to the Stuart court. In a
Commons speech of 1626, Sir John Eliot denounced Buckingham, Charles's
unpopular favourite, as a Sejanus, to which Charles responded, 'he must
intend me for Tiberius', and sent Eliot off to the Tower.[25] But it is necessary to remember that the play was first acted shortly after James's accession and that Jonson must have been working on it for some time earlier.[26]
It looks back to the last days of Elizabeth's rule, as well as forward. References to the fall of the Earl of Essex in 1601, and also to the trial of Sir
Walter Ralegh have been suggested,[27] but there is no critical agreement.
In any case, it is a simplification to see the play in total as a covert allegory.
What is important here is the play's depiction of state power and its handling of the abuse of power in a tyrannical regime, where the official
climate was one of the abhorrence of regicide and 'reverence for conse-
crated power'.[28]

A key device to illuminate the conditions of tyranny is Jonson's use of
commentator figures, the general Silius and the soldier Sabinus, both supporters of the family of Germanicus, and the senator Arruntius, commonly
seen as a mouthpiece for Jonson. They describe the degenerate state of
Rome and its decline from the days of 'god-like Cato' and 'the constant
Brutus, that . . . did strike / So brave a blow into the monster's heart / That
sought unkindly to captive his country' (1.93–6). They set out what life is
like under the current regime, the dangers of favourites and informers, the
atmosphere of fear and constraint: 'We shall not shortly dare to tell our
dreams, / Or think, but 'twill be treason' (1.69–70). But their understanding
of their situation gives them no protection. Sejanus, who has spies every-
where, recognizes the threat these men pose to his power and plans their
destruction carefully, beginning with Silius:

> He is the most of mark, and most of danger
> . . . His steep fall,
> By how much it doth give the weightier crack,
> Will send more wounding terror to the rest.
>
> (2.286, 290–2)

The disposal of Sabinus is less urgent, and in any case, as Sejanus tells
Tiberius, 'We must not pluck / At all together, lest we catch ourselves'
(1.297–8). But of particular danger is another man, the annalist Cremutius
Cordus,

a writing fellow . . .
A most tart and bitter spirit . . . who under colour
Of praising those, doth tax the present state,
Censures the men, the actions, leaves no trick,
No practice unexamined, parallels
The times, the governments; a professed champion
For the old liberty.

(2.304–12)

In the great central scene of Act 3, which takes place in the Senate, both men are arraigned on trumped-up charges, not by either Sejanus or Tiberius in person, but by minions who 'may better do it, / As free from all suspicion of a practice' (3.6). Silius, angered that his military service for the Roman state against foreign enemies is unacknowledged, speaks out boldly, well understanding why it is that Tiberius needs to get rid of him:

Since I have done thee that great service, Caesar,
Thou still hast feared me; and, in place of grace,
Returned me hatred.

(3.300–2)

In Stoic manner he takes his own life onstage, which gives the wily Tiberius the opportunity to say that Silius has 'abused our mercy, / Intended to preserve thee'. Cordus, accused of sedition on account of having too greatly honoured men of the past such as Brutus and Cassius, eloquently defends himself and the value of his chronicles by demonstrating how previous rulers like Augustus had understood the need to preserve history and acted magnanimously towards those who criticized him. But freedom of speech in Tiberius's regime is a threat not a right, and Cordus's books are ordered to be burnt. Later Sabinus is trapped by Sejanus's acolyte Latiaris, who tricks him into unguarded denunciation of Tiberius and then has concealed spies break in and arrest him.

The play's depiction of the operations of state terror is unrelentingly grim; virtuous characters exist, but they are all impotent, except in eloquence, and there is no image of a virtuous ruler, as in *Richard III* and *Macbeth*, to offset the viciousness of Sejanus and Tiberius. The play is of course entitled *Sejanus his Fall*, and the charting of the favourite's downfall, of which he is completely unaware until the last moment, provides one of its subtler satisfactions. Sejanus's own modus vivendi is that of a despot, and like the traditional tyrant he regards himself as entirely above the law and able to dictate his own moral terms. He pronounces magnificently:

> The coarsest act
> Done to my service I can so requite,
> That all the world shall style it honourable.
>
> (1.327–9)

He has the Machiavellian's attitude to the exploitation of others for his own ends, and an understanding of human weakness: 'Ambition makes more trusty slaves than need' (1.366). In confidence with Tiberius he admits to the belief that power justifies any act, and that rulers can only hold on to it by setting aside all moral standards:

> The prince, who shames a tyrant's name to bear
> Shall never dare do anything but fear.
>
> (2.178–9)

But the play's real Machiavellian is Tiberius, a deeply sinister figure, who both appears and speaks less than Sejanus, but is always in complete control. In Act 2, he allows Sejanus to express his philosophy of tyranny as fully as possible, encouraging the favourite to develop his plan for suppressing all opposition to the regime. Because Sejanus is the mouthpiece for the most outrageous views, Tiberius is able to remain in the background and appear, at least in public, as a man of impeccably proper sentiments. 'We would not kill, if we knew how to save' (2.270), he tells Sejanus gravely. But Sejanus always overestimates the degree of control he can exercise over his master, and underestimates Tiberius's understanding of realpolitik. The favourite overplays his hand when, taken in by Tiberius's apparent dependence on him, he proposes to marry into the Emperor's family. Tiberius's response at this point, expressed in the exclamation, 'H'mh?' (3.515), is, paradoxically, one of the most eloquent moments in this highly articulate play. He is by no means the 'dull, heavy Caesar' (3.586) that Sejanus, blinded by his own ambition, imagines, and from this moment the favourite's downfall begins.

The play is structured on the lines of 'fall of princes' tragedy, but, as Lever says, 'in essence it amounts to a denial of the moral principles underlying such concepts'.[29] Although Sejanus falls in one day from the height of fortune to ignominious death, torn literally to pieces by a fickle mob, this is not so much because fortune's wheel, set in motion by a universal impulse, has made its inevitable turn, as because the processes by which tyrannical power is maintained operate in this way. His fall is accompanied by the rise of Macro, a similarly ambitious servant of state, who, in historical actuality, was eventually obliged to take his own life. But Tiberius, safe in his retreat on the island of Capri to indulge his private perversions, survives, a 'malicious deity',[30] whose interests are so perfectly served by the outbreak of supernatural manifestations, and he continues to rule as before. One of the lessons of tyranny that the play teaches is that the successful tyrant always gets someone else to do his dirty work, and needs never be present to see it done. In the play's last act Jonson provides suggestions of providentialist intervention in the fate of Sejanus, with the 'supernatural melodrama'[31] of divine portents, evil omens, the black smoke belching from Sejanus's statue, ravens croaking all night long, and so forth. Terentius, who narrates Sejanus's bloody end, concludes in pious and orthodox fashion:

> Let this example move th'insolent man
> Not to grow proud, and careless of the gods.
>
> (5.908–9)

In the context of the play as a whole, this moralizing seems but a gesture, perhaps another indication of Jonson's need to hedge his subversive play around with a fence of orthodoxy. But, as Lever says, its uncomfortable message is that 'history is made by men; it is as ruthless and immoral as they'.[32]

Jonson's play was undoubtedly one of the influences on Massinger's depiction of tyranny in *The Roman Actor*. The debt is signalled early on, when in his dedication Massinger defends the 'gravity and height' of his play, borrowing the phrase from Jonson's dedication 'to the Readers' of *Sejanus*. Domitian became Emperor of Rome in AD 81, forty-four years after the death of Tiberius, and his reign, like that of the greater part of Tiberius's, is depicted in Tacitus's *Annals* as a reign of terror, although he espouses a different, and more theatrical, style of tyranny. As Bushnell puts it, Domitian is a 'full-blown version of the tyrant, crazed by desire and exploding into violence'.[33] Like Jonson, Massinger drew on Tacitus, and there is much similarity in the way in which tyranny's operations are represented in the two plays. Domitian's subjects recall better days in the later years of the Roman republic, under 'great Pompey', and like Tiberius Domitian has a virtuous brother, the previous emperor Titus, now dead, against whom his own wickedness is offset. State tyranny is similarly depicted. In the first scene the senators, later to become Domitian's victims, tortured onstage, outline the privations of the tyrant's subjects:

> we hardly sleepe
> Nay cannot dream with safetie. All our actions
> Are call'd in question; to be nobly borne
> Is now a crime; and to deserve too well
> Held Capitall treason.
>
> (1.1.71–5)[34]

The tyrant rules through a network of spies, scrupulous in rooting out opposition in any form, calling it, like the chronicles of Cordus in *Sejanus*, sedition. Here, Aretinus, Domitian's chief informer, accuses the actors of practices forbidden by the state:

> . . .   You are they
> That search into the secrets of the time,
> And under fain'd names on the Stage present
> Actions not to be toucht at.
>
> (1.3.36–9)

The play in fact does not present them in this role, and seems to show Paris, the lead actor, as too true a servant of the state, losing his life because he cannot resist acceding to the royal will, but it does pose some searching questions about the relations of tyranny and theatricality. Domitian, unlike Tiberius, enjoys playing the part of a tyrant. He is completely open about making an equation between his own will and the law;[35] when his servant Parthenius comes in 1.2 to seize Domitia, the wife of Lamia, to be Domitian's mistress, Domitia's momentary anxieties about the legality of this move are easily resolved: 'When power puts in its Plea the laws are silenc'd.' As Butler says, 'Domitian's is the only authority in the state, and he wields power as if it were his personal property',[36] unhesitatingly enslaving his people as he does so. 'His pleasures/ Are unconfin'd', Parthenius tells Domitia; 'this sillable, his will,/ Stands for a thousand reasons' (1.2.46–8). Returning in triumph from conquest, Domitian celebrates his own superiority, telling the Roman people how fortunate they are in having him as their emperor, and adds:

> I am above
> All honours you can give me: And the stile
> Of Lord, and God, which thankefull subjects give me,
> (Not my ambition) is deserv'd.
>
> (1.4.34–7)

The vision of absolute rule embodied in Domitian's conduct has been seen as particularly meaningful in the context of Stuart rule in the mid-1620s. In 1626, when the play was first performed, Charles I had succeeded to the throne, at once putting into practice a personal style even more ostentatiously imperial than his father's, and the way in which Domitian rides roughshod over the rights of his subjects, as he does with Domitia's husband Lamia, seems clearly 'to exemplify that early Stuart nightmare, that men's goods and liberties will all fall into the power of the prince, leaving him the only "freeman" left'.[37] But it is not the case, as in *Sejanus*, that resistance to this tyranny is impotent. In 3.2 Domitian has the senators Rusticus and Sura put to torture in public, as a display of his power, disregarding the advice of his toady Parthenius to act more discreetly. The two refuse to exhibit any signs of pain and suffering, awaiting death with smiling stoicism, and promising to 'appear in horror' to Domitian after their deaths. The tyrant is filled with amazement and fear, and can only regain composure when Domitia, to whom he is in turn in thrall through his passion for her, comes on to divert him with a theatrical entertainment put on by Paris. This in itself is ominous for Domitian, because Domitia is so enraptured by Paris's acting that she falls in love with him, and allows herself eventually to become part of the conspiracy against the emperor.

Domitian's enemies are thus not powerless; they are led by his female kinsfolk, including Domitilla, his cousin, Julia, his brother's wife, and Domitilla's servant Stephanos. Domitilla at one point fears to act against a legitimate ruler, and voices the doctrine of passive obedience, preferring to await divine vengeance on Domitian:

> The immortal Powers
> Protect a Prince though sould to impious acts
> And seem to slumber till his roaring crimes
> Awake their justice.
>
> (3.1.58–61)

The fall of Domitian is prefaced, like the fall of Sejanus, by a display of omens and portents, including an astrological prediction, at which he scoffs, of the date and hour of his death. The ghosts of the Senators Rusticus and Sura appear, as they foretold, to torment the sleeping emperor in a scene obviously modelled on *Richard III*. After this Domitian becomes convinced that 'the offended Gods . . . conspire against me' (5.1.282–4). The providentialist ideology that underlies 'fall of princes' tragedy is much more active in this play than in *Sejanus*, and the climax is achieved when a band of the tyrant's wronged subjects, including Domitia, Domitilla and Julia and two freedmen, come forward to enact a ritual stabbing, in a manner imitated from *The Maid's Tragedy*. As at so many points in this play, tyranny and theatricality come together. Domitian, whose fate is entwined with that of Paris, the other 'Roman actor', dies in a way that would be familiar to any theatregoer of the time, like the villain in a revenge tragedy. And while Paris's great speech in Act 1 is a defence of the theatre as a moral art which truly mirrors a vicious society to itself, the play's successful exploitation of evil and vice for dramatic ends cannot be ignored.

In exploring the relationship between tyranny and absolutism, Massinger also illuminates how absolutist rule challenges the rights and freedoms of the subject. In some tyrant plays, such as *The Second Maiden's Tragedy* (written 1611, probably by Middleton), where the tyrant figure is a usurper rather than a legitimate ruler, the issue is not problematized. In this play, the Tyrant (who is given no proper name) has without compunction sacrificed countless subjects to satisfy his desires: 'So many bodies have been hewn down,/ Like trees in progress, to cut out a way . . . for us and our affections' (1.1.179–81) is how he expresses it.[38] But the rightful king, Govianus, is a strong antagonist, and is in the end restored to the throne by his supporters, not without first having poisoned the Tyrant. In the process, however, Govianus's Lady, with whom the Tyrant is also in love, is obliged to kill herself in order to escape his power; and this, as it proves, unsuccessful attempt to appropriate to himself what belongs to another man, constitutes the major infringement of the subject's rights on which the play's main plot turns.

Sexual appropriation is also used in this way to represent a broader notion of tyrannical power in plays by Fletcher. Fletcher, who wrote, sometimes with Beaumont, sometimes with Massinger, and sometimes by himself, composed a considerable number of plays which handle this theme in comic as well as tragic modes. Two of the tragedies to which it is most central are *The Maid's Tragedy* (with Beaumont, 1610/11) and *Valentinian* (1610–14). In both cases the tyrant is a legitimate ruler, and the moral dilemma of the wronged subject who happens to espouse divine right beliefs creates the main tragic situation. *Valentinian* is another play which takes as its setting the reign of a degenerate Roman emperor, although Fletcher's source is not so much classical history as a contemporary French pastoral romance, *L'Astrée*, by Honoré D'Urfé, and consequently it is less involved with political problems than with the problems arising from the intersection of love and honour. Nonetheless, Valentinian is depicted as a corrupt classical tyrant following in the line of Tiberius, Nero and Caligula; the action is set against a background of military unrest during the collapse of the Roman empire, for which Valentinian's misrule is held largely responsible, and his frustrated soldiers long to pursue an aggressive expansionist policy like that of Julius Caesar or Germanicus. The military context is also important in *The Maid's Tragedy*, although the setting, Rhodes, with an unnamed King, seems almost deliberately dehistoricized, and it is from the military that opposition to the tyrant emerges. Fletcher's soldiers are figures of honour and rectitude; and both plays make the point that the ruler and his army are bound in a relationship of mutual dependence, with duties and obligations owing on both sides. Where the demands of court and army directly conflict, the generals Aecius in *Valentinian* and Melantius in *The Maid's Tragedy* bring military values to bear on their roles as resisters of tyranny. Fletcher is not interested, like Shakespeare, in the rise of the tyrant, nor, like Jonson and Massinger, in the relations between tyranny and the state, but rather in the conflict of wills between tyrant and subject. In both Fletcher plays this conflict stems from his desire for a woman.

In *Valentinian*, the Emperor desires Lucina, chaste wife to the great soldier Maximus, and when she resists all his efforts to seduce her he takes her by force. Lucrece-like, Lucina then kills herself. In the long-standing debate on the ethics of rape-victim suicide, going back to St Augustine, the conservative position was that a raped wife's honour could be vindicated only in this way. Maximus, in anguished discussion after the rape with his close friend, the general Aecius, claims to have been prevented from taking revenge on Valentinian because of the 'awe' a legitimate monarch commands, but in fact, in an ingenious twist, it is Aecius who really upholds the divine right ideology and will never countenance action against the prince, however wicked:

> On forraigne foes
> We are our own revengers but at home
> On Princes that are eminent and ours,
> 'Tis fit the Gods should judge us.
> (3.3.155–8)[39]

Maximus, however, privately determines on revenge and, realizing that the principled Aecius will forever stand in his way, decides with much heart-searching that his first step must be to kill his friend, though in the event he cannot do it. But a rapid moral decline starts up in Maximus, and the destruction ensues of what the play presents as the most intense and noble of human bonds, friendship between men. Aecius, who cannot bring himself to support his friend and take armed opposition against his emperor, kills himself because he cannot endure life under tyranny. In *The Maid's Tragedy* the King's appropriation of a woman is differently handled, though here, too, military values and male friendship are subsequently brought into play. The King has taken Evadne as his mistress, and to protect the secrecy of their relationship marries her off to Amintor. He obliges the innocent Amintor, who is this play's supporter of absolutist beliefs, not only to break a previous engagement to Aspatia, the tragic maid of the title, but also to conceal his degrading condition as cuckold by playing the part of a devoted husband. Evadne initially colludes in this arrangement, not because of love for the King, but, ironically, because of respect for his status:

> I swore indeede that I would never love
> A man of lower place, but if your fortune
> Should throw you from this hight, I bad you trust
> I would forsake you, and would bend to him
> That won your throne, I love with my ambition,
> Not with my eies.
>
> (3.1.171–6)

Amintor cannot contemplate revenging his dishonour; he is even more devoutly absolutist than Aecius:

> in that sacred name
> The King, there lies a terror, what fraile man
> Dares lift his head against it? let the gods
> Speake to him when they please, till when let us
> Suffer, and waite.
>
> (2.1.307–11)

But, like Aecius, he too has a close friend, the general Melantius, who does not subscribe to this ideology. Melantius is Evadne's brother, and on hearing what has happened his first thought is to revenge the family dishonour:

> The credit of our house is thrown away
> But from his iron den ile waken death
> And hurle him on this King; my honestie
> Shall steel my sword.
>
> (3.2.189–92)

But, in an interesting twist characteristic of this witty play, Melantius first converts his sister into a recognition of her own part in dishonouring their house, and then persuades her that it is her duty to carry out the revenge. And so, in a highly theatrical scene, victim confronts tyrant, mistress confronts lover, subject confronts king, and kills him, on the very bed where the act of dishonour has taken place. Although the King tries to exercise his royal prerogative, he cannot dissuade the vengeful Evadne from her mission; to her he is no longer a lover desirable because of his rank, but

> Such a tyrant
> That for his lust would sell away his subjects,
> I, all his heaven hereafter.
>
> (5.1.94–6)

She stabs him in ritual style:

This for my lord *Amintor*,
This for my noble brother, and this stroke
For the most wrong'd of women.

(5.1.109–11)

In both plays the tyrant is killed onstage, in a spectacle of sadistic violence. In *Valentinian* this is a prolonged public scene in which the Emperor, having been administered a slow-acting poison by Aretus, a loyal servant of Aecius, is brought onstage in a chair, visibly deteriorating, while courtiers and physicians attempt consolation. Aretus, who has taken the same poison ahead of Valentinian, gloatingly describes the physical torments that Valentinian can expect. This deliberate exhibition of the tyrant's mortal punishment demystifies the sacredness of royal power, and may have been especially significant to the original audiences after 1610. In that year Henry IV of France was assassinated, an event which caused alarm to the timorous King James, and resulted in a great increase in his own personal protection.

The plays make an equation between the sexual will of the tyrant and his legal power;[40] when Lucina threatens to cry for justice after Valentinian has raped her, he merely responds chillingly, 'Justice shall never heare ye, I am Justice' (3.1.34). The tyrant turns his private desires into political acts, and in each case his eradication is a political coup, as well as a personal vindication for his killer. Samuel Taylor Coleridge thought Beaumont and Fletcher 'the most servile *jure divino* royalists',[41] but these two plays seem designed to reveal how tyranny challenges the concept of royal absolutism. By showing how the tyrant invades his subjects' privacy and infringes on their rights, and by making these subjects members of a state institution, the army, on which the ruler depends to maintain his power, these plays raise difficult questions about the style of kingship the Stuarts sought to promote. They also implicitly propose a theory of government whereby the king derives his right to rule not from divine prerogative but from an acknowledgement of his obligations to provide for the welfare of his subjects. The failure to engage with this theory was one of the factors which brought Charles I's regime to its untimely end, culminating in an act which many regarded as justifiable tyrannicide.

7

Reading Revenge

Revenge is a pervasive theme in early modern English drama, directing plots and character motivation in comedy as well as tragedy. For instance it dominates the main plot of *The Dutch Courtesan* through the vengeful plotting of the spurned Franceschina, and in *The Roaring Girl* Moll's humiliation of the gallant Laxton is conducted as a kind of revenge against patriarchy by a woman reclaiming her honour. In Shakespearean comedy Beatrice in *Much Ado About Nothing* urges Benedict to 'kill Claudio' on her behalf in revenge for Claudio's dishonouring Hero, and Malvolio makes his exit from the reconciliatory finale of *Twelfth Night* by vowing, 'I'll be revenged on the whole pack of you.' But it is on the tragedy of revenge that this chapter will centre, to consider a selection of plays, many of them interrelated, which are structured by the concept of revenge, beginning with *The Spanish Tragedy* and continuing almost up to the closure of the theatres, with Shirley's *The Cardinal* of 1641. Revenge was the most popular plot-motif for tragedy in the period, and we need to think about why it had such continuous appeal. Although the term 'revenge tragedy' did not become current until the early twentieth century, it does not seem anachronistic as a way of categorizing plays like this in the early modern period, since they were written according to such specific and self-conscious conventions as to set them apart, and even to confer on them a kind of cult status. Revenge itself has an internal impulse towards structure, which lends itself towards dramatic enactment; there is a mimetic aspect, whereby the revenger imitates and pays back the initial offence, but also an incremental tendency, in that the retaliation may overgo that offence, and often cause widespread collateral damage. 'Besides, Revenge should have proportion', says Mathias of Saxony, one of the many wronged characters in Chettle's *The Tragedy of Hoffman*,

> By slie deceit he acted every wronge,
> And by deceit I would have him intrapt;
> Then the revenge were fit, just, and square.
> (2200–3)[1]

The object of revenge is a levelling out, and while it may at first stem from a moral impulse, as playwrights from the Greek tragedians and Seneca onwards recognized, the necessary recourse to violence runs the danger of compromising the revenger's integrity, not least because violence can become dangerously attractive in itself. 'When the bad bleed, then is the tragedy good', observes Vindice, the morally equivocal protagonist of *The Revenger's Tragedy*, with the implication that the more bleeding there is, the better. In Senecan tragedy, which was a formative influence on English revenge tragedy in its earlier years, notoriously, the act of revenge surpassed the original injury: 'Scelera non ulcisceris,/ Nisi vincis' (Injuries are not revenged except where they are exceeded) (*Thyestes*, 195–6).[2] The ghost of the murdered Andrugio in *Antonio's Revenge* incites his son to violence with this motto (3.1.51).

There is no denying that the impulse to take revenge for a perceived slight, injury or dishonour is a transhistorical one, not culturally restricted to particular periods of history or types of society. But revenge was particularly popular as a dramatic subject in Renaissance Europe, in the drama of France, Spain and Italy as well as of early modern England, where many of the best plays, and the best-known now, evolved around it. So it is worth asking the question as to whether there were particular tendencies in contemporary society with which plays about revenge might especially engage. Given that the dominant strain of Elizabethan tragedy, following neoclassical principles, is set in courts and concerns the ruling classes, it is inevitable that power structures and relationships between rulers and ruled will feature in actions of revenge. And while it may be the case that drama, because of its interactive mode of expression, operates in an indirect relationship to the dominant ideologies of the time, neither directly expressing or challenging them, it may nevertheless illuminate tensions within the existing social structures.

Historians concur in the view that in the sixteenth century the sovereign states of Europe were involved in a movement towards the centralization of power. Gordon Braden, in *Tragedy and the Senecan Tradition*, refers to 'the overarching political event of the day, the suppression of the feudal aristocracy by centralised monarchy and the newly unified modern state'.[3] In England, according to Ronald Broude, the Tudor monarchs took steps to consolidate that power by 'creating a central government strong enough to counteract the sort of baronial license which had led to the Wars of the Roses',[4] civil wars extensively dramatized by Shakespeare and others throughout the 1590s. The mystificatory identification by the Tudors and Stuarts of political order with cosmic order, as for instance in the much-quoted speech of Ulysses in *Troilus and Cressida*, was a strategy so successful that E. M. W. Tillyard accepted it as part of the popular ideology of the period in his influential, but now much challenged, book, *The Elizabethan World Picture*. The baronial classes resisted the attempt by the state to subsume authority under the crowned monarch and his officers, and noblemen continued to maintain bands of armed retainers, with whom they might appear at court. The traditional principles of family solidarity and the primacy of lineage and blood ties stood opposed to what Mervyn James calls 'the emergence of a "civil" society in which the monopoly of both honour and violence by the state was asserted'.[5] Honour was a key concept in the competitive world of early modern England, and in a society where violence was endemic its maintenance often took forms which challenged the ideals of order and civic behaviour that the Tudors wished to enforce. In Senecan tragedy the upholding of family or dynastic honour is an entrenched motif, which may account for some of its appeal to the Elizabethans. The conflict between the duty owed to family and kinsfolk and the allegiance claimed by the monarch and the forces of state control created dramatically exciting situations in plays like *The Spanish Tragedy* or *Hamlet*; and where the existing power structure was inefficient, morally compromised, or corrupt, as also in *Titus Andronicus, Antonio's Revenge, The Revenger's Tragedy* or *The Revenge of Bussy D'Ambois*, the resultant dilemma impacted on the moral status of the revenger himself.

As Katherine Maus notes, 'defectiveness of the status quo' is a precondition of revenge tragedy,[6] to which the revenge constitutes a response. This defectiveness is commonly inherent in the ruler himself, and in the condition of centralized and absolute authority he represents. The revenger, recognizing that he is unable to challenge such authority openly, must either resort to secret stratagems and concealment, 'dissembling quiet in unquietness' (3.13.30),[7] as Hieronimo in *The Spanish Tragedy* puts it, or take up a posture of stoic defiance and resistance to the imperfect world of fortune and change, like Bussy D'Ambois and his brother Clermont in *The Revenge of Bussy D'Ambois*. In either case, he finds himself alienated, spiritually as well as socially, from the society in which he has to operate. Hamlet's sense of the world as 'an unweeded garden that grows to seed' expresses the condition. The orthodox Christian position, based on the biblical injunction, 'Vengeance is mine; I will repay, saith the Lord' (Romans 12:19) is more of an 'ethical touchstone'[8] than a practical reality, except in the isolated instance of *The Atheist's Tragedy*, where Charlemont's forbearance in the face of the machinations of his doctrinairely atheist opponent D'Amville is, quasi-miraculously, vindicated. Although, as influential critics from the earlier twentieth century, such as Fredson Bowers and Lily B. Campbell have illustrated, there was an extensive body of moralistic and prescriptive literature concerning the taking of revenge, revenge tragedies tend to problematize the issue rather than taking a directly didactic line on it. Even if Clermont in *The Revenge of Bussy D'Ambois* and Charlemont in different ways follow the advice of the ghost in *The Atheist's Tragedy* to 'Attend with patience the success of things/ But leave revenge unto the King of Kings' (2.6.22–3),⁹ this is not a position open, for example, to Hieronimo, Titus Andronicus or Hamlet. It is complicated by questions of honour, both personal and familial, as well as the sceptical view of law and authority that underlies most of these plays. In such circumstances, the appeal of Senecan stoicism as a dignified and honourable stance in a world of unstable values is evident. Much has been made of Seneca's influence on revenge tragedy in terms of the mechanisms to activate horror, such as vengeful ghosts, scenes of excessive bloodshed and violence, and criminal protagonists; important as these aspects are, it is perhaps Seneca's lessons in philosophical detachment and self-sufficiency, along with his grand and hyperbolic rhetoric, what Sidney called 'the height of Seneca his style', that make the most profound impression on English tragedy of the period.

Revenge tragedies were always set abroad, partly because the regulation of the English stage made it impossible to deal with matters of politics or religion in the openness of a contemporary English setting, though it was recognized that foreign settings could easily be read as commenting on society at home. Heywood wrote in *An Apology for Actors* that 'if wee present a forreigne history, the subject is so intended, that in the lives of Romans, Grecians, or others, either the virtues of our Countrymen are extolled, or their vices reproved' (sig. F3v). But depictions of Spanish or Italian courts were not necessarily transparent, and they both reflect and endorse popular xenophobic attitudes to the great Catholic powers of Europe, against which the Protestant English nation was beginning to define itself. Italy especially was associated with the practice and passion of revenge, carried out with cruelty and violence, but often with cunning and deviousness. Nashe typically apostrophized the country: 'O Italie, the Academie of manslaughter, the sporting place of murther, the Apothecary-shop of poison for all nations: how many kind of weapons hast thou invented for malice?'¹⁰ Stories of the courts of the Borgias, often derived from Geoffrey Fenton's translation of Guicciardini, *The historie of Guicciardini containing the warres of Italy* (1579), created a background for plots of sensational and ingenious revenge involving poison, treachery and betrayal, and long-nursed grudges, only brought to fruition after long periods of brooding and contriving. In this context it is impossible to avoid the term 'Machiavellian'. The historical Machiavelli as a patriot and republican and political theorist was ignored in favour of the quasi-diabolic figure partially constructed from the well-known work of Gentillet, *A Discourse . . . Against Nicholas Machiavel* (translated into English 1608), and recognized from the plays of Kyd and Marlowe onwards as an atheist, hypocrite and ruthless power-seeker who acknowledged no bonds or allegiances, human or divine. As Machevil proclaims in the prologue Marlowe gives him to introduce *The Jew of Malta*,

> Many may talk of title to a Crowne:
> What right had *Caesar* to the Empery?
> Might first made Kings, and Lawes were then most sure,
> When, like the *Dracos*, they were writ in blood.
> (18–20)[11]

The Jew is his creature, and follows him in his love of treachery and contrivance, his total lack of conscience, his supreme egotism ('Ego mihimet sum semper proximus'),[12] and above all his smoothly deceptive exterior. As Maus says, the stage machiavel was so alarming a figure because he personified 'a radical, unprincipled estrangement of internal truth from external manifestation'.[13] The fear of the man whose exterior not only concealed but even belied his interior ran deep, and it is not accidental that this fear is often articulated in terms of role-playing and theatricality. Richard Gloucester, an early version of the machiavel, rejoices in the power conferred on him by his ability to play a part:

> Why, I can smile, and murder whiles I smile
> . . .
> Change shapes with Proteus for advantages
> And set the murderous Machiavel to school.
> (*Henry VI, Part 3*, 182, 192–3)

No revenge tragedy is without its Machiavellian plotter: Hieronimo and Lorenzo in *The Spanish Tragedy*, Piero in *Antonio's Revenge*, Hoffman in *The Tragedy of Hoffman*, Vindice in *The Revenger's Tragedy*, Francisco in *The White Devil*, Bosola in *The Duchess of Malfi*, to name but a few. The emergence of private plotting, concealed contrivance, solitary meditation into open and bloody vengeance and self-proclamation – ' "Tis I, 'tis Vindice, 'tis I' – creates a frisson peculiar to plays of this genre.

Revenge tragedy often climaxes in killing as a spectacle, sometimes in the form of ritualistic murder such as the bloody banquet of *Titus*

Andronicus or the masque of death in *The Revenger's Tragedy*, but also in forms closer to those taken by killings in real-life English society, such as the hangings of Horatio and Pedringano in *The Spanish Tragedy*, or the duel of honour in *Hamlet*. Death in the theatre and in real life were not unconnected. It has often been pointed out that James I drew on a parallel between state execution and the staging of monarchy in his remark that 'a king is as one set on a scaffold, whose smallest actions and gestures all the people do gazingly behold'.[14] In this connection Bate cites Heywood's *Apology for Actors*, where the playwright, attempting to defend the stage as a noble profession, points out how in imperial times tragedies were staged in which the real executions of condemned criminals took place, with the result, in his view, that the criminals, sited as the centrepiece of an aesthetic spectacle, 'would make suit rather so to dye with resolution, and by the hands of such princely *Actors*, then otherwise to suffer a shamefull and most detestable end' (sig. E3v). Conversely, in *The Spanish Tragedy* and *Titus Andronicus* it is members of the nobility who unsuspectingly take part in play-acting only to discover that the killing is for real. This was an era when public executions were common; it has been calculated that during the reigns of Elizabeth and James one person went to the gallows in England and Wales for every day of the year.[15] They were popular spectacles; for instance, hundreds of people turned out to witness the execution in 1572 of Anne Sanders and her confederates for the murder of George Sanders, who were, according to a contemporary account, displayed in 'the open Theater' before the public gaze, as they appeared on a specially erected stage to make their last confessions.[16] Executions and killings in the theatre of course differ in the most important respects from those in real life, but it seems safe to say that the enactment and displaying of death on the stage might cater to the voyeuristic fantasies of audiences whose appetite for the gruesome spectacle had been whetted by judicial killings witnessed at Tyburn. However, it may also be true that the similarities between revenge killings onstage and legalized killings in real life might prompt audiences to question the nature of the relationship between justice and the law. As Bate puts it, 'the necessity to revenge reveals the inadequacy of the law; the formalization of revenge in performance acts as a substitution for the law, simultaneously revealing the law to be itself nothing other than a performance'.[17] Those sardonically comic scenes in which condemned prisoners confidently await a pardon from friends at court, such as Pedringano in *The Spanish Tragedy* and Junior Brother in *The Revenger's Tragedy*, only to be disappointed at the last minute, may well have chimed with English audiences' experiences of the consequences of unfounded trust in the law, with strong implications of the law's emptiness and inadequacy. Revenge, as Bacon says, is 'a kind of wild justice', sidestepping the law or else subsuming its prerogative. The revenger's cause is the redemption of honour, which has been illegitimately taken from him by the actions of others.

Even if, as has been claimed, revenge is a feminine genre,[18] and revenge personified as Vindicta, a blood-stained female figure, revengers are normally male, and the honour which they seek to reclaim through their actions a necessary component of their masculinity. There has been much debate among social historians as to whether the period witnessed a crisis in gender relations, and if so, what form it took.[19] In a culture which was both patriarchal and misogynistic, any signs of independent or assertive behaviour by women was liable to be classified as deviant; and recent scholars have found much evidence of 'disorderly women and female power'[20] in England, especially in non-elite society. Concomitantly, 'anxious masculinity' has also become a focus of attention, illuminating not only the fears about women to which drama might give expression, but also the ways in which society operated to reinforce the ideology of patriarchy. In revenge tragedy a man's personal honour, as well as that of his family, is often in large part bound up with the conduct of his female relations, in *Hamlet*, *The Revenger's Tragedy*, *The Duchess of Malfi* and *The Maid's Tragedy*, for example. It is also defined in terms of his own ability to resist effeminization. Hamlet is disgusted with himself when he realizes that instead of taking action as a man would, he is compelled 'like a whore' to 'unpack my heart with words/ And fall a-cursing like a very drab,/ A scullion' (2.2.563–5). The reaffirming or reclaiming of masculinity is an important part of the revenger's project, sometimes because he is the representative of his family, the patriarchal figure who must guard and protect his womenfolk and dependents, like Vindice, sometimes because masculinity is essential to his own identity. The dying Hoffman accepts his fate at the hands of those enemies responsible for his father's death rather than rebelling against it, because he feels that his revenge has been compromised:

> You kild my father, my most warlike father,
> Thus as you deale by me, you did by him;
> But I deserve it that have slackt revenge
> Through fickle beauty, and a woman's fraud.
>
> (2609–12)

As he sees it, he has been emasculated by his pursuit of a woman, since his desire for her led him easily into a trap, and he has fallen into his enemies' hands through weakness. By contrast, the strength displayed by revenging women, such as Tamora in *Titus Andronicus* or Evadne in *The Maid's Tragedy*, is deviant and horrific; Tamora, though wronged and dishonoured, betrays her gender when she directs her anger against her Roman enemies:

> No grace, no womanhood – ah, beastly creature,
> That blot and enemy to our general name.
>   (2.3.182–3)

This is the accusation directed at her by Lavinia.

The significance of *The Spanish Tragedy*'s position as the first extant English tragedy centred on blood-revenge and its shaping influence on much of the drama to come, like its huge contemporary popularity, has never been disputed. It may have been preceded by the mysterious and ghostly *Ur-Hamlet*, the version of *Hamlet* that did exist, as we know from casual references by Lodge, Henslowe and others, from at least 1596 and possibly also written by Kyd, but, like so many plays of the period, this one has been lost for ever. In a number of ways, not least its social concerns, *The Spanish Tragedy* represents its genre; the conflict of interest between the desires of the individual and the authority of the state, the social tensions between the claims of the nobility and those of the meritocracy, the role and responsibility of the monarch, and the patriarchal anxiety over the transmission of heritage are all recurrent themes in revenge tragedy. *The Spanish Tragedy* is less typical in its use of a contemporary political setting involving the strained relations between Spain and Portugal in the 1580s, after the Spanish victory over the Portuguese at Alcantara in 1580, though the play is by no means historically accurate. Spain was England's greatest enemy at this time, and Hieronimo's curious masque presented to the King of Spain and the Portuguese Ambassador in 1.5 creates a fantasy of the English as historically victorious over both nations, allowing the audience a point of entry into the action. Hieronimo's role here as Master of the Revels, to be repeated in Act 4 when he organizes and presents the tragedy of Soliman and Perseda, enables him to obtain his revenge on the courts of Spain and Portugal through a dramatic performance. The ironic and metatheatrical quality of this scene, whereby both actors (with the exception of Bel-Imperia) and the audience are taken by surprise, the King of Spain, his brother and the Portuguese Viceroy commending as skilful acting what is in fact real dying, have never been surpassed. The moment at which Hieronimo reveals that the acting of death has been for real and not 'fabulously counterfeit' by producing the body of his own dead son brings home to both audiences, those onstage and those in the theatre, that drama is about real life. Hieronimo's triumph in revenge is sealed when, having bitten out his tongue to escape forced confession under torture, he manages to obtain a penknife and take with him another victim, the Duke of Castile, before claiming his own life. The last Chorus, spoken by the Ghost of Don Andrea and Revenge, who have presided, unseen, throughout the play, not only affirms the completeness of Hieronimo's revenge, but may also remind the audience in the theatre that they, too, may be providing the spectacle for unseen watchers, and the relationship between life and art is not clear-cut.

The social order that appears initially to exist in *The Spanish Tragedy* with the peace between Spain and Portugal, and the celebration of royal authority in the King of Spain, who is gracious in his treatment of his former enemy and eager to reward the loyal service of his subjects in the persons of Hieronimo and his son Horatio, is soon violently disrupted. Individual desire, manifested first by Bel-Imperia and then by Horatio, is at odds with the demands of patriarchy and hierarchy. Bel-Imperia, niece to the childless King of Spain and sister to Lorenzo, heir to the kingdom, is not content to accept her allotted role as dynastic trophy to be awarded to the suitor favoured by her male relations, in this case Prince Balthasar of Portugal, in order to forge a political alliance between the two nations. She has already attracted her brother's disapproving attention by conducting an affair with the lower-born Don Andrea, killed by Balthasar in battle, and now intends to take Horatio as a lover in his place. But first, Horatio's attraction to her must be put to use:

> How can love find harbour in my breast
> Till I revenge the death of my beloved?
> Yes, second love shall further my revenge!
> I'll love Horatio, my Andrea's friend
> The more to spite the prince that wrought his end.
>
> (1.4.64–7)

Horatio does not resist the charms of the beautiful and strong-willed Bel-Imperia, but their secret affair is betrayed to Lorenzo and Balthasar by Bel-Imperia's disloyal servant Pedringano, and he is murdered in the arbour where the two have hidden to make love. As the aristocrat's special caste insult to the low-born man who threatened his dynastic ambitions, Lorenzo has Horatio's body hanged in the arbour, and jokes cynically as he does so:

> Although his life were still ambitious proud
> Yet is he at the highest now he is dead.
>
> (2.4.60–1)

The grief-stricken Hieronimo's efforts to prove the identity of his son's murderer are thwarted by the cunning and influential Lorenzo, who has aristocratic power and status on his side, and can both silence underlings and sway the King, his uncle. Hieronimo, whose position as Marshal of Spain means that he is responsible for the administration of the law, is increasingly frustrated by the irony of his situation:

> Thus must we toil in other men's extremes,
> That know not how to remedy our own;
> And do them justice, when unjustly we
> For all our wrongs, can compass no redress.
>
> (3.6.1–4)

The man who has risen above the circumstances of his birth, like Don Andrea and Horatio, and has become a worthy servant of the state, is betrayed by the system when he had expected his dutiful service to be rewarded, just as the servant Pedringano is betrayed by his master Lorenzo. Social bonds and obligations have no currency; Hieronimo is driven back on his own sense of family loyalty and the archaic compulsion to revenge.

Hieronimo acknowledges the existence of the orthodox Elizabethan prohibition on private revenge in favour of attending on the fulfilment of God's purpose, but for him it is a kind of moral yardstick rather than practical reality. Senecan doctrine is more in accordance with the promptings of his grief-stricken heart:

> '*Per scelus semper tutum est sceleribus iter.*'
> Strike, and strike home, when wrong is offer'd thee;
> For evils unto ills conductors be.
>
> (3.13.6–8)

But revenge is much more than a mechanical impulse for Hieronimo; Kyd so movingly depicts the father's pride in his ambitious and talented only son and his outrage at the brutality of the murder that paternal grief becomes a sympathetic aspect of Hieronimo's motivation. His wife Isabella's suicide is the response of despair to the destruction of her hopes for the future; it makes Hieronimo's active vengeance the more necessary. The theme of broken heritage is echoed and re-echoed in the Portuguese Viceroy's sorrow for the loss of Prince Balthasar and the Spanish King's grief at the ending of his dynasty, and particularly in the plight of the old man, Bazulto, who comes as a petitioner before Hieronimo in his capacity of Marshal of Spain, to supplicate for justice for his murdered son. It is at this point in the play that Hieronimo is so overwhelmed by his own sorrow that he loses his hold on reason, momentarily identifying Bazulto with the dead Horatio, and then recognizing the old man as a mirror of his own condition:

> Thou art the lively image of my grief;
> Within thy face my sorrows I may see.
>   (3.13.160–1)

In the additions to the play, written by someone other than Kyd, perhaps Jonson, for the new quarto printed in 1602, the mirror effect is even more emphatically reproduced in a scene with a painter, Bazardo, also the father to a murdered son. Hieronimo requests Bazardo to reproduce Horatio's murder and his own response to it in a picture:

> Make me curse, make me rave, make me cry, make me mad, make me well again, make me curse hell, invoke heaven, and in the end leave me in a trance; and so forth.
> *Painter*: And is this the end?

7 Woodcut from the title page of the 1623 edition of *The Spanish Tragedy*, by Kyd.

Hieronimo: O no, there is no end; the end is death and madness! And I am
never better than when I am mad.

(Fourth Addition to *The Spanish Tragedy*, 154–59)

These scenes brilliantly create the quality of a world where nothing makes
sense, all order is lost, to which alienation and madness seem the only
responses. And if Hieronimo's carefully planned and violent revenge seems
excessive in that it eradicates the innocent along with the guilty, the Ghost's
concluding summary, listing the multiple deaths as an interconnected
series, has a certain restorative quality in its sense of vindication and
completion.

The *Spanish Tragedy* was imitated and parodied over several decades.
Shakespeare responded to it, probably quite rapidly, in *Titus Andronicus*,
his first tragedy, and again, in a more measured way, in *Hamlet*. Marston's
Antonio's Revenge and Chettle's *The Tragedy of Hoffman*, plays of uncertain
dating close in time to *Hamlet*, form part of this same group, all featuring
alienated protagonists bent on revenge for injuries to their family in the
context of a corrupt or ineffective sovereign power. Like Hieronimo, Titus
is a father driven to the verge of madness by the destruction of his family,
although he is not, unlike Hieronimo, guiltless to begin with. He finds
an image for his own condition of spiritual alienation, not in the plight
of another individual, but in the raging of a storm-tossed sea, which
deluges the earth in its violent motions, just as Titus's passions exceed
his capacity to control them. Again, the revenge is bloodthirsty and excessive, consisting first in the cutting onstage of the throats of Chiron and
Demetrius, brutish sons to the Goth Queen Tamora, and then in baking
them in a pie which Tamora unwittingly eats, after which Titus stabs her.
The classical setting Shakespeare chose for his revenge tragedy, consciously 'antique' though not in fact directly historical, enabled him to
draw on the Senecan motifs of the Thyestean banquet along with other
stories from classical literature, such as the rape of Philomela from Ovid
and the rape of Lucretia, in a way that marks *Titus Andronicus* off as
completely different from any other revenge tragedy of the period. But
as in *The Spanish Tragedy*, the play's world is one in which a mighty empire
is on the verge of collapse; and Titus, a man devoted, perhaps excessively,
to the pieties of ancient Rome whose military glory he has done so much
to uphold, is at a loss in a society where these values go for nothing. As
with Hieronimo, the form of his revenge involves the destruction of the
whole society in which he once played so vital a part. He is pushed to
the limits when, having sacrificed his own right hand to the Emperor
Saturninus to save the lives of his sons Quintus and Martius, falsely

accused of murder, their severed heads are brought back to him. Encircled by the few remaining members of his family he takes a ritual vow:

> You heavy people, circle me about,
> That I may turn me to each one of you
> And swear unto my soul to right your wrongs.
> (3.1.275–7)

This can only be achieved with outside aid. Thus he sends off his eldest son Lucius to raise an army from Rome's enemy, the Goths, to attack the city, although in the event the Goth invasion is less crucial to the denouement than is Titus's ability to outdo his chief antagonist, Tamora, in a battle of wits. Once again, there is no possibility of redress through legal means, since Rome is ruled by the corrupt Saturninus, and the scene in which Titus and his followers send petitions to the gods on letters attached to arrows satirically rejects the notion of divine justice. 'Terras Astraea relinquit', as Titus tells his brother Marcus. Blood revenge is the only option. But in the course of pursuing it, Titus's involvement in violence blurs the distinction between just revenger and murderer. His violation of taboos and codes of honour is no less than Tamora's. Before he kills Chiron and Demetrius, he gloatingly details the process of his vengeance on Tamora in a ritualistic speech where retaliation entirely submerges justice:

> Hark, villains, I will grind your bones to dust,
> And with your blood and it I'll make a paste,
> And of the paste a coffin I will rear,
> And make two pasties of your shameful heads,
> And bid that strumpet, your unhallowed dam,
> Like to the earth swallow her own increase.
> (5.3.186–91)

The same compromising of the revenger's moral identity occurs in *Antonio's Revenge* and *The Tragedy of Hoffman*, where issues of revenge for wrongs done to family members are also at stake. In both, revenge is a problematic concept because of its association from the start with evil rather than justice. The first revenger in *Antonio's Revenge* is Piero Sforza, a character of distinctly Senecan criminality, who celebrates his own 'topless villainy' (1.1.85) in planning a revenge on the royal house of Genoa: 'Poison the father, butcher the son, and marry the mother, ha!' (1.1.105). For him, vengeance is pleasurable destruction: 'Swell plump, bold heart,/ For now thy tide of vengeance riseth in' (2.2.217–18).[21] The young Antonio, son to the dead duke of Genoa and Piero's chief victim, although, like Hamlet, conscious of being greatly wronged and unable to regain legal redress, does not move towards active revenge until midway through the play, prompted by his father's angry ghost. Newly motivated by this vengeful apparition, Antonio's first acts as revenger transform him instantly from innocent victim to bloody criminal. In a sadistic scene he stabs to death the child Julio, Piero's son, and then enters his mother's bedchamber with 'his arms bloody, a torch and a poniard', rejoicing in the killing:

> Look how I smoke in blood, reeking the steam
> Of foaming vengeance. O my soul's enthron'd
> In the triumphant chariot of revenge.
> Methinks I am all air and feel no weight
> Of human dirt clog. This is Julio's blood;
> Rich music, father! This is Julio's blood.
>
> (3.2.79–84)

The image of the exultant Antonio is clearly intended to identify him visually with Piero as he appears at the start of the play, 'unbrac'd, his arms bare, smear'd in blood, a poniard in one hand, and a torch in the other'. For Antonio, revenge is a perversely life-enhancing act and when, at the end, having served up Julio's body to his father in a banqueting dish, Antonio combines with the other conspirators to torture and kill Piero, he again celebrates killing as triumph:

> I will not lose the glory of the deed
> Were all the tortures of the deepest hell
> Fix'd to my limbs. I pierc'd the monster's heart
> With an undaunted hand.
>
> (5.3.120–2)

The rituals of vengeance are fully subsumed into a political act of vengeance against a tyrant, whereby Antonio and his supporters are praised for 'ridding huge pollution from the state'; and the last speeches are pervaded by images of catharsis.

This apparent endorsement and moral approval of grotesque violence in *Antonio's Revenge*, which has made many of the play's critics uncomfortable, have been read in terms of the play's metatheatrical quality; more than once, the child actors in Marston's play are made to draw attention to their identities as performers. Old Pandulpho, for example, displaying like Hieronimo his dead son's body, weeps, then remarks:

> Man will break out, despite philosophy.
> Why, all this while I ha' but play'd a part,
> Like to some boy that acts a tragedy,
> Speaks burly words and raves out passion.
>
> (4.2.69–72)

The fact that the speaker *is* a boy that acts a tragedy acknowledges the illusion being created in front of the audience, and distances them from the emotion being expressed. As Barbara Baines suggests, Marston gives his characters a self-conscious dimension, as beings aware of themselves behaving like actors in a play.[22] Thus the dramatic technique 'creates an aesthetic detachment in the audience precisely at the moment of the intensification of emotional response. This dual response of the audience is made possible through a consciousness of the actors as characters who behave as actors.'[23] By substituting an aesthetic perspective on revenge for a moral one, and thus celebrating the bloodshed and violence deplored by the Christian position on revenge, Marston, in Baines's view, implies a critique of the revenge genre and of the audience approval which has fostered it. But how far the audience would have been capable of this double response is another matter.

Such a reading cannot be made of Chettle's *The Tragedy of Hoffman*, a play written very close in time to *Antonio's Revenge* and to *Hamlet*; the exact chronology of these three plays has never been conclusively established, although it is hard to believe, despite the tantalizing similarities between the three, that *Hamlet* was the earliest. The sustained metatheatrical dimension, which Marston perhaps elaborated from *The Spanish Tragedy*, is absent in *Hoffman*; although Hoffman's project is to gain revenge for his father's death it commands no ethical sympathy because his father was executed for the crime of piracy. Hoffman has no political mitigation for the bloodthirsty cunning with which he hunts down and despatches a series of enemies. His sidekick Lorrique, a villainous servant in the mould of Ithamore from *The Jew of Malta* or Aaron in *Titus Andronicus*, who take conscious delight in evil, draws attention to the excessive quality of Hoffman's revenge, remarking:

> I am halfe a Monarke: halfe a fiend
> Blood I begun in and in blood must end
> yet this *Clois* is an honest villaine, ha's conscience in his killing of men:
> he kils none but his fathers enemies, and there issue, 'tis admirable,
> 'tis admirable, 'tis well 'tis meritorious, where? in heaven? no, hell.
>
> (659–64)

Chettle has taken Kyd's motif of family pride and inverted it, turning Hieronimo's pathetic devotion to his dead son into Hoffman's obsessive desire to preserve his father's skeleton, which he has stolen from the gallows where it was hung, and to honour his father with a wide-sweeping tragic revenge which 'shall pass those of Thyestes, Tereus,/ Jocasta, or

Duke Jason's jealous wife' (409–10). Like Barabas in *The Jew of Malta*, Hoffman nurses a grudge against the ruling classes who he feels have victimized him, and aspires to displace them. He fantasizes to Lorrique about their future together, once his revenges are accomplished:

> That done; ile seat thee by my throne of state,
> And make thee rival in those governments,
> That by thy secrecy thou lift'st me to;
> Shalt be a Duke at least.
>
> (735–8)

But whereas Lorrique, like Ithamore, is fully conscious of his own villainy, Hoffman believes himself to be carrying out a justified revenge after the style of the classical models such as Thyestes. The impulse to revenge has gained its own momentum, losing sight of measure or proportion in the process. But Hoffman does not triumph in slaughter as Hieronimo does; he dies as his father did, killed by the imposition of a burning iron crown, regretting the incompletion of his own project. Chettle's play depicts revenge as a destructive and alienating impulse, which nurtures the revenger's obsessions and his sense of invulnerability. There is something of this notion in *Hamlet*, except that fatalism substitutes for invulnerability, but it is explored more fully in *The Revenger's Tragedy*.

Initially Vindice, whose name of course suggests that he is an embodiment of the impulse to revenge, seems at least partially justified in his hatred of the corrupt ducal family, and in particular in his wish for vengeance on the old Duke, who some years earlier had poisoned Vindice's lover, Gloriana, when she would not consent to his sexual advances. When the Duke's son and heir Lussurioso attempts to replicate his father's depredation of Vindice's family by plotting to seduce his sister, Castiza, Vindice's anger knows no bounds. Lussurioso compounds his offence by proposing to bribe Castiza's mother to act as bawd to her daughter. After Lussurioso has hired the disguised Vindice to make the initial approaches as his pander, the revenger makes a solemn vow:

> Sword, I durst make a promise of him to thee;
> Thou shalt disheir him; it shall be thine honour.
>
> (1.3.174–5)[24]

At this point he is horrified by Lussurioso's predatory behaviour and almost unable to comprehend his cynical misogyny, believing his mother and sister to be impregnable against Lussurioso's advances. He and his brother Hippolyto have been drawn into court corruption through poverty; Hippolyto is an attendant in the Duke's chamber, dependent on royal favour because their father, now dead, was robbed of due recognition for his service by the Duke and thus unable to provide adequately for his family. So the hatred of the Ducal family has a material basis, and Vindice's view of himself and his brother at this point as 'innocent villains' (1.3.170) need not be read ironically. But the play shows how his progressive involvement in the planning of revenge is in itself corrupting, especially since the moral impulse modulates into an aesthetic one. In the play's central scene, where Vindice displays to Hippolyto his masterstroke, dressing up the skull of Gloriana in rich robes, poisoning its jaws, and presenting it as a 'country lady' to satisfy the old Duke's lust, his joy in the cunning of the contrivance takes even Hippolyto by surprise. 'O sweet, delectable, rare, happy ravishing', exclaims Vindice.

> *Hippolyto*: Why, what's the matter, brother?
> *Vindice*:   O, 'tis able
> To make a man spring up, and knock his forehead
> Against yon silver ceiling.
>
>   (3.5.1–4)

Although his use of the skull as the instrument of its own revenge is essentially fitting to the ethical and aesthetic style of revenge as retaliation for lost honour, the sadism of the scene combines with the revengers' pleasurable observation of the Duke's agonizing death to complicate the audience response to revenge as an act of justice; and Vindice's triumphant summation, 'Now nine years' vengeance crowd into a minute' (3.5.123), might have recalled the English dislike of long-harboured revenge and of the cunningly contrived style of revenge which they imputed to 'Machiavelli's nation':

> Indeed, there is nothing wherin they take greater delectation, pleasure, and contentment, than to execute a vengeance; insomuch as, whensoever they can have their enemie at their pleasure, to be revenged upon him after some strange & barbarous fashion, and in murdering him they put him in remembrance of the offence done unto them, with many reproachful words and injuries to torment the soule and the bodie together; sometimes they wash their hands and their mouthes with his blood, and force him with hope of his life to give himselfe to the divell; so they seeke in slaying the bodie to damne the soule, if they could.[25]

Hippolyto applauds 'the quaintness of thy malice', and in the second half of the play the brothers become preoccupied with achieving the perfect revenge. They are disappointed at the loss of a 'sweet opportunity' to kill Lussurioso in 5.1, when he comes to view what he expects to be the body of Piato (the name Vindice assumes in disguise), and finds instead that of his own father. 'Here was the sweetest occasion, the fittest hour, to have made my revenge familiar with him' (5.1.15–16), claims Vindice punningly; but Lussurioso has not come alone, so the brothers must delay. And when at last the killing is achieved, it is only Vindice's and Hippolyto's pride in their achievement that betrays them; Antonio is baffled at the extraordinary way in which the Duke has been despatched, until Vindice enlightens him: ''Twas somewhat wittily carried, though we say it. 'Twas we two murdered him'. Although Vindice expects to be congratulated on his achievement, and is momentarily taken aback by Antonio's horrified response, the revengers' final emotion is satisfaction; but their success is figured rather as a triumph of wit than of honour or justice, and it is not a misrepresentation to call the play's ending 'cheerful'.[26]

The play's exploration of revenge is complicated by the range of revenge actions depicted, 'the most elaborate plot ever seen on the stage of the Globe',[27] as it has been called: Vindice's, on the Duke, for the murder of Gloriana, and, following that, on Lussurioso, for the attempted seduction of Castiza; the Duke's bastard son, Spurio's, on the Duke, for the social exclusion brought on him by his bastardy; Antonio's, on the Duke's family, for condoning the rape of his wife; Ambitioso's and Supervacuo's, on Lussurioso, for contriving the execution of their brother Junior; Lussurioso's, on Piato for making him look a fool in front of his father; and, overarching all this, the revenge that Vindice envisages in 5. 2 when he marshals his supporters against Lussurioso:

> Let our hid flames break out, as fire, as lightning,
> To blast his villainous dukedom, vexed with sin.
>
> (5.2.5–6)

A lord responds: 'Our wrongs are such,/ We cannot justly be revenged too much.' The effect of the play has sometimes been judged to be didactic, a moralistic exposure of human depravity and a warning against assuming God's prerogative by taking revenge into one's own hands. Certainly, the playwright, whether Middleton, as now widely accepted, or some other, has pulled no punches in his depiction of corruption. Every member of the ducal family is sinful, and the conscienceless lust displayed by the Duke and his son Lussurioso can perhaps be read as representative of tyrannical power in a broader sense. The Duke's regime is guilty, too, of social sins against the people, of injustice and failure to reward service, suggested in the neglect of Vindice's father which contributes so strongly to the family's resentment of its rulers. The background of a society which has lost all moral standards along with any conception of a stable hierarchy, where law is so ineffectual and biased as to be completely disregarded, is filled out in terms suggestive of Jacobean England and the court of King James, regularly satirized for its extravagance and loose morality. Vindice's extraordinary speech on the transience of mortal things in 3.5, beginning 'Does the silk-worm expend her yellow labours / For thee?' brilliantly illustrates this vision of a world out of kilter. It is a conservative vision, informed, as John Peter has pointed out,[28] by the medieval tradition of Complaint with its awareness that all human life is vanity. Yet this reading of *The Revenger's Tragedy* as a kind of late morality is easily unsettled by the play's parodic, sceptical qualities, its humour, its black comedy effects, which operate to subvert a straight-faced moralistic account. The self-conscious, even playful, dramatic style of the play suggests an ambiguous attitude not just towards the taking of revenge but also towards the genre of the revenge tragedy. The play has been seen as 'an exercise in theatrical self-abandonment', the real subject of which is not revenge at all, but an extended commentary on *Hamlet*.[29] There is a sense in which the revenge play is beginning to feel played out.

Another way in which this sense might be thought to express itself is the move towards a drama of anti-revenge. The two plays *The Revenge of Bussy D'Ambois* (1610), by Chapman, and *The Atheist's Tragedy* (1611), by Tourneur, were written after what Bowers called 'the golden age of the true Kydian revenge tragedy',[30] and as he sees it both plays are 'in revolt against the bloodthirsty and hysterical Kydian hero'.[31] In neither case are the 'retaliatory prerogatives'[32] of the wronged man central to the outcome. *The Revenge of Bussy D'Ambois* is a play loosely based on recent French history, and written as a sequel to *Bussy D'Ambois* (1607), which followed quite closely the eventful life of a colourful, somewhat anarchic French nobleman at the court of Henry III, who was, like the character in the play, killed by the angry husband of the woman he had seduced. In the sequel it is Bussy's fictional brother, Clermont D'Ambois, who is cast in the role of revenger. His motivation has been rather differently construed; for Bowers, if it is strictly viewed, it is tainted because 'conceived in an unjust cause',[33] since Bussy died for committing adultery, but neither play makes much of this fact, whereas for Broude it is 'most nearly in accordance with divine purpose', since Clermont is an honourable man and his antagonist a sadistic coward, the killing is carried out openly in fair fight and the dying man forgives his killer at the point of death. The revenge, undertaken to appease the restless ghost of Bussy, is not in fact the climax of the play, nor is revenge its central focus, since Clermont's conflict with the authoritarian state of Henry III and his unscrupulous ministers is Chapman's real interest. After Clermont has revenged his brother's death he discovers that his friend and patron, the Duke of Guise, has been murdered at the behest of the King; the loss of the Guise strikes at Clermont's heart, but the possibility of revenging his death is unquestioningly dismissed:

> There is no disputing with the acts of Kings:
> Revenge is impious on their sacred persons.
>
> (5.5.151–2)[34]

Clermont, whose greatest loyalty has been to the Guise, therefore kills himself. Far from being an obsession, as it becomes for Hieronimo or Vindice, revenge for Clermont is what Bowers calls 'a repugnant duty'; his greatest preoccupation in life is to study 'how to be truely noble, truely wise' (1.1.151), and he despises actions such as revenge undertaken in passion: 'Nor can we call it Vertue that proceedes/ from vicious Fury' (3.2.108–9). Although his brother's ghost appears in 5.1 to put the view that in this instance revenge would be justifiable because it makes good a deficiency in the law, the ghostly appearances here and elsewhere in the play come across as remnants of an outworn dramatic mode, in which the playwright has no real dramatic confidence. Clermont does the best he can, undertaking a gentlemanly revenge in the fairest possible way, but it is in the stoic manner of his death that his honour is truly confirmed.

Unusually, it is the women characters in this play who demonstrate the greatest commitment to revenge. Tamara, the bereaved lover of the dead Bussy D'Ambois, calls on revenge, with all its familiar associations of blood, passion and retribution, to take possession of her spirit; Charlotte, sister to Bussy and Clermont, finding her brother's attitude 'foggy-spirited', disguises herself as a man, having decided to 'strip off my shame with my attire' to take over the task of revenge herself (3.2.163). The Countess of Cambrai, Clermont's lover, who has literally wept herself blind through grief at the news that he has been betrayed and captured, is the third in this female triad, embodying that appeal to passion and violence that Clermont abjures.

Where Chapman's play seeks to demonize Kydian revenge by feminizing it, Tourneur, who also defines heroism in terms of stoical virtue rather than the pursuit of honour through blood, marginalizes revenge still further, by associating it with the surrender to passion and base natural impulse that Christian belief deprecates. In *The Atheist's Tragedy*, as in *The Revenge of Bussy D'Ambois*, the world is a morally more straightforward place than in *The Revenger's Tragedy*, one where traditional values still maintain and codes of honour are recognized and acknowledged. In *The Revenge of Bussy D'Ambois* monarchy is not an institution in which the honourable individual can place any trust, but at least honourable individuals can exist and hold on to their integrity in spite of it. *The Atheist's Tragedy*, unusually, is a play in which the court is absent and the institutions of state have little place. There is no tyrant, and the threat to order and stability comes not from above but from below, and is represented in the protagonist, D'Amville, a discontented younger brother motivated by the desire to improve the material fortunes of his family and create a dynasty regardless of anyone who stands in his way. Because, like Edmund in *King Lear*, he is a younger brother, he has no rights to the patrilineal fortunes, and no respect for the traditions of inherited order; he believes only in the primacy of the individual will, which, like Edmund, he identifies with nature. As his name might have implied, he is an atheist, committed to a materialist view of reality, which is, in the play's terms, not just untenable but spiritually abhorrent. D'Amville, his sons and those minor characters like the adulterous Levidulcia, his sister-in-law, and the lecherous Puritan chaplain Languebeau Snuff, whose lives are dedicated to the satisfaction of the senses, are all deviants destined to extinction in a world ultimately governed by a beneficent providence. D'Amville's Machiavellian schemes to acquire wealth and status are directed against the family of his brother Montferrers. He murders Montferrers, and falsely reports the death of Montferrers's son, Charlemont, in action; then, having persuaded the honourable Charlemont to take up military service abroad, he marries off Castabella, an heiress and Charlemont's betrothed, to his diseased elder son Rousard. Charlemont is confronted on the battlefield by his father's ghost. But whereas ghosts in revenge plays conventionally appear to advocate revenge, in the mode of Senecan drama, this one has a different agenda. His message is terse and unequivocal:

> Return to France, for thy old father's dead
> And thou by murder disinherited.
> Attend with patience the success of things,
> But leave revenge unto the King of Kings.
> (2.6.20–23)

And when, later, Charlemont is about to kill Sebastian, D'Amville's younger son, in revenge for the wrongs committed by D'Amville, the ghost again intervenes:

> Hold, Charlemont!
> Let him revenge my murder and thy wrongs
> To whom the justice of revenge belongs.
> (3.2.32–4)

Charlemont's impulse to retaliate is thwarted, and once he has managed to submit himself to fate and find comfort in stoic resignation, a protective providence takes control over his fortunes, and those of Castabella. Charlemont's passivity is set against D'Amville's frenetic machinations. The triumph of stoicism is crowned when D'Amville knocks out his own brains with the axe intended for Charlemont, and Charlemont speaks the play's message:

> Only to Heav'n I attribute the work,
> Whose gracious motives made me still forbear
> To be mine own revenger. Now I see
> That *patience is the honest man's revenge.*
>
> (5.2.274–7)

In both moral and social terms the play articulates a profoundly conservative vision, sidestepping all the challenges and ambiguities of the earlier revenge plays.

Although the simplifications of *The Atheist's Tragedy* might suggest that revenge had become unfashionable as a dramatic subject, this was by no means the case. Tragedies written between 1611 and 1641 return regularly to an exploration of the revenge ethic, notable examples being *The White Devil*, *The Duchess of Malfi*, *Women Beware Women*, *The Changeling* and *'Tis Pity She's A Whore*, all plays discussed elsewhere in this book, though it is never the moral centre of the action. Exploration of the kind of social issues which so dominated *The Spanish Tragedy* takes other forms. Shirley's *The Cardinal* (1641), performed less than a year before the closure of the theatres in 1642, is almost certainly the last such play, and it revisits many themes and motifs from earlier revenge tragedies, beginning with *The Spanish Tragedy*, with what has been praised as 'unJacobean simplicity'.[35] Its model is *The Duchess of Malfi*, from which the conflict between authority and individual desire is taken. The revenge situation is created by the conflict between the courageous Duchess Rosaura, who determines to marry the man she loves, Alvarez, and the Cardinal, a monster of vice, who wishes her to marry his nephew Columbo. Rosaura is, like the Duchess of Malfi, a widow, and feels herself as a woman and a duchess compromised by her sex and her rank:

> Misery
> Of birth and state! That I could shift into
> A meaner blood, or find some art to purge
> That part which makes my veins unequal!
>
> (1.2.198–202)

When Alvarez is murdered by Columbo, in a supposed marriage masque, reminiscent of the death-by-playacting in *The Revenger's Tragedy*, she longs passionately for the chance to revenge his death herself. Although she is a forceful woman – the only person bold enough to confront the Cardinal to his face with an account of the ways in which he has abused his office – she is not, like the revenging women in *The Revenge of Bussy D'Ambois* or *The Maid's Tragedy*, demonized for her vengeful desires; for her, revenge is a quasi-religious obligation, referred to as 'tragic duties' to her husband's hearse, for which she will 'sacrifice to that hovering ghost / Columbo's life' (4.2.147–8). In the event, she falls back on the feminized resource of pretend madness, although the true extent of her madness, as in Hamlet's case, remains ambiguous. At any rate, the Cardinal is deceived, and also angered by the thought that he cannot now take his own revenge on her, because it will be wasted on someone incapable of appreciating what it means; her new-found docility, or as he puts it, 'her loss of brain', makes her an unfit antagonist:

> She's
> So much a turtle, I shall lose by killing her,
> Perhaps do her a pleasure and preferment.
> That must not be.
>
> (5.1.43–5)

The problem of achieving a just revenge, which troubled Hamlet when confronted with Claudius apparently at prayer, remains an issue, if not a strictly ethical one. However, the play does find an honourable revenger in Hernando, a colonel who has been insulted on the battlefield by Columbo, but more importantly admires Alvarez and loves the Duchess. He takes up her cause, killing Columbo and then confronting the Cardinal. In Hernando revenge is purged of its connotations both of violence and of self-satisfaction; his encounter with Columbo is a fair fight, carefully choreographed, with seconds present, and in the final confrontation with the Cardinal, he reverts to the expiatory rhetoric of the earliest revenge plays, invoking the spirit of the murdered Alvarez to present himself as 'the man / When the world's justice fails, shall right thy ashes, / And feed their thirst with blood!' (5.3.78–80). Although the circumstances are quite different, this recalls Hieronimo being forced to take revenge to compensate for the failure of the law. When, on behalf both of Alvarez and of the Duchess, Hernando rushes out from behind the arras to stab the Cardinal, he transforms the killing into an act of purgation:

> Your blood
> Is much inflam'd: I have brought a lancet wi' me
> Shall open your hot veins and cool your fever.
>
> (5.3.174–7)

The Cardinal then seems to acknowledge the justice of his fate in a confession to the King:

> My life hath been prodigiously wicked;
> My blood is now the kingdom's balm; O sir,
> I have abus'd your ear, your trust, your people,
> And my own sacred office.
>
>   (5.3.198–202)

But he also contrives, in a last act of Machiavellian cunning, to kill the Duchess by getting her to drink her health with him from a bowl of poisoned wine. As it transpires, it is this poison which kills him, since the wounds he received turn out not to be fatal. 'Then I have caught myself in my own engine', he observes, summing up the demise of so many revengers. In this play it is the Cardinal onto whom tyrannous authority is displaced, and the King is a secondary figure, well-intentioned but quite easily swayed. The Cardinal, though apparently based on Cardinal Richlieu, then, in 1641, at the height of his power in France, in all probability referred also to the much-hated Archbishop Laud, at the time awaiting trial in the Tower.[36] The play has recently been read as an intervention in the 'fierce debate about the power wielded by the Anglican prelacy in both church and state',[37] which seems plausible, given the historical moment of its performance. In the play, revenge accomplishes restoration, but perhaps at this dangerous time for the English monarchy, the King's final realization that he should have made a better choice of advisors was somewhat wishful thinking. He gets the play's last, gnomic, line: 'None have more need of perspectives than kings.'

8

Comedy and the City

London is the capital of England and so superior to other English towns that London is not said to be in England, but rather England to be in London.

Thomas Platter

The women have much more liberty than perhaps in any other place; they also know well how to make use of it.

Duke of Wirtemberg

The inhabitants of early modern London were, like those of today, self-conscious about their city, and foreign visitors always felt it necessary to make some comment, usually admiring, about the capital. 'We may well understand by the relation of Travellers, as by our owne experience, that London is not alone the Honour of our Nation, but by others reputed the Mirror of Europe, for Civill Government, and stately building, and the unparalel'd patterne of vertue, in her many grave Senators and Citizens.'[1] So wrote the pamphleteer Richard Rawlidge, although in its context this view of London as a prototype of civic glory for all Europe to admire is in fact the prelude to a denunciation of the proliferation of 'alehouses, Tipling-houses, Tobacco-shops etc. in London and the skirts thereof',[2] that had manifested itself in recent times. This was a period of rapid change in the city; its population was increasing, from about 50,000 at the beginning of the sixteenth century to five times that number at the end, and almost doubling again by 1660.[3] Immigration from mainland Europe, particularly significant in the 1560s and early 1570s, was a major cause. As Stow and other chroniclers record, one result of the Reformation visible to all was the destruction of monasteries and priories and the erection of grand houses on what had formerly been church lands by those families ennobled and enriched by Henry VIII; and after the fall of Antwerp in 1576 London became the greatest trading city of Europe. The legend of its foundation by the Trojan Brutus, a descendant of Aeneas, 'increasingly became a legitimising myth for England's national and imperial ambitions',[4] and enabled the city to represent itself as a synecdoche for the whole country, not least in terms of the huge material transformation of English society in this period.[5] The concentration of power and wealth in London was regarded with some ambivalence, as an epigram of 1628 by John Owen, 'London's Loadstone', suggests:

> As Thames devours many small brooks and rills,
> So smaller towns with their wealth London fills;
> But though that Thames empts itself in the sea
> Wealth once in London never runs away.[6]

'With time England will be only London', King James had observed. The growth of trade, the importation of exotic products and substances, silver from Spanish America, silks and spices from the East, the 'sugar, civet, almonds, cambrick' that provide the basis for Simon Eyre's rapid rise to wealth and fame in *The Shoemakers' Holiday*, was an important and highly visible aspect of the city's increasing prosperity. Donald Lupton, in *London and the Country Carbonadoed* (1622), characterized the city as 'the great Bee-hive of Christendome', a centre of industry and production. But London was also, in a notorious phrase, a 'centre of conspicuous consumption'.[7] Such consumption might be celebrated in the praise of abundance; but, conversely, the swarming plenitude evoked in Jonson's comedies such as *The Alchemist* and *Bartholomew Fair* might result in a transformation of the urban landscape into what has been called 'an Elizabethan junkyard'.[8] Expressions of pride in the city's glories were invariably tempered with an awareness of the other side of the coin:

> O London, thou art great in glory, and envied for thy greatnes: thy Towers, thy temples, and thy Pinnacles stand upon thy head like borders of fine gold, and thy waters like frindges of silver hang at the hemmes of thy garments. Thou art the goodliest of thy neighbours, but the prowdest; the wealthiest, but the most wanton. Thou hast all things in thee to make thee the fairest, and all things in thee to make thee the foulest.[9]

Here Dekker invokes the bi-fold character of the city in generalities, glamorizing it in the sort of register a preacher might have used; but what the drama of the period explores is particularities, which can be more simply defined in secular terms. Manley refers to 'a sense of moral, social, and economic crisis' arising out of 'the distortion of human values and relationships by the power of money.'[10] As Jean-Christophe Agnew has shown, it was not just the power of money that created an unprecedented social anxiety, but the proliferation of many forms of unregulated commerce, resulting in what he calls 'the placeless market': 'A new extraterritorial zone of production and exchange sprang up outside London's ancient marketplaces and thus out of reach of their juridical, ceremonial and talismanic protections – and regulations.'[11] Agnew goes on to argue that the theatre itself, operating as it did from the suburbs of the city and its liberties, was such a new form of commercial exchange, and thus shares 'elective affinities' with the market.[12]

It is also true that, of all the literary forms of the period, the drama is the one that gives most scope to an exploration of the contradictions and ambivalences of city life more broadly, and in particular the comedy that developed at the turn of the sixteenth and during the first decades of the seventeenth century. It has been thought surprising that plays in which 'London anatomised its own evolving and sprawling self'[13] were not written earlier, in view of the domination that London theatre achieved over the provinces. But it was the end of sixteenth century which saw the appearance both of history plays about the lives of Londoners and of city comedy. The term 'city comedy' is now a familiar one, and much in use after the publication of Brian Gibbons's *Jacobean City Comedy: A Study of Satiric Plays by Jonson, Marston and Middleton* in 1968 gave it a kind of official status. But as Gibbons's subtitle indicates, his interest was in a very specific group of plays that might be categorized as a genre; and it is misleading to assume that only the comedies of these named writers were concerned with the representation of the city. The concept of comedy generally as an urban genre has a long ancestry;[14] and as Manley puts it, for writers of the time, 'the ancient proverbial analogy between life and stage was epitomised by the urban environment'.[15] But the ways in which London playwrights of the period, writing specifically for London theatres and an audience of Londoners explore the urban condition emerge directly from their experience of this particular city. And even if they might encode aspects of it under other names, such as Vienna in *Measure for Measure* (1604), or Florence in the first version of Jonson's *Everyman in His Humour* (1598) or Milan in Dekker's *The Honest Whore* (1604), this was a convention readily understood. Jonson had only to alter a few characters' names in the Folio text of *Everyman in His Humour* (1616), and Florence was instantly transformed into London. One critic says that 'city comedy' is a concept that has outgrown its usefulness because the social analysis of the plays is now more concerned with what he calls 'material life' than with place.[16] But I would urge that what gives the London comedies in this period their energy and contemporary appeal is that they are both local and topical.

> Our scene is London, 'cause we would make known,
> No country's mirth is better than our own.[17]

wrote Jonson in the satirical prologue to *The Alchemist*, stressing that his typically urban cast of characters, 'your whore, bawd, squire, imposter', are especially well represented in the London of his time. And so selfconsciously topical is this play that its time references, and even the duration of the action, can be shown to refer to the actual period of its composition, late in 1610, when the theatres had reopened after a four-month closure due to plague. The action is also precisely located. 'The Blackfriars of the play and the Blackfriars in which Jonson's theatre stood are inseparable.'[18] In *Bartholomew Fair* Jonson uses the Induction to insist on the localization of the play in the here and now, when the Scrivener produces articles of agreement between the theatre audience (this time at the Hope) and the author on 'the one and thirtieth day of October, 1614'; the audience must agree not to 'look back to the sword-and-buckler age of Smithfield but content [themselves] with the present' (118–19). *The Knight of the Burning Pestle*, also a Blackfriars play, though this time by a children's company, the Children of the Queen's Revels, is another example where play and action are self-referentially conjoined. The play depicts the performance of a play by a children's company at a theatre which is probably the Blackfriars, and may well be set in the year of its performance. When Nell, the Citizen's wife, asks one of the boy actors, 'Were you never one of Master Moncaster's scholars?' (1.2.25),[19] Beaumont is using her to make an in-joke, referring to the Children of the Revels's main rivals, the Children of Paul's. In effect, the Blackfriars audience is seeing a play set in the theatre where they are sitting, which is about themselves seeing a play. Few plays of the period are anchored in quite this way, but in most comedy the London setting is much more than just local colour.

Initially a novelty, the contemporary London scene rapidly became the standard setting for comedy from the end of the sixteenth century. William Haughton's play, *Englishmen for my Money* (1598), is usually regarded as the first play to set the fashion. Londoners were clearly eager to see their society and their city depicted on stage, even if the depictions were not always flattering. They showed Londoners shaping themselves and their communities in various ways, defining their identity against outsiders such as strangers and foreigners from other countries, or even dwellers in the suburbs, but also from other parts of England. In *The Alchemist* Kastril the Angry Boy and his sister, the rich widow Dame Pliant, come up to London specifically to learn London fashions in dress and behaviour. They want to be up with latest trends. In Massinger's *The City Madam*, Plenty is 'a rough-hewn gentleman, and newly come / to a great estate'[20] in the country, who comes to the city to woo one of the fashionable daughters of Sir John

Frugal. The city, like a magnet, draws money to it. Occasionally foreigners may be welcomed, like the Dutch shoemaker Hans in *The Shoemakers' Holiday*, but he is actually the aristocrat Roland Lacy in disguise so as to escape enlistment in the French wars and to be near his lover, Rose. The workmen in Simon Eyre's shoe shop are delighted with him: ''Fore God, a proper man, and I warrant a fine workman' (1.4.59), declares Hodge. But more commonly (and more realistically) they are mocked and ostracized, like Franceschina in *The Dutch Courtesan*, whose otherness is denoted by her imperfect command of English, or the three suitors, French, Dutch and Italian, who come to woo London girls in *Englishmen for my Money*, and are made to look ridiculous. Nicer distinctions also come into play. Stow noted with displeasure the growth of the London suburbs and their encroachment on the fields and pastures of his youth. For him the essential London was demarcated by walls and gates. The expansion of London was a source of anxiety and the suburbs were regarded as a dangerous extra-territorial zone of often unregulated activity. Dekker put this view of the suburbs in extreme terms: 'How happie were Citties if they had no Suburbs, sithence they serve but as caves, where monsters are bred up to devowre the Citties themselves?'[21] The distinction between city and suburbs features significantly in *The Knight of the Burning Pestle*, one of the most socially conscious plays of the period.[22] The Prologue's bold statement, opening the play, locates the action outside the realm of court satire:

> From all that's neere the Court, from all that's great,
> Within the compasse of the Citty-wals
> We now have brought our sceane.
>
> (1.1–3)

But while the play's framing action is specifically confined to the theatrical space within the Blackfriars, inside the city walls, the actions of 'The London Merchant' and of the play improvised by Rafe move out into the suburbs, which are marginal locations, 'other' to the city proper. Nell, the Citizen's wife, characteristically praises Humphrey as a 'fair-spoken man': 'I beleeve thou hast not thy fellow within the wals of *London*; and I should say the Suburbes too, I should not lie' (2.38–9). The innocence of the bewildered child Michael appears when he asks Mistress Merrythought, 'Is not all the world Mile-end, mother?' (2.68), Mile End being a suburb just outside Aldgate, where city bands, like the one Rafe describes in Act 5, assembled to train. But Michael's sense of the suburbs as a vast desert is developed in the play's comically domesticated chivalric landscape; Luce and Jasper wander through Waltham Forest, which becomes Waltham

Down, 'in whose bottom stands the inchanted Valley' (2.105), and later the Waltham desert of Rafe's chivalric imagination, where he encounters the giant Barbarosso and delivers Barbarosso's captives, who have travelled 'North-ward from *London*' (3.371) to be treated for venereal disease. The reputation of the suburbs as the place of recreation for Londoners is cynically played with here. For all his adventures, Rafe is at heart a London boy, thinking constantly of home, of Susan, his love, who is a cobbler's maid in Milk Street, of his friends the London apprentices, of Moorfields, and, as he dies, his last thoughts are of Grocers' Hall to which he hopes his soul will ascend.

In *Westward Ho* by Dekker and Webster (1604) the identification of the suburbs is more explicitly with sexual freedom and licence. The city wives, Mistresses Tenterhook, Wafer and Honeysuckle plan an excursion with their gallants by river to Brainford in Essex, a well-known suburban location for such trysts. The merchant Justiniano attempts to seduce Mistress Honeysuckle, telling her to think herself a woman outside the city limits, 'because the Suburbes, and those without the bars, have more privilege then they within the freedome' (2.1.163–4).[23] But in the surprise denouement, where the women deny the gallants the pleasures that they had led them to expect, the city wives distinguish themselves from their suburban counterparts. They refuse to take offered aphrodisiacs of burnt wine and eggs because 'thats an exercise for your sub-burbe wenches' (5.1.115), and insist that they are capable of being 'as fantasticke and light-headed to the eye, as fether-makers, but as pure about the heart, as if we dwelt amongst em in Black Fryers' (4.1.161–2). The wives would even like to expel the bawd Birdlime from London altogether and confine her to 'the place of six-penny Sinfulnesse, the suburbes' (5.4.250), but she cannily points out this is impossible because of the location of her customers: 'Tis wel knowne I have up-risers and downe-lyers within the Citty' (5.4.252). The city authorities attempted to keep prostitutes from operating within the city limits, but were unable to do so. Even if the wives, unexpectedly, regulate their sexual activity, the play acknowledges that boundaries are not impermeable.

London plays are peppered with place names, often creating the effect of mapping the city through their action. In the first act of Dekker's *The Shoemakers' Holiday* companies of soldiers train for the French wars at Mile End, Tothill-Fields, and Finsbury, drilling grounds to the east, west and north of the city walls; the Earl of Lincoln sends his nephew Lacy to the Guildhall, but instead he joins Simon Eyre's workshop in Tower Street. Eyre praises his workmen as the best in the parish, 'the flower of saint

Martins, the mad knaves of Bedlem, Fleetstreete, Towerstreete and White-chapell' (1.1.213–14).[24] Jane, believing her husband Rafe to be dead in France, finds work in a seamster's shop in the Old (or Royal) Exchange, to the west of St Paul's church. Hammon, the rich city gentleman, hopes to marry her at St Faith's church under Paul's, a nearby chapel, where the shoemakers loyal to Rafe (who is of course not dead), having assembled at the Woolsack in Ivy Lane, waylay him. Meanwhile, Rose and Lacy are secretly wed at the Savoy in the Strand. The final feasting takes place at 'the great new hall in Gratious [Gracechurch] street corner, which our Maister the new lord maior hath built' (5.2.181–2), in fact the Leadenhall, a London covered market. The convergence of the various groups of characters on a site of festivity, where the King is present to honour Eyre and join in the Shrove Tuesday celebrations, marks this play's affirmative portrayal of the relationship between monarch and city, as well as its honorific image of London and Londoners.

London topography is used in a more satirical vein in *Eastward Ho* (1605), by Chapman, Jonson and Marston, where the grand visions of travel and exploration cherished by the insolvent knight Sir Petronel Flash and his new wife Gertrude, he to sail to Virginia, she to go by coach to his (non-existent) castle in the country, extend only to the ignominious Cuckolds' Haven, a point on the insalubrious Surrey side of the Thames between Southwark and Deptford, and opposite Wapping on the other bank. The action of the play moves eastwards from the rich merchant Touchstone's city house in Goldsmith's Row, a point of stability for himself and his virtuous apprentice Golding, who becomes a deputy alderman at the nearby Guildhall. Petronel, Quicksilver, Touchstone's prodigal apprentice, and an assortment of adventurers meet at the Blue Anchor Tavern, Billingsgate, just below London Bridge, before setting out on their voyage to Virginia. But the river Thames, an important symbol of Elizabethan London, takes an active part in aborting the voyage in a storm. Slitgut, a butcher from Eastcheap, climbing a pole at Cuckold's Haven to erect a ceremonial pair of ox-horns on it for St Luke's Day, looks out over the river to observe the shipwreck: 'Let me discover from this lofty prospect, what pranks the rude Thames plays in desperate lunacy' (4.1.19–20),[25] he comments as the half-drowned voyagers drag themselves ashore. Quicksilver reaches land at Wapping, the location of a gallows where pirates were hanged, Petronel on the Isle of Dogs, known as a refuge for debtors and cutpurses;[26] 'The last money we could make, the greedy Thames has devoured', he laments (4.1.186). Where *The Shoemakers' Holiday* draws its characters into the heart of festive London, *Eastward Ho* sends its prodigals and spendthrifts to congregate in prison. In this play Touchstone's work-place at the city's commercial heart stands in contrast to its outposts and liminal sites, Moorfields, where Golding envisages Quicksilver reduced to beggary by his prodigal ways, Tyburn, Wapping, the Isle of Dogs, St Katherine's Hospital, and the various London prisons. Petronel, Quicksilver and the usurer Security fetch up at the Counter, a debtors' prison. This urban landscape is the obverse to the familiar, comforting city topography of *The Shoemakers' Holiday*.

The city of comedy is defined through its particular geography, which playwrights can draw on selectively, to create specific kinds of landscape, both physical and moral, but also through the perceived affinity between city and theatre. 'The Cittie is like a Commodie', observes the title character, a duke in disguise, in Sharpham's *The Fleire* (1606),

> both in partes and apparell, and your Gallants are the Actors: for hee that yesterday played the Gentleman, nowe playes the Begger; shee that played the Wayting-woman, nowe playes the Queane; hee that played the married-man, nowe playes the Cuckolde; and shee that played the Ladie, nowe playes the Painter. Then for their apparell, they have change too: for shee that wore the Petticote, nowe weares the Breech; he that wore the Coxcombe, nowe weares the feather; the Gentleman that wore the long Sworde, nowe weares the short Hanger; and hee that could scarce get Velvet for his cape, has nowe linde his Cloake throughout with it.
>
> (2.124–34)[27]

Justinian in *Westward Ho*, a jealous city husband determined to prove his belief that he is a cuckold, addresses the audience in soliloquy: 'Have amongst you Citty dames? You that are indeed the fittest, and most proper persons for a Comedy' (1.1.225–6). The idea that city structures comedy through 'the formulation of social types'[28] appears in Jonson's Induction to his late play, *The Magnetic Lady* (1632), where the Boy advertises the forthcoming production to two sceptical gentlemen: 'What is't you lack? Any fine fansies, figures, humors, characters, ideas, definitions of lords, and ladies? Waiting-women, parasites, knights, captaines, courtiers, lawyers?' (1–5).[29] The Boy might have extended his list of characters to be found in both city and theatre still further to include such figures as the usurer, the country visitor, the citizen and his wife, and the whore, all of whom become stereotypes central to comedy. The quotation from Sharpham suggests other ways in which the city resembles comedy: the character types play different parts, in which they act out scenarios of transformation based on social mobility, upwards as well as downwards. The city is a realm of opportunity: for role-playing and disguise; for finding a wife or husband; for money-making and profiteering. This vision links the city with the theatre as a kind of playground where life is structured like a game, and the standard plots are acted out, commonly involving trickery, gulling and deception. It reveals 'how precarious social identity was'.[30] Oppositions both moral and social are set up: city against country, gentry against citizens, wives against seducers, those with money against those who would take it from them.

Money is a major element of the playwrights' response to the material transformation of the city in this period. These comedies show money being made through honest as well as dishonest activity, being spent, being lent, being lost, constantly changing hands. *The Shoemakers' Holiday* is unusual in its depiction of a world of work, a vision of the artisan workshop as a centre of energetic activity among men and women, where the body of the artisan is 'inscribed into the sphere of élite power and written as vigorous, vital, and crucial to the nation'.[31] Although Eyre achieves his social rise to the status of Lord Mayor by borrowing money (from the disguised Lacy) and also a disguise (an alderman's robe) in order to acquire trading commodities at a cheap rate, the play evades any possible element of chicanery here, instead insisting on Eyre's balance of crowd-pleasing individualism with commercial good sense and acceptance of artisan co-identity with his workmen. But the antagonistic relationship between the goldsmith Touchstone and his apprentice Quicksilver in *Eastward Ho* is more typical of comedic attitudes to work and wealth. Quicksilver mocks Touchstone's comfortable citizen morality – 'Touchstone, keep thy shop, and thy shop will keep thee' (1.1.49) – perceiving instead the exploitative and predatory nature of financial dealings in the city which is also the basis of Touchstone's wealth:

> I am entertained among gallants, true! They call me cousin Frank, right! I lend them moneys, good! They spend it, well! But when they are spent, must they not strive to get more? Must not their land fly? And to whom? Shall not your worship ha' the refusal? Well, I am a good member of the City, if I were well considered. How would merchants thrive, if gentlemen would not be unthrifts? How could gentlemen be unthrifts, if their humours were not fed? (1.1.26–34)

Quicksilver's prodigality is in turn a source of profit for the usurer Security, though he also provides Security with further customers, through his dealings with the gallants, getting them into debt and thus forcing them to borrow at Security's inflated rates. London is a city of trade, and trade means competition. 'No trade or vocation profiteth, but by the losse and displeasure of another', as the trickster Coccledemoy in *The Dutch Courtesan* points out (1.2.41–2). The fluidity of money is perceived as threatening. Aristocrats and gentlemen, members of the traditional ruling classes, are the losers. Monopoly in *Westward Ho*, nephew to an earl, is insouciant in his dealings with the prosperous citizen Tenterhook, not even wanting his bags of borrowed cash to be sealed, because 'I must disburse instantly: we that be Cutters have more places to send money to, then the divell hath to send his spirits' (1.2.7–8). In Middleton's *A Chaste Maid in Cheapside* Sir Walter Whorehound plans to marry Moll Yellowhammer, daughter of a goldsmith, to replenish his dissipated fortunes, and while he makes his entrance into Yellowhammer's shop the goldsmith is seen at work beating down a needy gentleman trying to make some money by selling off his gold chain. Whorehound aims to marry off his cast-off mistress to the goldsmith's son, telling her:

> I bring thee up to turn thee into gold, wench, and make thy fortune shine like your bright trade. A goldsmith's shop sets out a city maid.
>
> (1.1.99–101)[32]

In a society so concerned with commercial exchange, everything has its price, and sex is readily commodified. In Massinger's *The City Madam*, Mary Frugal tells her country gentleman suitor Plenty, 'Since you'l marry / In the city for our wealth, in justice, we / Must have the countries Soveraignty' (2.2.177–9).[33] She recognizes the purchasing power she commands as a city merchant's daughter, and intends to use her considerable financial credit to obtain status and domination over her husband. The transference of wealth and power from the country, where it is identified with traditional aristocracy, to the greedy city world of finance is a constant theme for lamentation in the conservative thinking of the age. The impoverishment of landowning peers who could not keep up with inflation and the pace of economic change was a reality, as Lawrence Stone has shown.[34] When Luke Frugal, younger brother to Sir John Frugal, believes himself to have inherited Sir John's wealth, he soliloquizes, Volpone-like, over Sir John's treasure chests, about the transformative power of money and the forms it takes:

> Here lay
> A mannor bound fast in a skin of parchment,
> The wax continuing hard, the acres melting;
> Here a sure deed of gift for a market-town,
> If not redeem'd this day, which is not in
> The unthrifts power. There being scarce one shire
> In *Wales* or *England*, where my moneys are not
> Lent out at usurie.
>
> (3.3.35–42)

Luke is a monstrous figure, more a moral type of avarice and excess than a social type, but his lines here evoke not only familiar fears about the predatory city of merchants and usurers devouring the enfeebled country aristocracy, but also the anxieties aroused by the spectre of the fluid and unregulated market.

Jonson's city comedies *The Alchemist* and *Bartholomew Fair* are more concerned with the circulation of money in the city, but here the transference of wealth is between those who are well enough off, to different degrees, but undeserving and gullible, and those who are indigent but cunning. In *The Alchemist* both groups are motivated by greed, the cheaters as much as their victims, though the wit and self-awareness of the cheaters, the 'venter tripartite', Face, Subtle and Doll, win them, if not the moral high ground, at least the audience's dramatic support. Although many of the gulls are seeking to transform their lives into something more exciting and glamorous, like Dapper, a lawyer's clerk, who wants to become a gambler and man-about-town, and Drugger, the novice tobacco seller, who wants a prosperous business and a rich wife, the play depicts a society so dedicated to acquisition by any means that morality and reason are easily set aside.[35] This play typifies the view that gulling is city comedy's 'master structure (the structure that organises sexual and financial relations)'.[36] But in this context gulling is not necessarily an easy way of life. The three cheaters are involved in a constant frenzy of activity, and they work hard for their living. Because the action is set during plague-time, the freedom of Face, Subtle and Doll to use Lovewit's house for their own purposes is only a temporary one; Lovewit will return from his Kentish hop-fields, where he has taken refuge from the plague, as richer Londoners tended to do, and Face will resume his familiar (and commonplace) identity as Jeremy the butler, while Subtle and Doll, the outsiders, must return to the margins of city life from which they came. 'Pray heaven/ The master do not trouble us this quarter', exclaims Subtle when he hears the doorbell ring (1.1.180–1). So, time is short, and they must work to make their profit.

The play contrasts their unceasing activity with the expectations of their victims of making money the easy way. Subtle is sought by a steady stream of clients, who must all be kept apart from one another, and when they start to appear without due appointments trouble ensues. Mammon's unexpected return, for instance, means that Dapper must be hastily thrust into the privy while he awaits the appearance of the Fairy Queen; and Face must be deployed to delay the eager knight while Subtle changes from his disguise as 'Priest of fairy' back into the priestly alchemist, and Doll transforms herself into a lord's sister. All three are regularly involved in costume changes, and it is only through their energy and quick-wittedness that seven different comic sub-plots are kept going until the last act. The gulls remain blissfully unaware of all this effort. When Surly points out that the man seeking to profit from the philosopher's stone 'must be *homo frugi,*/ A pious, holy, and religious man' (2.2.97–8), Mammon, with a fine stroke of casuistry, replies that Subtle's austerity does the job vicariously: 'That makes it, sir, he is so. But I buy it,/ My venture brings it me' (2.2.100–1). Ananias and Tribulation, the Puritans, similarly believe that they can pay Subtle to do the work for them. 'The Saints/ Throw down their purse before you', Tribulation tells Subtle expansively (3.2.18).

Gulling takes a lot of effort, but for Face, Subtle and Doll, born actors all, the activity of changing identities and taking on new roles is itself pleasurable. Doll enjoys the chance to play 'my Lord what's – hum's sister':

> I'll not forget my race, I warrant you.
> I'll keep my distance, laugh and talk aloud;
> Have all the tricks of a proud scurvy lady,
> And be as rude's her woman.
>
> (2.4.8–11)

Face observes her skilful performance with relish: 'Why, this is yet/ A kind of modern happiness, to have/ Doll Common for a great lady' (4.1.22–4). Surly does not know Face's real identity, but takes him, not unreasonably, for an expert brothel-keeper:

> Don Face! Why he's the most authentic dealer
> I'these commodities! The superintendent
> To all the queinter traffickers in town.
>
> (2.3.301–3)

Subtle is equally convincing in his role as the scholarly alchemist, 'a notable, superstitious, good soul,/ has worn his knees bare and his slippers bald,/ With prayer and fasting' (2.2.101–3). In the city social identity is fluid, and 'frequently fraudulent'.[37] Skilful role-players like these three can (almost) efface their origins. Everyone seeks transformation of one kind or another.

In Act 5, Face tots up the spoils that the three of them have accumulated, money from Mammon, the Puritans, Dapper and Drugger, and a miscellaneous collection of goods: 'the jewel of the waiting maid's/ That stole it from her lady . . . the fish wife's rings . . . the whistle that the sailor's wife/ Brought you, to know an her husband were with Ward [a famous pirate] . . . silver beakers and tavern cups . . . French petticoats/ and girdles and hangers . . . bolts of lawn' (5.4.110–120). The play is characterized by such a profusion of material things that it seems to express what has been termed 'a new and almost novelistic interest in personal detail'.[38] City life is made concrete in all its variety and abundance, and rendered with an attention to the trivial and everyday that would have created for the Black-friars audience a complex reflection of their own society in a way that no earlier play had attempted. The commonplace lives of men like Dapper and Drugger are deftly sketched in with quotidian observations about Dapper's doting grandmother, his ability to 'write six fair hands', and his modest intellectual pretensions, and Drugger's care to keep his tobacco fresh, not 'wrapp'd up in greasy leather or piss'd clouts', his sufferings from worms and indigestion, caused by 'a piece of fat ram-mutton to supper/ That lay so heavy on my stomach' (3.4.114), his anxiety at being overtaxed for his water-rates.

 Bartholomew Fair, too, depicts a richly textured world in minute material detail, a world peopled by an even wider range of London types and of local trades and activities. The Fair, an event that took place every August in Smithfield, just outside the city limits, brings together tradespeople, entertainers, prostitutes, gamblers, eager to profit from the appetites of an undiscriminating public greedy for pleasure, especially in the forms of food and sex. Recent critics have observed how the traditional view of the 'festive marketplace', celebrated by Bakhtin as the place where the 'lower bodily stratum' could be given due acknowledgement and 'the popular subversive tradition of laughter, parody, scepticism and utopian hope . . . preserved'[39] was breaking down. The play brings the fair to life in sensuous detail, with its vivid evocation of sights, sounds and smells, epitomized in the booth of Ursula, the pig-woman; Ursula not only sells roast pork, priced variably according to the extent of the customer's hunger (pregnant women pay more), short measures of ale and adulterated tobacco, but her booth also provides relief for those taken short (like the embarrassed Mistress Winwife) and an organization for supplying prosti-tutes. 'Here you may ha' your punk, and your pig in state, sir, both piping hot' (2.5.36–37),[40] Knockem the horse dealer tells Quarlous. The goods and services offered by the other tradespeople of the fair are equally debased – Joan Trash's gingerbread made of 'stale bread, rotten eggs, musty ginger, and dead honey' (2.2.10), Leatherhead's overpriced toys, Nightingale's ballads sung to distract the crowd's attention while Edgworth picks their pockets. The visitors to the fair are too greedy to be careful how they spend their money. The foolish Bartholomew Cokes, an Esquire of Harrow and a landed gentleman, is fleeced at every turn as he dashes from one attraction to another, recklessly emptying his purse on hobby horses, gingerbread and ballads; he loses his money, his cloak and his hat, his sword and his cut-work handkerchief, as well as Grace Wellborn, his fiancée, and even his way home. He tries to induce Troubleall, the madman, to take him back to his house: 'Thou shalt see, I have wrought pillows there, and cambric sheets, and sweet bags too' (4.2.87–8). But Troubleall is the last person who can help, obsessed as he is with obtaining the warrant of justice Overdo before he can do anything at all.

The gentry and bourgeois characters, like Overdo and his wife and the Littlewits, are outsiders, either socially or geographically, to the world of the fair, lured in to satisfy various sorts of appetites – Overdo, for instance, to spy out 'enormities' and detect false trading, Littlewit, who fancies himself as a man of fashion, 'one o' the pretty wits o' Paul's', to get his play put on by Leatherhead's puppet theatre. They are all exposed and humiliated. Mistress Overdo and Mistress Littlewit become separated from their husbands; the former, because she is drunk, the latter, because she is pregnant, need to use the toilet facilities in Ursula's booth, where her associates, Knockem and Whit, both bawds, quickly seize the opportunity to recruit them as prostitutes to supplement the dearth of available women in the fair. 'Here will be Zekiel Edgeworth, and three or four gallants with him at night, and I ha' neither plover nor quail for 'em', complains Ursula to Knockem (4.5.12–14). In the last scene the two husbands, each preoccupied with the pursuit of his own agenda, are exposed to ridicule when their wives are revealed. Mistress Littlewit, newly attired in a prostitute's green gown, is unmasked by Overdo himself, while Mistress Overdo reveals herself, calling for a basin in which to vomit. Thus the women from respectable society in their transformation into whores have found themselves, rather literally, commodified, though, as Brian Gibbons says, all the characters 'obey society's market forces and its rules of commerce'.[41] Grace Wellborn, though not humiliated in the same way as the two wives, plays another typically female part in the commerce of society. As a rich ward she is initially under the control of Overdo, who has bought her wardship and plans to profit from it by selling her as a wife to the wealthy Cokes; however, she ends up under the control of Winwife, who has acquired her by getting the cutpurse Edgworth to steal the marriage licence from Cokes's guardian. Thus the boundary between respectable and criminal society melts away; the two are connected not only in their bondage to market forces but by the fact that the continuance of the social institutions of the former is based on the complicity of the latter.

Bartholomew Fair dramatizes the 'commodification of the personal'[42] generally, but other plays expose the commodification of women more specifically. The nature of marriage as a property transaction is brilliantly dramatized in Middleton's best city comedy, *A Chaste Maid in Cheapside*, where the Yellowhammers, prosperous and aspiring citizens, are bent on marrying their reluctant daughter Moll to the unsavoury knight Sir Walter Whorehound. Yellowhammer and his wife are crudely obsequious in his presence, making it clear how highly they value his status, which for Mistress Yellowhammer has a quasi-sexual allure in itself. As she tells him,

> You have a presence, sweet Sir Walter,
> Able to daunt a maid brought up i'th' city;
> A brave Court spirit makes our virgins quiver,
> And kiss with trembling thighs.
>
> (1.1.118–21)

Although, as her father acknowledges, Moll as a citizen's daughter is 'no gentlewoman', this is of no account to Sir Walter, who is concerned only with the Yellowhammer money, which he needs to bolster his precarious lifestyle and shaky finances; his reference to Moll as 'my love the gold-smith's daughter' denotes her significance for him. He looks forward to receiving 'two thousand pound in gold/ And a sweet maidenhead/ Worth forty' (4.2.92–3) on his marriage. But Moll has other plans, and tries to escape to marry her lover, Touchwood Junior. When her parents capture her in the nick of time, Yellowhammer vows, 'I will lock up this baggage,/ As carefully as my gold' (3.1.50–1). In similar ways, all the plots in this play revolve around the equation between money and sex. Marriages are contracted to secure financial interests, and offspring are both produced and disclaimed to the same end. The Kixes must get a child in order to disinherit Sir Walter; and since Sir Oliver Kix is impotent, he will allow his wife to be serviced by the over-fertile Touchwood Senior, who in turn has had to live apart from his wife because they cannot afford to maintain any more children. While Sir Walter needs to marry Moll for her money, and to secure her brother Tim as a husband for his cast-off mistress, Mistress Allwit must prevent Sir Walter's marriage in order to preserve the status quo in her own household, where Sir Walter is her long-term lover, father of her many children and provider for the whole family. As Allwit declares in the shocking and complacent soliloquy with which he enters the play:

> I thank him, h'as maintained my house this ten years,
> Not only keeps my wife, but a keeps me,
> And all my family; I am at his table,
> He gets me all my children, and pays the nurse,
> Monthly, or weekly, puts me to nothing.
>
> (1.2.16–20)

His wife co-operates contentedly in this arrangement, which Allwit acknowledges without shame as a commercial transaction, describing himself as a cuckold who makes his living in the same way 'as other trades thrive, butchers by selling flesh,/ Poulters by venting conies, or the like' (4.1.240–1). Mistress Allwit epitomizes the wife as both consumable and consumer. Her husband admires the conspicuous expense of her lying-in, borne of course by Sir Walter:

> A lady lies not in like her; there's her embossings,
> Embroiderings, spanglings, and I know not what,
> As if she lay with all the gaudy shops
> In Gresham's Burse about her.
>
> (1.2.32–5)

And the Puritan gossips at the christening feast of her new baby, grabbing for sweetmeats, drunk and incontinent on the abundant wine, testify to the hypocrisy of this materialistic society, obsessed with appetite.

Although chaste maid characters like Moll and Luce in *The Knight of the Burning Pestle* refuse to participate, city wives are complicit in this consumerist ethos. In *The Shoemakers' Holiday*, Margery Eyre's relish of the social advancement that her husband's promotion will bring is satirized in her greed for new, high-status clothes, such as a French hood and a farthingale, and is contrasted with Simon Eyre's dismissal of them as 'trash, trumpery, vanity' (5.1.17). Gertrude in *Eastward Ho* shares Margery's sense of style, and despises her sister's plain dress:

> Do you wear your coif with a London licket [lace], your stammel gown with the tuf-taffety cape, and the velvet lace. I must be a lady, and I will be a lady. (1.2.14–17)

The devotion to upward mobility of Lady Frugal and her daughters in Massinger's *The City Madam* takes the same form; the profusion of expensive and exotic commodities, gowns of satin, velvet petticoats, shoes of perfumed Spanish leather, the 'Caroche/ Drawn by six Flanders mares', and the 'French, and Italian Cooks; Musicians, Songsters' (2.2.111–12, 115) that Anne Frugal desires as part of her marriage settlement, all of these define the city as a centre of extravagance and consumption where fantasy in the form of infinite acquisition is displaced on to women, characterized by their capacity to spend money they have not worked for. Lady Frugal and her daughters, vain, greedy and aggressive, are the monstrous women attacked in contemporary pamphlets such as the notorious *The Arraignment of Lewd, Idle, Froward, and Unconstant Women* (1615) by Joseph Swetnam. Karen Newman has summarized the misogynistic representation of women's roles in city comedies: 'Traditionally excluded from public life, from government affairs, law courts, and the pulpit, women enter the public sphere of early seventeenth-century London by going to market, both to buy and to sell.' She adds, 'the city woman tropes urban vice: the noise, the crowd, sexuality, and consumerism'.[43]

The city wife is probably the major female role within the gender discourse of these plays, and Leinwand has usefully pointed out how 'role' functions as a 'structuring principle' for women in place of the demarcations according to status that operate for men. 'Women were anatomised as virgins, wives, widows, and whores. And each role had economic, moral, and social implications.'[44] The categories are not necessarily distinct; Mistress Allwit in *A Chaste Maid*, like the wives in *Bartholomew Fair*, scandalously crosses the boundary between wife and whore. And there are variations within the stereotype; while the city wives in *Westward Ho* typically depend on their husbands' money and their own wit as key resources, in their refusal to cuckold their husbands they sever the 'expected link between spending and wantonness'.[45] They also show women able to turn their husbands' misogynistic expectations of them to their own advantage, and get a lot of fun out of doing it:

> Tho we are merry, lets not be mad . . . It were better we should laugh at these popin-Jayes, then live in feare of their prating tongues: tho we lye all night out of the Citty, they shall not find country wenches of us: but since we ha brought them thus far in to a fooles Paradise, leave em int: the jest shal be a stock to maintain us and our pewfellowes in laughing at christenings, cryings out, and upsittings this twelve month. (5.1.160, 168–73)

But marriage is the institution to which almost all female roles are related. When the Duke in *Measure for Measure* interrogates Mariana as to her status, and she tells him that she is neither maid, wife nor widow, he concludes, 'Why, you are nothing then' (5.1.176). Lucio interposes another possibility: 'My lord, she may be a punk, for many of them are neither maid, widow, nor wife.' The punk, or prostitute, is a familiar figure in city comedy, as she probably was in the society of what has been called 'the disorderly poor'[46] in early modern London, an essential element of the culture of commodification, openly trading sex for money, and queering the pitch for women who will only trade sex for marriage. But as Freevil in *The Dutch Courtesan* points out, prostitution can also serve to protect marriage. For him, brothels are 'most necessary buildings'. Asked his reason for this assertion, he responds:

> I would have married men love the stews as Englishmen lov'd the Low countries: wish war should be maintain'd there lest it should come home to their own doors. (1.1.59, 62–5)

Freevil's argument here is positioned as a witty paradox, and can thus be written off. The prostitute is a figure on to whom anxieties about trade, regulation and social order can readily be displaced. Characters like Franceschina, Luce in *Westward Ho*, Doll Common in *The Alchemist*, Punk Alice in *Bartholomew Fair* or Shave'em in *The City Madam* are grasping and disorderly, utilizing their status outside respectable society to flout constraints on proper female conduct, cursing, drinking and fighting like men. The quasi-exploitative partnership between the prostitute and her pimp or bawd (Mary Faugh in *The Dutch Courtesan*, Birdlime in *Westward Ho*, Secret in *The City Madam*) is never developed to suggest the prostitute's vulnerability, since the interests of the two are identified. Birdlime, in fact, is a resourceful entrepreneur, not only looking out for Luce but negotiating with her various clients, who include an earl and his nephew as well as Inns of Court men and citizens, and attempting to procure new recruits to satisfy the customers. Conscious of her position on the margins of society, she observes it with a keen eye, telling Luce of the rowdy Inns of Court gentlemen, that 'they might have bin taken for Cittizens, but that they talke more like fooles' (4.1.16–18). She also dismisses the tailor's admiration for social status: 'Taylor, you talk like an asse, I tel thee ther is equality inough between a Lady and a Citty dame, if their haire be but of a colour' (1.1.24–5). Sindefy the prostitute in *Eastward Ho* is also a shrewd social commentator, with a clear-eyed sense of reality; she points out to her fanciful lover Quicksilver that his romantic vision of court life ignores the reality of a world where promotion and success have to be worked for by the same acceptance of self-abasement that her own profession demands, 'not only humouring the lord, but every torch-bearer, every groom that by indulgence and intelligence crept into his favour' (2.2.74–6). She is also the voice of good sense when the flighty Gertrude Touchstone, abandoned by her impoverished new husband Petronel Flash, casts about for ways to drum up some money and finally suggests pawning her newly acquired title: 'I'd lay my Ladyship in lavender – if I knew where', to which Sindefy responds, 'I make question who will lend you anything upon it' (5.1.54–5, 61). She can see Gertrude's fantasies for what they are, 'pretty waking dreams' (5.1.88).

These plays show how women in the city can be witty and resourceful as well as wanton, greedy and extravagant. In an era of anxiety about the threat posed by masculine women to men's authority, when King James spoke in the Star Chamber in 1616 against 'the pride of women' who prevailed upon their menfolk to bring them up to London 'because the new fashion is to be had no where but in London'[47] and commanded the clergy to preach against 'the insolencie of our women' and their aggressive behaviour,[48] these dramatic depictions of London women responded to current debate, but not necessarily in a way that offered comfort to conservative ideas about women's place in society. That the city itself was usually gendered female, in pamphlets and city pageantry, connects it with the complex roles women were allotted in London comedies, custodians of chastity, the family and its wealth, but also capable of squandering resources and ready to evade control. Comedies of London life are closely in touch with contemporary perceptions of the city, not only with the fears and anxieties about change and control that were in circulation but also with the awareness of new opportunities available.

The Place of Shakespeare

Shakespeare's role within the theatrical culture of his day is an interesting one; and although his current reputation and status, now those of a global phenomenon, confer on all contemporary references to him a peculiar significance denied to any other playwright of the period, in a number of ways his relationships with them and with the institution of theatre generally were not atypical of the time. For instance, he made use of pre-existing plays, as well as of non-dramatic texts, as sources for his own work, particularly at the beginning of his career, he collaborated with other playwrights and took inspiration from them, even, it is possible to argue, competing with them. Although his early years can still be characterized as 'lost', he worked as an actor as well as a playwright, was involved with more than one theatre company, and wrote poems to a noble and influential patron at times when plague closed the London theatres. But, on the other hand, he did become the richest and most successful playwright of his day, and the fact that he was, from early in its formation, the leading dramatist of the Lord Chamberlain's, later the King's, Men, and a sharer in the company is not unconnected with this. His work was the mainstay of their repertoire until the closure of the theatres, and his plays exerted an influence on the work of his contemporaries in a way that no one else's plays did.

However, it is not so much influence as Shakespeare's interrelationships with contemporary playwrights that will be the focus of this chapter. How can the kind of dialogue he maintained with them, and they with him, be characterized? In part, it is what is known as intertextual, from the term coined by Julia Kristeva to refer to the process by which writers make texts out of those which already exist, a process seen as a matter of inevitability rather than a matter of personal choice. But, I would argue, it is, from the start, also a conscious relationship. As Russ McDonald says, 'Shakespeare the professional was always conscious of what his fellows were doing and what the public was demanding.'[1] But in the case of two particular playwrights, Marlowe and Jonson, Shakespeare's relationship with them was more active and intentional, even reciprocal, a matter of creative exchange. Marlowe, born in the same year as Shakespeare, established himself as a presence in the London theatres several years earlier, his first play probably being *Dido, Queen of Carthage* for the Children of the Chapel in about 1584–5; but for him, and for the English stage, the turning point came with *Tamburlaine the Great*, part 1, performed by the Admiral's Men around 1587 and published, anonymously, with the second part, in 1590. 'The general welcomes Tamburlaine received', as the Prologue to part 2 puts it, spurred the young playwright to produce his second part, playwrights such as Greene, Peele and Lodge quickly latched on to Marlowe's formula, and Shakespeare, whatever else he was doing at the time, took notice. Marlowe's next plays, *Dr Faustus* and *The Jew of Malta*, probably followed in fairly quick succession, both written before 1590 and not, as far as we know, printed in his lifetime.

The generally accepted chronology of Shakespeare's works attributes nothing to him before 1590, although some scholars have conjectured that his first plays date from about 1586.[2] But if, as I believe, Marlowe's work gave a strong impetus to Shakespeare, Shakespeare responded to it quickly and also for some time to come. The plays now known to us from the titles given to them in the First Folio as the second and third parts of *Henry VI* are much influenced by Marlowe, and the first part, probably written later, opens in Marlovian style with the Duke of Bedford's thunderously rhythmic cosmological injunctions:

> Hung be the heavens with black! Yield, day, to night!
> Comets, importing change of times and states,
> Brandish your crystal tresses in the sky,
> And with them scourge the bad revolting stars
> That have consented unto Henry's death.
>
> (1.1.1–5)

To strengthen the connection, it has even been suggested that the hearse used here for the body of Henry V might have been the one used for Zenocrate's body, so conspicuous in *Tamburlaine*, part 2.[3] The plays were probably written for the same company, Lord Strange's Men. Marlowe's mighty line runs through all Shakespeare's 1590s history plays, sometimes to parodic effect, as for instance in Northumberland's exaggeratedly rhetorical proclamation of chaos in *Henry IV, Part 2* (1.1.153–69), or the ancient Pistol's ranting speeches in the same play, extending even to Henry V's encouragements to his troops. According to Nashe, who was probably Shakespeare's collaborator on the play, *Henry VI, Part 1* was a huge success, witnessed by patriotic audiences of 10,000 or more who admired brave

Talbot, the terror of the French. Marlowe responded to the *Henry VI* plays by drawing, as Shakespeare had done, on the recent edition of Holinshed's chronicles, and producing an English history of his own which also focused on the dilemma created for the nation when a weak king was on the throne. In *Edward II*, his last play, Marlowe made some radical adjustments to his characteristic dramatic structure, and instead of a play dominated by a single towering figure had his king surrounded by contentious barons, as Henry VI is, and accompanied by self-seeking hangers-on, first Gaveston, then Spenser. 'It is perhaps the only time in [Marlowe's] career as a dramatist that he shows how powerfully a rival had influenced him', James Shapiro believes.[4] As Marlowe had learnt from the *Henry VI* plays, so Shakespeare 'reclaimed the debt'[5] in *Richard II*, depicting a Plantagenet king like Edward, an unworthy descendant of a conquering ancestor and a weak ruler who has allowed favourites too much influence and imperilled his country by selfish and ill-conceived policies. Not only is the situation of the king similarly conceived in the two plays, but his career follows the same dramatic trajectory, as he disregards wise counsel, involves his country in civil war and is deposed, imprisoned and murdered. In each case the king regains some tragic status in the last hours of his life, allowing for a complexity of response to the downfall of an inadequate and irresponsible ruler who is nevertheless a legitimate king. The debt of *Richard II* to *Edward II* is a very obvious one and exemplifies how Shakespeare was able to build on and develop further ideas from the earlier play. While *Edward II* is an end in itself, and no expectation is created that the child-king Edward who succeeds to the throne at the end might have had his own play, in *Richard II* Shakespeare seems to have realized early on that his material could be extended; and Bolingbroke, the apparently competent and conscienceless usurper who is also the father of an 'unruly son', has a story of his own that will extend into the two parts of *Henry IV*.

But, nevertheless, at the time of his death in 1593 Marlowe was capable of things that Shakespeare had still to achieve. Jonathan Bate suggests that the homage he pays to Marlowe's famous speech from *Dr Faustus*, 'Was this the face that launched a thousand ships,/ And burnt the topless towers of Ilium?', in Richard's address to himself in the mirror, 'Was this face the face/ That every day under his household roof/ Did keep ten thousand men?' (4.1.271–3) betokens 'dramatic anxiety'.[6] Shakespeare, Bate says, had not yet achieved anything like the tragic impact or the challenge to orthodoxy of *Dr Faustus*. Perhaps his truest homage to that play, which is also, like *Richard II* to *Edward II*, a realization of the potential for the development of some of its best elements, comes only in the much later *Macbeth*.

Shakespeare's first tragedy, *Titus Andronicus*, published in 1594 but perhaps written in 1592 or earlier, is strongly influenced by Marlowe, but by the tragicomic *The Jew of Malta*, not by *Dr Faustus*, which does not seem to have spoken directly to Shakespeare in his early years. *The Jew of Malta*, on the other hand, clearly inspires the figure of Aaron in *Titus*, both generally in his Machiavellian energy and relish for villainy, and also in specific instances. The most obvious of these are his opening soliloquy (2.1.1–24) in its celebration of aspiration, its classical comparisons, its very un-Shakespearean extended simile, its delight in glitter; and in his boastful catalogue to Lucius of sadistic deeds (5.1.125–44), concluding unrepentantly,

> And nothing grieves me heartily indeed
> But that I cannot do ten thousand more.
>
> (5.1.143–4)

This is obviously derived from the passage in *The Jew of Malta* where Barabas and Ithamore, his Turkish slave, vie with one another in listing ingenious acts of wickedness they have delighted to commit. While Marlowe's scene is unequivocally black comedy, and looks distantly back, perhaps to the comedy of evil explored in the medieval Vice, the tone of Shakespeare's, placed at a very late moment in the play, immediately preceding the tragic denouement, is more problematic; laughter seems to be invited, but simultaneously requires to be suppressed. But the comically inflected Machiavellian of *The Jew of Malta* continued to fascinate Shakespeare, who reworked it in Richard of Gloucester in *Henry VI, part 3*, and more fully in the same character in *Richard III*. This character's pleasure in evil is a sardonic, self-protective response to the world in which he finds himself, an attempt to construct a position of control by someone who would naturally figure as an underdog. To an extent, this is also the situation of Marlowe's Barabas, but Richard faces more challenges and stronger antagonists. His ambition and his desire to overgo classical precedents (in *Henry VI, Part 3*, 3.2.186–90) evoke Tamburlaine too.

In the 1590s Shakespeare's representations of ambition always seem to recall Marlowe. Even in the very unMarlovian *The Taming of the Shrew*, probably about 1592 or earlier, the ridiculous competition between rich old Gremio and Tranio, actually a servant in disguise with no money at all, to make the best offer for Bianca plays on the Marlovian fascination with exotic material wealth. Gremio can provide a house 'richly furnished with plate and gold', 'hangings all of Tyrian tapestry', 'ivory coffers . . . cypress chests . . . Turkey cushions . . . valence of Venice', and even an argosy, but when Tranio, absurdly, boasts of 'no less / Than three great argosies, besides two galliasses/ And twelve tight galleys' (2.1.339–71), he knows he is outdone. Material wealth features most centrally in another of Shakespeare's Marlowe-indebted plays, *The Merchant of Venice*, which was, interestingly, called *The Jew of Venice* in the Stationers' Register of 1598; *The Jew of Malta* and *The Merchant of Venice* were the only two plays of the time to feature a Jew as the central character. By this time, about 1596, Shakespeare's relationship to Marlowe is confident and no longer anxious; Marlowe is no longer a competitor. Shakespeare's Shylock, like Marlowe's Barabas, is a Jewish usurer who behaves treacherously, despises Christians, loses a beloved daughter to a Christian lover and is tricked out of his wealth by Christians. Shylock, too, believes himself to be a victim whose rights are ignored by those who do not accept his common humanity. Shylock lives and conducts his business in Venice, a city which like Malta was something of a cultural melting pot, and both plays explore the clash of cultures involved. There are verbal echoes too, as for instance from Barabas's exclamation of pleasure when Abigail retrieves his money for him – 'O my girl,/ My gold, my fortune, my felicity . . . / O girl! O gold! O beauty! O my bliss' – to Shylock's (reported) outrage on discovering Jessica's elopement with Lorenzo – 'My daughter! O, my ducats! O, my daughter' (2.8.15). But there the connections cease to be important. Shakespeare's situating of his Jew in the kind of romantic comedy of courtship, cross-dressing and feminine initiative that he made his own turns this into a completely different sort of play, and one that has no interest in the comic cruelty and cynicism which informs the latter part of Marlowe's.

In *As You Like It*, possibly first performed in early 1599,[7] Shakespeare directly alludes to his dead rival, when he makes Phoebe, passionately smitten by the sight of Rosalind disguised as the boy Ganymede, quote from his poem *Hero and Leander* (first published posthumously in 1598):

> Dead shepherd, now I find thy saw of might:
> 'Who ever loved that loved not at first sight?'
>
> (3.5.82–3)

The 'dead shepherd' alludes to the title of Marlowe's already well-known poem, 'the passionate shepherd to his love', which first appeared in print that same year in a collection entitled *The Passionate Pilgrim*, which was, ironically, ascribed to 'W. Shakespeare' on its title-page. Other references attest to Marlowe's vivid presence in Shakespeare's imagination at this time. In the next scene, Rosalind-as-Ganymede (who was a character in *Dido, Queen of Carthage*) recalls Marlowe's poem again, in debunking spirit, when she says that Leander drowned from the effects of cramp while swimming in the Hellespont to cool himself, rather than on his way to a rendezvous with Hero. Earlier, Touchstone, complaining to Audrey that in the forest of Arden he feels like an exile, 'Ovid . . . among the Goths', remarks,

> When a man's verses cannot be understood, nor a man's good wit seconded with the forward child, understanding, it strikes a man more dead than a great reckoning in a little room. (3.3.9–12)

To an alert audience, the lines might recall Barabas's 'great riches in a little room', and, juxtaposed with the 'reckoning' over the tavern bill in Deptford which supposedly brought about Marlowe's premature death, evoke again the ghost of Shakespeare's rival. Marlowe's most recent biographer, David Riggs, goes still further in suggesting that Touchstone's words implicitly relate Ovid's banishment by Augustus Caesar to the events of June 1599, when a considerable collection of licentious and satirical recent publications, including Marlowe's translations of Ovid's *Elegies*, were publicly burned outside St Paul's church.[8] The reference may not be so specific, but nonetheless the issues of free speech and the right to make satires are aired in *As You Like It*, particularly in the demand of the melancholy cynic Jacques for 'liberty/ Withal, as large a charter as the wind,/ To blow on whom I please' (2.7.47–8), although Jacques's assertively foul-mouthed style may have related more broadly to the current debate over satirical licence, which the burning of the books was intended to close down, rather than to Marlowe.

As You Like It was not the last play in which Shakespeare engaged with Marlowe's work; 'Aeneas's tale to Dido', which Hamlet wants to have recalled by the Players, and perhaps the rant and rhetoric of the first Player's speech, may hark back to *Dido, Queen of Carthage*, and speculative interconnections could be extensively prolonged.

Shakespeare's relationship with Marlowe was unique in his career, and if not formative, was at least highly significant. Marlowe found himself as a playwright at a younger age than Shakespeare, and Shakespeare took more time to achieve the same confidence. The other contemporary with whose work Shakespeare became actively involved was Jonson, although the relationship was a very different one. It may have begun, as Shakespeare's did with Marlowe, when the two were working for the same theatrical company, in Marlowe's case, Lord Strange's Men, and in Jonson's the Lord Chamberlain's Men. In 1598 Jonson's *Everyman in His Humour* in its original Italianate setting was performed by the Lord Chamberlain's Men; Shakespeare as a sharer in the company acted in it, and according to a not particularly reliable tradition, had in fact recommended it to the company when they were about to turn it down.[9] The lives and work of the two men were most closely connected over the next three or four years, when they might well have been seen as 'two authors writing for the same actors, acting in each other's plays, and developing new theatrical modes together'.[10] Jonson reacts, and even alludes to Shakespeare in plays of this period and Shakespeare (much less, and more debatably) to Jonson, and in 1603 Shakespeare acted in Jonson's *Sejanus*, possibly at the new king's court. After this Shakespeare's part in the dialogue seems to have lapsed, although he remains an important presence in Jonson's imagination, more significant, perhaps, in the critical than in the creative side of it. While the rivalry of Shakespeare and Marlowe is implicit, the relationship between Shakespeare and Jonson is shaped and constructed by the younger writer; and although scholars argue as to whether Jonson's attitude to Shakespeare can be characterized as an obsession,[11] he clearly set himself up in opposition to Shakespeare as his 'great rival',[12] and defined his own theatrical practice in distinction to Shakespeare's. Marlowe, cryptic in everything, left no comment on Shakespeare; Jonson, however, had a great deal to say, including the generous tribute to his genius in the First Folio, in which the resonant epithet 'gentle' is attached to Shakespeare's name for the first time; he also said, more informally, 'I loved the man'.

After *Everyman in His Humour* came *Everyman out of His Humour*, performed in 1599, where Jonson's first recorded reactions to Shakespeare find expression, largely in critical form; there may be some degree of homage to Shakespeare in the dog which accompanies the foolish knight Sir Puntarvolo on his travels – perhaps played by the same animal that made a hit as Crab in *Two Gentlemen of Verona* – and in the play's last line, where Macilente/Asper, the author-surrogate, asks the audience for applause which 'may, in time, make lean Macilente as fat as Sir John Falstaff' (5.11.77–78),[13] but there is also a personal sneer at the coat of arms Shakespeare had acquired for his father in 1596. The family motto, given as 'Non sanz droict'(not without right) is referred to when Sogliardo, a clown with social aspirations, pays thirty pounds for a coat of arms, described at some length, to which Sir Puntarvolo suggests as a motto, 'Not without mustard' (3.4.86). More problematic in relation to Shakespeare is a wooing scene, again involving the fantastic Sir Puntarvolo, which bears clear resemblance to passages in *Twelfth Night*. Wishing to play the knight-errant, he prepares to woo his wife at a window, but begins his addresses to her waiting gentle woman by mistake. His ineptitude distinctly recalls Sir Andrew Aguecheek. Later in the scene he interrogates

the waiting gentlewoman (who has to pretend not to recognize him) about
the knight (himself) who has come to woo Lady Puntarvolo. 'Of what
years is the knight, fair damsel?' he asks; and she replies, 'Faith, much about
your years, sir'. The dialogue continues with further verbal similarities to
the first scene between Viola and Olivia in *Twelfth Night*, and the immediate assumption is that Jonson was parodying Shakespeare. This seems to
be reinforced by a discussion about the nature of comedy between Mitis,
the commentator, and Cordatus, in which Mitis defines the sort of comedy
that Jonson rejected with what seems to be a parody of the plot of *Twelfth
Night*, involving 'a duke . . . in love with a countess, and that countess . . . in
love with the duke's son, and the son to love the lady's waiting-maid: some
such cross-wooing' (3.6.170–2). But the usual date given for *Twelfth Night*
is later 1601, and *Everyman out of His Humour* was certainly on the stage in
1599, so that Mitis's speech, and Sir Puntarvolo's wooing, must be seen in
the light of an anticipation, and Shakespeare here the borrower;[14] perhaps
he was reacting to Jonson's mocking denigration of romantic comedy of
the sort he had written many times, and transformed Sir Puntarvolo's
fantastical wooing in disguise into something much more rich and strange.[15]
Twelfth Night also seems to glance back at *Everyman in His Humour*; in each
play the foolish gull (Stephano in Jonson, Sir Andrew Aguecheek in Shakespeare) is anxious to act convincingly as a gentleman, learning the right
pursuits, how to swear in the right style, and what sort of stockings to
wear. Sir Andrew is hopeful that his leg 'does indifferent well in a diverse-
coloured stock'· (1.3.113–14). Stephano, urged by Musco to display his
'excellent good leg' to best advantage, looks forward to obtaining a pair of
silk stockings: 'I think my leg would show well in a silk hose' (1.2.44, 41).
This evident interaction with Jonson's work accords with the view that
Shakespeare's turn of the century plays (including *As You Like It*) reflect a
distinctive engagement with current theatre. Although he did not involve
himself deeply in the 'War of the Theatres' taking place between 1599 and
1601, in which Jonson, Marston and Dekker were chief participants, he was
not unaware of its existence. Both the First Quarto and the Folio texts of
Hamlet allude briefly though anxiously (in the 'little eyases' speech) to the
current popularity of the children's troupes, at a time when the Children
of Pauls were competing with the Lord Chamberlain's Men for audiences.
More to the point in this context, however, the anonymous author of the
university play known as *The Second Part of The Return from Parnassus*,
a Cambridge undergraduate who was a witty and well-informed commentator on the contemporary cultural scene alludes directly to the
Shakespeare/Jonson rivalry. He introduces the actors Kemp and Burbage

as characters, and Kemp, well-known as a performer of comic parts for the Lord Chamberlain's Men in the 1590s, gives his opinion:

> Why here's our fellow *Shakespeare* puts them all down, ay and *Ben Jonson* too: O that Ben Jonson is a pestilent fellow. He brought up *Horace* giving the Poets a pill, but our fellow *Shakespeare* hath given him a purge that made him beray his credit.[16]

To get the point of this it is important to understand that Kemp and Burbage are presented as illiterate and ignorant professional actors who scorn both 'university men' and the kind of Inns of Court students who were performers in and audience to these plays. The Parnassus plays in fact sympathize with Jonson, not with Shakespeare, and the references to Shakespeare that cluster in the *First Part of the Returne* are to him as a popular writer of romantic poetry, appealing to undiscriminating followers of fashion.

What actually constituted his 'purge' has never been agreed, but the implication is that Shakespeare was in some way responding to Jonson's play *The Poetaster* (1601), in which Horace, representing Jonson, causes Crispinus, representing Marston, to vomit up some of that playwright's more recondite diction. In 1601–2 Shakespeare wrote *Troilus and Cressida*, and in the figure of the armed Prologue, recalls the Prologue to *The Poetaster*, who enters 'hastily, in armour' to defend the embattled Jonson; Shakespeare's Prologue, unlike Jonson's, appears 'not in confidence of author's pen'. This Prologue has been called 'one of the rare instances in which Shakespeare glances disapprovingly at Jonson's work'.[17] Critics have speculated as to whether *Troilus and Cressida* itself was intended as the purge, or more specifically the character of Ajax,[18] or whether Shakespeare left it to another of Jonson's targets in *The Poetaster*, Dekker, to answer back in *Satiromastix* (1601), performed by both the Lord Chamberlain's Men and the Children of Paul's. In any case, the creative relationship between Shakespeare and Jonson now became one-sided, although, as Shakespeare's biographer has suggested, his introduction of a new style of 'lying or boasting railers', such as Thersites in *Troilus and Cressida*, Parolles in *All's Well that Ends Well* and Lucio in *Measure for Measure*, may have taken a cue from Jonson and his clown Carlo Buffone in *Everyman out of His Humour*.[19] But Jonson's competitive stance towards the work of his rival continued, even after Shakespeare had retired from writing plays. He seems always to have been aware of Shakespeare and his work as constituting some kind of challenge to the kind of writer he wanted himself to be.

In his Jacobean plays, however, Shakespeare entered into dialogue with two younger playwrights, Beaumont and Fletcher, the latter of whom was to become his successor as chief playwright to the King's Men. They began to write plays about 1605/6, at first for the Blackfriars children's company, and from about 1608/9 for the King's Men also, by which time they would have become personally acquainted with Shakespeare when writing for his company. Beaumont, however, knew Jonson first, and was already on friendly terms with him in the last years of Elizabeth's reign.[20] Perhaps it was in the light of this association that Beaumont made a jibe in his early play *The Woman-Hater* (1606) about Shakespeare as a social climber, recalling Jonson's 'not without mustard' joke in *Everyman out of His Humour*. Count Valore, telling his sister Oriana satirically what 'fine sights' are now on display at court mentions the legs of a man, 'once sockeless', but now 'very strangely become the legges of a Knight and a Courtier', and continues:

> Another payre you shall see, that were heire apparant legges to a Glover, these legges hope shortly to bee honourable; when they passe by they will bowe, and the mouth to these legges, will seeme to offer you some Courtship. (1.3.13–21).[21]

This is a glancing allusion, perhaps something of a private joke; for Beaumont's two early plays, the other being *The Knight of the Burning Pestle*, are so permeated by allusions to Shakespeare's plays that it is almost as if he were on the lookout for Shakespearean phrases to incorporate into his own work. In *The Woman-Hater*, the obsessively hungry Lazarello, modelled on a Jonsonian 'humour' character, parodies lines from *Hamlet*, *Much Ado About Nothing*, *Othello* and *Antony and Cleopatra*, the last of which was first staged only in late 1606 or early 1607 and was not yet in print: 'I will die bravely, and like a Roman', boasts the foolish courtier. The First Intelligencer, spying on him, pricks up his ears: 'I will die bravely, like a Roman: have a care, mark that: when he hath done all, he will kill himself' (3.2.115–16). The central situation of the disguised Duke seems to echo *Measure for Measure*, another very recent play not yet in print. Beaumont was equally quick off the mark in *The Knight of the Burning Pestle*, which contains allusions to or quotations from a wide range of plays, including *Henry VI, Part 3*, *Romeo and Juliet*, *Henry IV, Part 1*, and *Macbeth*, another play on stage in 1606 but not in print. Jasper, 'his face mealed' and supposedly a ghost, makes fun of Banquo's ghastly appearance at Macbeth's banquet; Ralf, the grocer's stage-struck apprentice, called upon to display his talents in a 'huffing part', nearly manages five whole lines from Hotspur's boasts in

Henry IV, Part 1 (1.3.201–5). Using Shakespeare in this way in the form of comic parody, Beaumont implicitly acknowledges his senior's pre-eminence on the contemporary stage, even if, like the author of the Parnassus plays, his tone is one of mockery.

But the plays of the 'Beaumont and Fletcher canon' are much more evidently works of homage, in their wholesale reliance on Shakespeare for character-types and dramatic situations. Indeed, Fletcher deliberately 'writes back' to Shakespeare in his play *The Woman's Prize, or The Tamer Tamed* (?1611), which imagines an afterlife for Petruchio from *The Taming of the Shrew*. In this play Petruchio's second wife, Maria, turns the tables on him, enlisting the support of other women to baffle and torment her husband, devising various stratagems to render him 'easie as a child/ And tame as fear' (1.2.113–14). She denies her husband sex, and withdraws with her sister into an upper part of the house where they gather a band of women to behave riotously. Eventually Petruchio feigns death, Maria repents her bad behaviour, and the two are reconciled. Although the play positions itself as pro-feminist by comparison with *The Taming of the Shrew*, and the Epilogue states that it is 'apt meant/ To teach both sexes due equality,/ And, as they stand bound, to love mutually', the misogynistic speeches given to Petruchio and his servants stress the monstrousness of female sexuality in a manner quite foreign to Shakespeare, answering back to him in another way.[22] No other contemporary play (by any writer) bears quite this relation to one of Shakespeare's, and other Beaumont and Fletcher plays which clearly look back to a source in Shakespeare, such as *The False One* (1620) to *Antony and Cleopatra* and *The Sea Voyage* (1620) to *The Tempest*, offer no challenge to their predecessors. Indeed, the Prologue to *The False One* disingenuously denies any intent to compete with earlier plays (not naming Shakespeare), because it deals with 'Young Cleopatra' and not 'her fatal love to Antony'. It might be argued that writing back to Shakespeare in the way Fletcher does it in *The Woman's Prize* was not commonly done until after the Restoration.

In an important instance, however, Shakespeare can be seen in dialogue with the writers whose work was, for a period in the later seventeenth century, considerably more popular with theatre-goers than his own. Debate continues as to whether Shakespeare's turn towards romance in the years after the King's Men had acquired the use of the Blackfriars Theatre in 1608 was influenced by Beaumont and Fletcher's plays in this style; it focuses especially on the relationship between two clearly connected plays, *Philaster* and *Cymbeline*. The dating of both, neither of which is published in a contemporary edition, is uncertain enough to allow that either might have been the first, and also to give scope for critics to derive their arguments for priority in part on their attitude to Beaumont and Fletcher as innovators. Those unable to accept that Shakespeare might have taken his cue from playwrights several years his junior stress Beaumont and Fletcher's status as 'prentice dramatists' who in 1608 or thereabouts were 'struggling to keep failure at bay', and also the undeniable debt of *Philaster* to other Shakespeare plays, such as *Twelfth Night* and *Hamlet*. More open-minded critics allow that 'Beaumont and Fletcher influenced Shakespeare's work, as he did theirs',[23] and that priority cannot finally be proven.[24] Even if Beaumont and Fletcher had had no distinct theatrical success by this time, they were hardly prentices, having had between them more plays staged than Marlowe ever did. One of those was *Cupid's Revenge*, generally accepted without debate as an early play, probably 1607/8, and preceding *Cymbeline*. The figure of Urania in this play, a princess who wants to escape a forced marriage to a foreign prince and disguises herself as a boy to follow the man she loves, has much in common with Imogen in *Cymbeline*. In *Philaster* the princess Arethusa stands in danger of a forced marriage, but the male disguise is assumed by Euphrasia, whose 'travels and sufferings'[25] greatly resemble Imogen's. There are also verbal connections between the two plays, of which the most notable is a speech by Iachimo, finding reasons for his defeat by Posthumus (at that point in disguise as a peasant), and some lines of Philaster, wounded by a 'Country Fellow' after he has attacked Arethusa. Iachimo says:

> I have belied a lady,
> The Princess of this country; and the air on't
> A very drudge of nature's, have subdu'd me
> In my profession.
>
> (5.2.2–6)

Philaster says, more tersely and with less complexity:

> The gods take part against me, could this boor
> Have held me thus else?
>
> (4.5.102–3)

The situations of the two speakers and their response are so similar that it was clear one playwright was echoing the other. Arethusa and Imogen are both princesses slandered by their lovers; and so too is Hermione in *The Winter's Tale*, another play that seems involved, if more tangentially, in this nexus. Themes of 'royal lineage and genealogy' make up another thread in the web.[26] Shakespeare was clearly engaged with the younger playwrights in a series of plays, probably over a period of three to four years. *Cymbeline* in turn may well have created the impetus for Fletcher's exploration of Romano-British relations in *Bonduca* (*c*.1610), which also draws on the misogyny Shakespeare allots to Posthumus.

Shakespeare's relationship with Fletcher culminated in the last plays of his career, *The Two Noble Kinsmen* and *Henry VIII*, both probably in 1613. These, it is now generally accepted, were co-written with Fletcher, as was *Cardenio* (1612/13), now lost, which was performed at least twice at court. This was not Shakespeare's first collaborative work, nor was it a final option with which to end his theatrical career; he had collaborated with other playwrights at different stages of his life, early on with Gorge Peele on *Titus Andronicus*, much later with George Wilkins on *Pericles* and probably with Thomas Middleton on *Timon of Athens*. None of these amounted to a sustained professional relationship. In both *Henry VIII* and particularly *The Two Noble Kinsmen* it seems as if Fletcher's influence induced Shakespeare to experiment, even though both plays relate to work he had done earlier. *Henry VIII* harks back to the English histories he had written in the 1590s which rely on Holinshed's *Chronicles* as a major source, but with more evident engagement with topical political issues such as divorce and England's destiny as a Protestant nation.[27] The celebration of the birth of Elizabeth, with which the play ends, and the fulsome compliment to King James – 'Wherever the bright sun of heaven shall shine,/ The honour and the greatness of his name/ Shall be, and make new nations' (5.4.50–2) – would for an audience of the time relate also to the marriage of James's daughter Elizabeth to the Elector Palatine in February 1613, a dynastic union made to consolidate the Protestant powers of Europe. But *Henry VIII* also shares features with Shakespeare's other late plays, such as the focus on the father–daughter relationship in which the daughter's role is to restore what the father has lost, an element of the supernatural in Queen Katherine's death-bed vision, and the idea expressed in Cranmer's long last-scene speech of cyclical time and redemption. The closeness of the working relationship between the two playwrights may be assumed from the fact that the last two components appear in scenes generally accepted as Fletcher's. Generically, the play is a hybrid, like *Cymbeline*, *The Winter's Tale* and *The Tempest*, and also like *Cupid's Revenge* and *Philaster*. Shakespeare is usually credited with rather more of it, though in one major scene (3.2) it appears that Fletcher took over half way through, and wrote the fine soliloquy in which Wolsey realizes that his star is on the wane:

> Nay then, farewell.
> I have touched the highest point of all my greatness,
> And from that full meridian of my glory

> I hast now to my setting. I shall fall
> Like a bright exhalation in the evening,
> And no man see me more.
>
> (3.2.222–7)

Fletcher wrote a larger part of *The Two Noble Kinsmen*, a play ascribed at its first entry in the Stationers' Register, which was not until 8 April 1634, to both playwrights; perhaps he also put together the final draft.[28] This may give support to the view that whereas in *Henry VIII* 'the dramatists' influence on each other's style was reciprocal . . . in *The Two Noble Kinsmen* the influence appears to have been one way'.[29] This does not mean, however, that *Two Noble Kinsmen* emerges as a seamless whole; far from it, and critics still take delight in pointing out how Fletcher, still regarded as inexperienced, trivializes the characterization of the kinsmen, Palamon and Arcite, and the object of their love, Emilia, and goes all out for sensation and immediate, rather than sustained, dramatic effect.[30] The re-shaping of Chaucer's source-story, *The Knight's Tale*, into a tragicomic romance, its high chivalric tone modified by the addition of the subplot centring on the Jailor's Daughter, seems perhaps more like Fletcher's style than Shakespeare's. Although the Jailor's Daughter clearly has an ancestor in Ophelia, it is possible to see her as 'richly synthesising Fletcherian and Shakespearean traditions'.[31] But the play's ending, with its brutal climax in the sudden violent death of Arcite and the emotional ambivalence of Palamon's acceptance that he has, after all, won Emilia, is Shakespeare's. 'O cousin', he exclaims as his beloved kinsman's body is borne off,

> That we should things desire, which do cost us
> The loss of our desire! That nought could buy
> Dear love, but loss of dear love.
>
> (5.4.109–12)

There is no redemption or reconciliation in this dark vision of human life with its painful paradox,[32] probably the last thing Shakespeare wrote for the stage.

Later in 1613 the Globe theatre burnt down, when the thatch caught fire at a performance of *Henry VIII*; the rebuilding was to be very expensive, and it may have been this that prompted Shakespeare to sell his shares in the company. He did not hasten to return to Stratford, but his active involvement in the life of the London theatre was now over. The influence his work exercised on the imaginations of contemporary playwrights, already evident in plays from the early seventeenth century, such as Marston's *The Malcontent* (1603), Middleton's *The Family of Love* (1602) and *The Revenger's Tragedy*, not to mention the plays of Jonson, intensified and diversified in the years up to the closing of the theatres. Plays by Webster, Middleton, Ford, Massinger, Shirley and many others are permeated by echoes and reminiscences, and structured as imitations of Shakespeare. Decades ago, a critic compiled a list of more than 100 plays written between 1600 and 1642 containing allusions to *Hamlet*, his most imitated play.[33] That he was central to the theatre of his age is evident from his usefulness both to other playwrights and to the commercial interests involved in printing and producing plays. Two plays from the 1620s, both by playwrights much indebted to Shakespeare, will demonstrate something of the variety of forms taken by the inspiration his work provided.

Massinger, who worked extensively with Fletcher and took over his role as chief playwright to the King's Men after Fletcher's death in 1625, was steeped in Shakespeare. *A New Way to Pay Old Debts* (1625/6), a late city comedy, rewrites *The Merchant of Venice* for a new age, taking over character relationships and plot elements; and the mighty figure of Sir Giles Overreach, a 'cruel extortioner' as the dramatis personae has it, relates back to Shylock (via Volpone), in his subversively anti-Christian attitudes to wealth, and similarly overwhelms his play. As in *The Merchant of Venice*, there are separate but overlapping groups of characters; on the one hand, Shylock, his runaway daughter Jessica and her Christian lover Lorenzo find parallels in Overreach, his daughter Margaret, who refuses to comply with her father's plans for her, and Tom Allworth, the page with whom she plans to run away in order to marry; on the other, the wealthy and munificent Portia, the generous Antonio and the adventurer Bassanio are echoed in the rich and gracious Lady Allworth, the benevolent aristocrat Lord Lovell and Wellborn, the prodigal who is redeemed by the patronage of Lady Allworth.[34] Massinger's distinctive concerns with the social order of Jacobean England modify the nature of his characters and their interrelationships; Wellborn, for instance, who has squandered family money to fund a lifestyle of 'Hawkes and Hounds,/ With choice of running horses; Mistrisses/ of all sorts, and all sizes' (1.1.45–6),[35] is more culpable for his prodigality than Bassanio, whose financial irresponsibility is rather casually written off as gentlemanly insouciance about material things. *A New Way* is a more explicitly moral comedy than *The Merchant of Venice*, and Wellborn, having played his part in bringing about Overreach's downfall, must then restore his reputation fully by serving in the army. Overreach is not a hoarder or a miser like Shylock; and whereas Shylock is desperate to preserve his own social (and racial) identity separate from the community in which he must, unwillingly, live, Overreach longs for power and status, believing that his money can buy his family gentility and a place in society:

'All my ambition is to have my daughter/ Right honorable' (4.1.99–100). But both characters expose the rift between a society nostalgically depicted as based on traditional values, whereby the possession of wealth is identified with inherited status, and a newer, more acquisitive one. Like *The Merchant of Venice, A New Way* evokes 'the pangs of transition to a capitalist, cash-nexus society'.[36] Overreach's creed that the only bonds between people are those forged by money ultimately derives from Shylock's, and both are unable to accept the codes of honour and dutiful obligation which govern the conduct of the other characters. Finally, both must be forced into compliance with the society whose values they have rejected; Shylock must convert to Christianity, and Overreach be confined to a 'dark room' for the cure of his lunacy.

In John Ford's tragedy *'Tis Pity She's a Whore* (?1625) the major characters have more obvious Shakespearean equivalents in the play which Ford has taken as his starting point, *Romeo and Juliet*; Giovanni and Annabella are the star-crossed lovers, there is a friar in each play, a nurse, a father concerned about his daughter's marital prospects and an unwanted suitor. The existence of these parallels is deliberately pointed up from the play's second scene, which begins with street-fighting between men of opposed factions, interrupted by the patriarch Florio, who appears, like the Prince of Verona in *Romeo and Juliet*, to express his outrage at 'these sudden broils so near my doors' (1.2.22). The parallels create a shock effect, tantalizingly suggesting similarity but exposing difference. Giovanni woos Annabella in a poetic style that recalls Shakespeare's Petrarchanism and the rhyming idiom he used for Romeo and Juliet's first meeting:

> *Giovanni*: . . . The poets feign, I read
> That Juno for her forehead did exceed
> All other goddesses, but I swear
> Your forehead exceeds hers, as hers did theirs.
> *Annabella*: Troth, this is pretty.
> *Giovanni*:   Such a pair of stars
> As are thine eyes, would, like Promethean fire,
> If gently glanced, give life to senseless stones.
> *Annabella*: Fie upon 'ee.
> *Giovanni*: The lily and the rose, most sweetly strange,
> Upon your dimple cheeks do strive for change.
> Such lips would tempt a saint.
>
> (1.2.192–202)[37]

By making his lovers brother and sister Ford not only turns Shakespeare's tragedy of the grudge between 'two households both alike in dignity' upon its head, but even seems to write back to and to challenge the earlier play's vision of social reconciliation achieved through sacrifice. His Parma is a darker and more corrupt city than Verona; the lovers may be the most principled characters within it, but they are not innocent, and the marriage into which Annabella enters to conceal her pregnancy is the opposite of the secret but 'holy' act by which Shakespeare's Friar Laurence hopes to 'turn your households' rancour into pure love' (2.2.92). Where Juliet refuses a suitor more socially acceptable than her lover and risks death to escape him, Annabella concedes to social pressure. Juliet's final gesture is to take the dead Romeo's dagger and bury it in her own body, a metaphorical re-enactment of coition. In *'Tis Pity She's a Whore* Giovanni uses the lover's dagger to rip open Annabella's body and cut out her heart, thus translating the Petrarchan conceit of possessing a lover's heart into 'grim reality'.[38] The play ends with the Cardinal's hypocritical summary:

> Of one so young, so rich in nature's store,
> Who could not say, *'Tis pity she's a whore?*
>   (5.6.158–9)

Massinger and Ford both return to Shakespeare writing consciously from a changed society; Massinger can find parallels between the 1620s and the 1590s, but for Ford the differences are more significant.

Then, as now, Shakespeare's work afforded his successors a seemingly inexhaustible fund on which to draw. It was basic, too, to the commercial interests of the theatre. In his lifetime, as Roslyn Knutson has shown, Shakespeare's plays were of major importance to the repertoire of the King's Men, and his output reflected contemporary tastes: 'Shakespeare supplied the kind of plays that audiences liked, with stories that they liked, in dramatic formulas that they liked.'[39] The Oxford scholar Leonard Digges observed, in verses published in an edition of Shakespeare's works printed in 1640 (though written earlier), how Shakespeare's plays, in contrast with those of Jonson, filled the theatre; the audience did not care for the speeches 'Of tedious (though well laboured) *Catalines*' and '*Sejanus* too was irksome', whereas

> Let but *Falstaffe* come,
> *Hall, Poines*, the rest you scarce shall have a roome
> All is so pester'd: let but *Beatrice*
> And *Benedicke* be seene, loe in a trice
> The Cockpit galleries, Boxes, all are full
> To heare *Malvoglio*, that crosse garter'd Gull.[40]

Shakespeare was also popular in print; it has been calculated that between 1594 and 1660 nineteen of his plays were published in separate texts, and of these there were sixty-six editions.[41] This may not sound a large number, but we should remember that it was not for the most part in the interests of the King's Men to have the work of their most popular playwright available in printed form for the use of other companies. The point has been made recently that printed plays were not in fact particularly profitable to the book trade.[42] Nonetheless, it has been convincingly shown that Shakespeare, like Jonson, wrote for the page as well as the stage, and that from quite early on, about 1598, he emerged as an author of plays, and these plays 'stopped having an existence that was [merely] confined to the stage'.[43] For Shakespeare (as for Jonson) there were also two folios before 1642, and after the publication of the second in 1632 William Prynne remarked with annoyance that play texts got far too much attention, and that 'Shackspeers Plaies are printed in the best Crowne paper, far better than most Bibles.'[44] Numbers of Shakespeare's plays were published in unauthorized or surreptitious copies, and many of these were falsely ascribed to him, often with title pages that claimed that they were by 'W. S', which printers and booksellers clearly recognized as a winning formula.[45] His name sold books as early as 1599. In this year a small collection of poems called *The Passionate Pilgrim* by 'W. Shakespeare' appeared; the majority of them were not by Shakespeare. A third edition of the popular collection came out in 1612, this time including poems by Thomas Heywood, who was upset by this, not wanting readers to get the impression that he had stolen from Shakespeare; he claimed that Shakespeare was 'much offended with Master Jaggard [the publisher] that altogether unknown to him, presumed to make bold with his name'.[46]

The meaning attached to Shakespeare's name had been transformed since the first printed reference to it was made in a riddling form to be decoded by the cognoscenti, by one of Shakespeare's contemporaries who evidently did not admire him. In his pamphlet *Greenes Groatsworth of Witte* (1592) Robert Greene, playwright and University wit, warns three playwriting friends, usually identified as Marlowe, Nashe and Peele, against actors in general and one actor in particular:

> For there is an upstart Crow, beautified with our feathers, that with his Tygers hart wrapt in a Players hyde, supposes he is as well able to bombast out a blanke verse as the best of you: and being an absolute Johannes fac totum, is in his owne conceit the onely Shake-scene in a countrey. (sig. E4v)

Here Shakespeare is mocked by the jealous Greene as a player pretending to be a writer, laying claim to what is not his right ('our feathers'), by implication because he is not a university man like Greene and the others.

Greene betrays the fact that this upstart has already written something worthy of quotation by his recollection of a line from *Henry VI, Part 3* (picked out in italics from the rest of the black-letter text). Greene died a few days before the publication of this pamphlet, but his jeering reference to a 'Johannes fac totum', the earliest recorded use of the expression, meaning as the *OED* has it, 'a would-be universal genius' was to be translated into reality in ways he could not have envisaged.

Epilogue

In recent years the early modern professional theatre has been defined as a marginal institution, both geographically and culturally, in its relation to those institutions which constituted the heart of the community.[1] But far from being a disadvantage, this isolation has been seen as empowering, enabling the theatre to use its 'ideologically removed vantage point' as a licence, the better to reflect on and explore the tensions and contradictions of its times. This has proved a very fruitful line of enquiry, particularly into the productive ambivalences of drama; and, undeniably, players were always marginal, if no longer masterless, men, and as much the focus for anti-theatrical prejudice as the materials they staged. But the stress on marginality should not obscure the fact that theatre as a social process was also central to its age, which was one of limited literacy and access to knowledge. Theatre was accessible to all levels of society and in its unique representational role capable of creating new ways of understanding what has been called 'social experience'[2] through its dramatization of human action and interaction. As an artistic medium theatre is expressive and volatile; its power to communicate is never controlled by any one element, and its reception is not determined by the intention of the author or creator. Meanings can be created by audiences, and may differ from time to time according to such variables as performance conditions and topical events, not to mention the special contributions made by performers. Drama sprang from debate, and has always maintained an openness, a readiness to engage with significant issues but without enforcing conclusions. Its essential nature as playing at new identities reflected much that was intrinsic to the culture of early modern London, in a period of rapid and confusing social change, when rank and social status were liable to fluctuation, and social identity was fluid and precarious. The theatricality of the Stuart court, with its attention to masques, displays and spectacles of power, even its effeminacy, was evident to contemporary observers. Theatre's theatricality was regarded with ambivalence, of which Shakespeare's disgusted comment in Sonnet 111 about being indelibly tainted, like the 'dyer's hand', by his profession, is the best-known example. The power of the stage to transform the moral into the aesthetic, as in revenge drama, was a subject of distrust, as was its infatuation with power itself. Its relation to the monarchy was uncomfortably poised. As Richard Wheeler puts it, 'If the theatre helped to create the social and political awareness that would bring to an end the age of absolutism, it was nonetheless enamoured of the vision of life's grandeur it associated with royal power.'[3] But, undeniably, the stage did shape such an awareness, enabling audiences not only to become conscious of themselves as onlookers but also to see how they might become participants in the scenes which the players represented before them.

Notes

Chapter 1 Introduction

1 Glynne Wickham, *Early English Stages: 1300–1660* (London: Routledge & Kegan Paul, 1959–81), III, xix.
2 Glynne Wickham, Herbert Berry and William Ingram (eds), *English Professional Theatre, 1530–1660* (Cambridge: Cambridge University Press, 2000), 68.
3 Ibid., 69.
4 Ibid., 51.
5 From Edward Hall, *Hall's Chronicle: The Union of the Two Noble and Illustre Famelies of York and Lancaster*, ed. Henry Ellis (1809), quoted by Graham Parry, 'Entertainments at Court', in John D. Cox and David Scott Kastan (eds), *A New History of Early English Drama* (New York: Columbia University Press, 1997), 196.
6 William Gager, quoted in David Mann, *The Elizabethan Player: Contemporary Stage Representation* (London and New York: Routledge, 1991), 132.
7 Cox and Kastan, *New History*, 69.
8 William Ingram, *The Business of Playing: The Beginnings of Adult Professional Theatre in Elizabethan England* (Ithaca and London: Cornell University Press, 1992), 139.
9 Wickham et al., *English Professional Theatre*, 292.
10 Quoted in ibid., 297.
11 Margreta de De Grazia, 'World Pictures, Modern Periods, and the Early Stage', in Cox and Kastan, *New History*, 17.
12 G. E. Bentley, *The Profession of Dramatist in Shakespeare's Time* (Princeton: Princeton University Press, 1971), 4.
13 Quoted in Bentley, *Profession of Dramatist*, 7.
14 E. K. Chambers, *The Elizabethan Stage*, 4 vols (Oxford: Clarendon Press, 1923), IV, 267.
15 Ibid., 200.
16 Ibid., 267.
17 Ibid., 300.
18 M. C. Bradbrook, *The Rise of the Common Player: A Study of Actor and Society in Shakespeare's England* (Cambridge: Cambridge University Press, 1962), 41.
19 From the Act of 1572 'for the punishement of Vacabones', in Chambers, *Elizabethan Stage*, IV, 269–71.
20 Bradbrook, *Rise of the Common Player*, 37.
21 Wickham et al., *English Professional Theatre*, 205.
22 Ibid., 206.
23 Bradbrook, *Rise of the Common Player*, 55.
24 Wickham et al., *English Professional Theatre*, 179.
25 Chambers, *Elizabethan Stage*, IV, 287.
26 Scott McMillin and Sally-Beth MacLean, *The Queen's Men and their Plays* (Cambridge: Cambridge University Press, 1998), 24.

27 Wickham et al., *English Professional Theatre*, 123.

28 Richard Dutton, *Mastering the Revels: The Regulation and Censorship of English Renaissance Drama* (Basingstoke: Macmillan, 1991), 157.

29 Ibid., 157.

30 James Shapiro, *1599: A Year in the Life of William Shakespeare* (London: Faber & Faber, 2005), 131.

31 Ibid., 47, quoting Everard Guilpin, *Skialetheia* (1599).

32 Andrew Gurr, *The Shakespearean Stage, 1574–1642*, 2nd edn (Cambridge: Cambridge University Press, 1982), 85, quoting Stow's *Annales*.

33 Bradbrook, *Rise of the Common Player*, 172.

34 Philip Edwards et al., *The Revels History of Drama in English*, vol. 4, 1613–1660 (London and New York: Methuen, 1981), 78.

35 Wickham et al., *English Professional Theatre*, 181.

36 Quoted in Bradbrook, *Rise of the Common Player*, 65.

37 Jean E. Howard, *The Stage and Social Struggle in Early Modern England* (London: Routledge, 1994), 23.

38 Thomas Heywood, *An Apologie for Actors* (1612), sig. B4v .

39 Quoted in Lisa Jardine, *Still Harping on Daughters: Women and Drama in the Age of Shakespeare* (Brighton: Harvester Press, 1983), 17.

40 Gurr, *Shakespearean Stage*, 196.

41 Martin Butler, *Theatre and Crisis 1632–1642* (Cambridge: Cambridge University Press, 1984), 300.

42 Ibid., 209.

43 Ibid., 299.

44 Ibid., 69.

45 Ibid., 201.

46 L. B. Wright, *Middle-Class Culture in Elizabethan England* (London: Methuen, 1935), 609.

47 Webster, 'To the Reader', in *The White Devil*, in *Selected Plays of John Webster*, ed. Jonathan Dollimore and Alan Sinfield (Cambridge: Cambridge University Press, 1983), 7.

48 Andrew Gurr, *Playgoing in Shakespeare's London* (Cambridge: Cambridge University Press, 1987), 31.

49 Ibid., 179.

50 Quoted from Gurr, *Playgoing*, 205.

51 Geoffrey Bullough, *Narrative and Dramatic Sources of Shakespeare*, 8 vols (London: Routledge & Kegan Paul, 1957–75), VII, 181.

52 Jeremy Lopez, *Theatrical Convention and Audience Response in Early Modern Drama* (Cambridge: Cambridge University Press, 2003), 32.

53 A. L. Rowse (ed.), *The Casebooks of Simon Forman. Sex and Society in Shakespeare's Age* (London: Weidenfeld & Nicolson, 1974), 311.

54 Gurr, *Playgoing*, 209.

55 Ibid., 223.

56 Ibid., 71.

57 Edmund Gayton, *Pleasant Notes upon Don Quixot* (1654), 271.

58 Quoted in Gurr, *Playgoing*, 219.

59 Lopez, *Theatrical Convention*, 33.

60 Angela Stock and Anne-Julia Zwierlein, 'Our Scene is London', in Dieter Mehl, Angela Stock and Anne-Julia Zwierlein (eds), *Plotting Early Modern London: New Essays on Jacobean City Comedy* (Aldershot: Ashgate, 2004), 9.

61 Quotation taken from *The Complete Plays of Ben Jonson*, ed. G. A. Wilkes, 4 vols (Oxford: Clarendon Press, 1981–2), IV.

62 M. C. Bradbrook, *Themes and Conventions of Elizabethan Tragedy* (Cambridge: Cambridge University Press, 1931), 112.

63 Ibid., 116.
64 Gurr, *Shakespearean Stage*, 111.
65 Michael Hattaway, *Elizabethan Popular Theatre: Plays in Performance* (London: Routledge & Kegan Paul, 1982), 77.
66 Wickham et al., *English Professional Theatre*, 182.
67 Quoted from *The Norton Shakespeare*, ed. Stephen Greenblatt et al. (New York and London: W. W. Norton, 1997), 3336.
68 Howard, *Stage and Social Struggle*, 31.
69 Franco Moretti, '"A Huge Eclipse": Tragic Form and the Deconsecration of Sovereignty', in Stephen Greenblatt (ed.), *The Power of Forms in the English Renaissance* (Norman, Okla.: Pilgrim,1982), 7, 9.
70 Quoted in Chambers, *Elizabethan Stage*, IV, 247.
71 Quoted in Gordon McMullan (ed.), *King Henry VIII*, The Arden Shakespeare (London: Thomson Learning, 2000), 59.
72 Ibid., 61.
73 Dekker, *The Gull's Hornbook*, in *Thomas Dekker: Selected Writings*, ed. E. D. Pendry (Cambridge, Mass.: Harvard University Press, 1968), 98.
74 Robert Weimann, *Shakespeare and the Popular Tradition in the Theater* (Baltimore and London: Johns Hopkins University Press, 1978), 212.
75 Ibid., 212.
76 Gurr, *Shakespearean Stage*, 113.
77 Ibid., 114.
78 Butler, *Theatre and Crisis*, 181.
79 Ibid., 183.
80 Gurr, *Playgoing*, 183.
81 Ibid., 233–4.

Chapter 2 Monarchy and the Stage

1 Howard, *Stage and Social Struggle*, 31.
2 McMullan, *King Henry VIII*, 59.
3 Stephen Orgel, 'Making Greatness Familiar', *Genre*, 15 (4) (1981), 41–8, 47.
4 From *The Scholemaster* (1570), quoted from Chambers, *Elizabethan Stage*, IV, 191.
5 Given in Chambers, *Elizabethan Stage*, IV, 263–4.
6 J. Leeds Barroll, 'A New History for Shakespeare and His Time', *Shakespeare Quarterly*, 39 (1988), 441–64.
7 Alexander Leggatt, *Shakespeare's Political Drama. The History Plays and the Roman Plays* (London and New York: Routledge, 1988), 76.
8 Wickham et al., *English Professional Theatre*, 195.
9 E.g. by Barroll, 'New History'.
10 John Chamberlain, *The Letters of John Chamberlain*, ed. Norman Egbert McLure, 2 vols (Philadelphia: American Philosophical Society), II, 578.
11 Dutton, *Mastering the Revels*, 236–46, Annabel Patterson, *Censorship and Interpretation: The Conditions of Reading and Writing in Early Modern England* (Madison: University of Wisconsin Press, 1984).
12 F. P. Wilson, *The English Drama 1485–1585* (Oxford: Clarendon Press, 1969), 40–3.
13 Quotation taken from *Gorboduc*, ed. Irby B. Cauthen, Jr (London: Edward Arnold, 1970).
14 Richard Dutton, 'Censorship', in Cox and Kastan, *New History*, 293.
15 Sandra Billington, *Mock Kings and Medieval Society in Renaissance Drama* (Oxford: Clarendon Press, 1991), 223.
16 Ibid., 222–31.

17 Quotations from *Thomas of Woodstock, or King Richard The Second, Part One*, ed. Peter Corbin and Douglas Sedge, *The Revels Plays* (Manchester: Manchester University Press, 2002), 147.
18 Chambers, *Elizabethan Stage*, IV, 323.
19 Dutton, *Mastering the Revels*, 109.
20 Janet Clare, *'Art Made Tongue-tied by Authority': Elizabethan and Jacobean Dramatic Censorship* (Manchester: Manchester University Press, 1990), 139.
21 Chambers, *Elizabethan Stage*, I, 325.
22 *State Papers Domestic, James I*, 31, 73, quoted in Clare, *'Art'*, 141.
23 Chambers, *Elizabethan Stage*, I, 326.
24 Ibid., 327.
25 Ivo Kamps, *Historiography and Ideology in Stuart Drama* (Cambridge: Cambridge University Press, 1996), 142.
26 Margot Heinemann, *Puritanism and Theatre: Thomas Middleton and Opposition Drama under the Early Stuarts* (Cambridge: Cambridge University Press, 1980), 166–70.
27 Clare,*'Art'*, 190–9.
28 T. A. Dunn, *Philip Massinger: The Man and the Playwright* (London: Thomas Nelson, 1957), 44.
29 Ibid., 43.
30 Richard Dutton, 'The Dating and Contexts of *Henry V*', *Huntington Library Quarterly*, 28 (2005), 173–204, 182.
31 S. R. Gardiner, 'The Political Element in Massinger', *The Contemporary Review*, 28 (1876), 495–507 .
32 Butler, *Theatre and Crisis*, 136.
33 From J. Quincy Adams (ed.), *The Dramatic Records of Sir Henry Herbert* (New Haven: Yale University Press, 1917), quoted in G. E. Bentley, *The Jacobean and Caroline Stage*, 7 vols (Oxford: Clarendon Press, 1941), I, 333.
34 Butler, *Theatre and Crisis*, 220–29, Bentley, *Jacobean and Caroline Stage*, I, 332–34.
35 Mary Beth Rose, *The Expense of Spirit: Love and Sexuality in the English Renaissance* (Ithaca, N.Y.: Cornell University Press, 1986), 12–42.
36 *Lyly: The Complete Works*, ed. R. W. Bond, 3 vols (Oxford: Oxford University Press, 1902), II, 208. All quotations from Lyly are taken from this edition.
37 Philippa Berry, *Of Chastity and Power: Elizabethan Literature and the Unmarried Queen* (London and New York: Routledge, 1989), 127.
38 Quotations from *Cynthia's Revels* taken from *Ben Jonson*, ed. C. H. Herford and Percy Simpson, 11 vols (Oxford: Clarendon Press, 1932), IV.
39 Anne Barton, *Ben Jonson, Dramatist* (Cambridge: Cambridge University Press, 1984), 80.
40 Helen Hackett, *Virgin Mother, Maiden Queen: Elizabeth I and the Cult of the Virgin Mary* (London: Macmillan, 1995), 227.
41 Quotations taken from Thomas Heywood, *If You Know Not Me, You Know Nobody, Part 1*, ed. Madeleine Doran, Malone Society Reprints (Oxford: Oxford University Press, 1935).
42 Michael Dobson and Nicola J. Watson, *England's Elizabeth: An Afterlife in Fame and Fantasy* (Oxford: Oxford University Press, 2002), 59.
43 Julia Gasper, *The Dragon and the Dove: The Plays of Thomas Dekker* (Oxford: Clarendon, 1990), 96 .
44 McMullan, *King Henry VIII*, 63.
45 Clare, *'Art'*, 114.
46 Quotations taken from *The Malcontent*, ed. Bernard Harris, New Mermaids (London: Ernest Benn, 1967).
47 Quotations taken from *Eastward Ho!*, ed. C. G. Petter, New Mermaids (London: Ernest Benn, 1973).
48 Clare, *'Art'*, 117 and n. 42, 147–8.

49 Quotations taken from *The Fawn*, ed. Gerald A. Smith (Lincoln: University of Nebraska Press, 1965).

50 John Harington, *The Letters and Epigrams of Sir John Harington*, ed. N. E. McClure (Philadelphia: University of Pennsylvania Press, 1930), 119–121.

51 Quoted from Chambers, *Elizabethan Stage*, III, 257. Translation by John Margeson in George Chapman, *The Conspiracy and Tragedy of Charles Duke of Byron*, ed. John Margeson (Manchester and New York: Manchester University Press,1988), cited in Dutton, *Mastering the Revels*, 183.

52 Quoted in Philip Finkelpearl, ' "The Comedians' Liberty": Censorship of the Jacobean Stage Reconsidered', *English Literary Renaissance*, 16 (1986), 127.

53 Butler, *Theatre and Crisis, passim*.

Chapter 3 Sex, Marriage and the Family

1 *Christian Oeconomie*, trans. Thomas Pickering (1618), quoted in Catherine Belsey, *The Subject of Tragedy. Identity and Difference in Renaissance Tragedy* (London: Methuen, 1985), 143.

2 William Averell, *A Dyall for Dainty Darlings, rockt in the cradle of Securitie* (1584), 32–3.

3 *A Discourse of Marriage and Wiving, and of the greatest Mystery contained, How to choose a good Wife from a bad*, by Alexander Niccholes, 'Batchelour in the Art he never yet put in practise' (1615).

4 Quoted from Elaine V. Beilin, *Redeeming Eve: Women Writers of the English Renaissance* (Princeton: Princeton University Press, 1987), 315.

5 Ibid., 315.

6 Quoted from Sara Mendelson and Patricia Crawford, *Women in Early Modern England* (Oxford: Clarendon Press, 1998), 135.

7 Averell, *Dyall*, 46 .

8 William Haller and Malleville Haller, 'The Puritan Art of Love', *Huntington Library Quarterly*, 5 (1941–2), 242.

9 Lawrence Stone, *The Family, Sex and Marriage in England 1500–1800*, abridged edn (Harmondsworth: Penguin Books, 1979), 101.

10 Niccholes, *Discourse*, 6.

11 Stone, *Family, Sex and Marriage*, 128.

12 Niccholes, *Discourse*, 10.

13 Ibid., 32.

14 Quoted from Susan Baker, 'Sex and Marriage in *The Dutch Courtesan*', in Dorothea Kehler and Susan Baker (eds), *In Another Country: Feminist Perspectives on Renaissance Drama* (Metuchen, N. J., and London: Scarecrow, 1991), 227.

15 Baker, 'Sex and Marriage', 218.

16 Quotations from John Marston, *The Dutch Courtesan*, ed. M. L. Wine, Regents Renaissance Drama Series (Lincoln, Nebr.: University of Nebraska Press, 1965).

17 Alexander Leggatt, *Citizen Comedy in the Age of Shakespeare* (Toronto: University of Toronto Press, 1973), 151.

18 Quotations from *The Scornful Lady*, in *The Dramatic Works in the Beaumont and Fletcher Canon*, gen. editor Fredson Bowers, 10 vols (Cambridge: Cambridge University Press, 1966–), II.

19 M. D. Bristol, *Carnival and Theater: Plebeian Culture and the Structure of Authority in Renaissance England* (New York and London: Methuen, 1985), 164.

20 Quotations from *Dramatic Works in the Beaumont and Fletcher Canon*, VI.

21 Edward M. Wilson, '*Rule a Wife and Have a Wife* and *El Sagaz Estacio*', *Review of English Studies*, 24 (1948), 187–94.

22 Quotations from *Dramatic Works in the Beaumont and Fletcher Canon*, VI.

23 Ibid.
24 Kathleen McLuskie, *Renaissance Dramatists* (Hemel Hempstead: Harvester-Wheatsheaf, 1989), 222.
25 David Farley-Hills, *Jacobean Drama: A Critical Survey of the Professional Drama, 1600–25* (Basingstoke: Macmillan, 1988), 187.
26 Catherine Belsey, *The Subject of Tragedy: Identity and Difference in Renaissance Drama* (London and New York: Methuen, 1985), 198.
27 Quotations from *The Selected Plays of John Webster*, ed. Jonathan Dollimore and Alan Sinfield (Cambridge: Cambridge University Press, 1983).
28 Kate McLuskie, 'Drama and Sexual Politics: The Case of Webster's Duchess', in James Redmond (ed.), *Drama, Sex and Politics* (Cambridge: Cambridge University Press, 1985), 87.
29 Quotations taken from *Women Beware Women*, ed. J. R. Mulryne, The Revels Plays (Manchester: Manchester University Press, 1975).
30 Quotations from Thomas Middleton and William Rowley, *The Changeling*, ed. N. W. Bawcutt, The Revels Plays (Manchester: Manchester University Press, 1970).
31 Jonathan Dollimore, *Radical Tragedy: Religion, Ideology and Power in the Plays of Shakespeare and his Contemporaries* (Brighton: Harvester, 1984) 178.
32 Christopher Ricks, 'The Moral and Poetic Structure of *The Changeling*', *Essays in Criticism*, 10 (1960), 290–306.
33 Richard McCabe, *Incest, Drama and Nature's Law 1550–1700* (Cambridge: Cambridge University Press, 1993), 248.

Chapter 4 Journalistic Plays

1 M. Clark, *Thomas Heywood* (Oxford: Blackwell, 1931), 120.
2 Alison Findlay, 'Sexual and Spiritual Politics in the Events of 1633–34 and *The Late Lancashire Witches*', in Robert Poole (ed.), *Rewriting the Lancashire Witches: Histories and Stories* (Manchester: Manchester University Press, 2002), 146–65, 151.
3 Viviana Comensoli, *Household Business: Domestic Plays of Early Modern England* (Toronto: University of Toronto Press, 1996), 173.
4 Sidney Lee, 'The Topical Side of Elizabethan Drama', *Transactions of the New Shakspere Society*, ser. 1 (1887–92), pt 1, 20.
5 Philip Henslowe, *The Diary of Philip Henslowe*, ed. R. A. Foakes and R. T. Rickert (Cambridge: Cambridge University Press), 123, 124.
6 C. J. Sisson, *Lost Plays of Shakespeare's Age* (Cambridge: Cambridge University Press, 1936), 80–124.
7 Diane Purkiss, *The Witch in History: Early Modern and Twentieth-Century Representations* (London and New York: Routledge, 1996), 233.
8 Arthur Golding, *A briefe discourse of the late murther of master George Sanders* (1573), in Charles Dale Cannon (ed.), *A Warning for Fair Women: A Critical Edition* (The Hague: Mouton, 1975), 218).
9 H. H. Adams, *English Domestic or Homiletic Tragedy, 1575 to 1642* (New York: Columbia University Press, 1943), 7.
10 J. M. R. Margeson, *The Origins of English Tragedy* (Oxford: Clarendon, 1967), 67.
11 See Lena Cowen Orlin, 'Familial Transgressions, Societal Transition on the Elizabethan Stage', in Carole Levin and Karen Robertson (eds), *Sexuality and Politics in Renaissance Drama* (Lewiston, Queenstown and Lampeter: Edwin Mellon, 1991), 34.
12 Quotations from this play are taken from *The Tragedy of Master Arden of Faversham*, ed. M. L. Wine, The Revels Plays (London: Methuen, 1973).
13 Peter Houlbrooke, *Literature and Degree in Renaissance England: Nashe, Bourgeois Tragedy, and Shakespeare* (Newark: University of Delaware Press; London and Toronto: Associated University Presses, 1994), 91.

14 *Tragedy of Master Arden of Faversham*, ed. Wine, lxxvi.

15 Frances Dolan, 'Gender, Moral Agency, and Dramatic Form in *A Warning for Fair Women*', *Studies in English Literature*, 29 (1989), 211. Alexander Leggatt, '*Arden of Faversham*', *Shakespeare Survey*, 36 (1953), 121–33.

16 *Tragedy of Master Arden of Faversham*, ed. Wine, lx.

17 Quotations from this play taken from Robert Yarrington, *Two Lamentable Tragedies* (1610), Students' Facsimile Edition (Amersham: John S. Farmer, 1913).

18 J. A. Sharpe, '"Last Dying Speeches": Religion, Ideology, and Public Execution in Seventeenth Century England', *Past and Present* 107 (1985), 148.

19 Lena Cowen Orlin, *Private Matters and Public Culture in Post-Reformation England* (Ithaca and London: Cornell University Press, 1994), 12.

20 Martin Ingram, '"Scolding Women Cucked or Washed": A Crisis in Gender Relations in Early Modern England?', in Jenny Kermode and Garthine Walker (eds), *Women, Crime and the Courts in Early Modern England* (London: UCL Press, 1994), 48–80; Joy Wiltenburg, *Disorderly Women and Female Power in the Street Literature of Early Modern England and Germany* (Charlottesville and London: University of Virginia Press, 1992), 214; Sandra Clark, *Women and Crime in the Street Literature of Early Modern England* (Basingstoke: Palgrave Macmillan, 1993), 34, 192; Frances Dolan, *Dangerous Familiars: Representations of Domestic Crime in England 1550–1700* (Ithaca and London: Cornell University Press, 1994), 17–18.

21 Quotations from George Wilkins, *The Miseries of Enforced Marriage* (1607), The Malone Society Reprints (Oxford: Oxford University Press, 1964).

22 Stone, *Family, Sex and Marriage*, 130.

23 Quotations from *Three Elizabethan Domestic Tragedies*, ed. Keith Sturgess (Harmondsworth: Penguin Books, 1969).

24 Orlin, *Private Matters and Public Culture*. 68.

25 Quotations from Thomas Dekker, John Ford and William Rowley, *The Witch of Edmonton*, ed. Arthur F. Kinney, New Mermaids (London and New York: A&C Black and W. W. Norton, 1998).

26 Quotations from this play are taken from Thomas Heywood and Richard Brome, *The Late Lancashire Witches*, ed. Laird Barber (New York and London: Garland Publishing, 1979).

27 Herbert Berry, 'The Globe Bewitched and *El Hombre Fiel*', *Medieval and Renaissance Drama in England*, 1 (1984), 212–13.

Chapter 5 History Plays

1 Jean Howard, 'Other Englands: The View from the Non-Shakespearean History Play', in Helen Ostovich et al. (eds), *Other Voices, Other Views: Expanding the Canon in English Renaissance Studies* (Newark and London: Associated University Presses, 1999), 135.

2 T. Hoensellaars, 'Shakespeare and the Early Modern History Play', in Michael Hattaway (ed.), *The Cambridge Companion to Shakespeare's History Plays* (Cambridge: Cambridge University Press, 2002), 32.

3 Ian W. Archer, 'Discourses of History in Elizabethan and Early Stuart London', *Huntington Library Quarterly*, 68 (2005), 205.

4 Matthew H.Wikander, *The Play of Truth and State: Historical Drama from Shakespeare to Brecht* (Baltimore: Johns Hopkins University Press, 1986), 8–9.

5 Dominique Goy-Blanquet, 'Elizabethan Historiography and Shakespeare's Sources', in Hattaway, *Cambridge Companion*, 65.

6 Richard Dutton, '"Methinks the truth should live from age to age": The Dating and Contexts of *Henry V*', *Huntington Library Quarterly*, 68 (2005), 173.

7 F. J. Levy, 'Hayward, Daniel and the Beginnings of Politic History in England', *Huntington Library Quarterly*, 50 (1987), 1–34.

8 Goy-Blanquet, 'Elizabethan Historiography', 69.

9 Quoted in Phyllis Rackin, *Stages of History: Shakespeare's English Chronicles* (Ithaca, N.Y.: Cornell University Press, 1990).

10 D. R. Woolf, *The Idea of History in Early Stuart England: Erudition, Ideology and 'The Light of Truth' from the Accession of James I to the Civil War* (Toronto: University of Toronto Press, 1990), xiii.

11 Ivo Kamps, *Historiography and Ideology in Stuart Drama* (Cambridge: Cambridge University Press, 1996), xiii.

12 David Bevington, *Tudor Drama and Politics: A Critical Approach to Topical Meaning* (Cambridge, Mass.: Harvard University Press, 1968), 192.

13 Alison Findlay, *Illegitimate Power: Bastards in Renaissance Drama* (Manchester and New York: Manchester University Press, 1994), 205.

14 Ibid., 207.

15 Julia Briggs, 'Marlowe's *Massacre at Paris*: A Reconsideration', *Review of English Studies*, n.s. 34 (1983), 258.

16 Quotations from *The Massacre at Paris* in *The Complete Works of Christopher Marlowe*, ed. Edward J. Esche et al., 5 vols (Oxford: Clarendon Press, 1998), V, and from *Edward II*, ibid., III.

17 Raphael Holinshed, *Description of Scotland* (1587), quoted in *Edward II*, ed. Richard Rowland in *Complete Works of Christopher Marlowe*, III.

18 Alan Stewart, *The Cradle King: A Life of James VI and I* (London: Chatto & Windus, 2003), ch. 4.

19 Ian W. Archer, 'Discourses of History in Elizabethan and Early Stuart London', *Huntington Library Quarterly*, 68 (2005), 219.

20 Lister M. Matheson, 'The Peasants' Revolt through Five Centuries of Reporting: Richard Fox, John Stow, and their Successors', *Studies in Philology* , 95 (2) (1998), 121–51.

21 Quotations from *The Life and Death of Jack Straw*, ed. Kenneth Muir, Malone Society Reprints (Oxford: Oxford University Press, 1957).

22 Irving Ribner, *The English History Play in the Age of Shakespeare* (Princeton: Princeton University Press, 1957), 78.

23 See *Woodstock, A Moral History*, ed. A. P. Rossiter (London: Chatto & Windus, 1946).

24 Quotations taken from *Thomas of Woodstock or Richard the Second, Part One*, ed. Peter Corbin and Douglas Sedge (Manchester: Manchester University Press, 2002).

25 Billington, *Mock Kings*, 227.

26 Macdonald P. Jackson , 'Shakespeare's Richard and the Anonymous *Thomas of Woodstock*', *Medieval and Renaissance Drama in England*, 14 (2001), 17–65.

27 Henslowe, *Diary*, 218, 219.

28 S. T. Bindoff, *Tudor England* (Harmondsworth: Penguin Books, 1950), 173.

29 Bevington, *Tudor Drama and Politics*, 293.

30 Quotations taken from *The Dramatic Works of Thomas Dekker*, ed. Fredson Bowers, 4 vols (Cambridge: Cambridge University Press, 1953), I.

31 Bevington, *Tudor Drama and Politics*, 292.

32 Gasper, *Dragon and the Dove*, 48.

33 E.g. Gasper, *Dragon and the Dove*; Muriel Bradbrook, *John Webster, Citizen and Dramatist* (London: Weidenfeld & Nicolson, 1980); Judith D. Spikes, 'The Jacobean History Play and the Myth of the Elect Nation', *Renaissance Drama*, n.s. 8 (1977).

34 Kathleen E. McLuskie, *Dekker and Heywood . Professional Dramatists* (London: Macmillan, 1994), 40.

35 Quotations from Thomas Heywood, *The First and Second Parts of King Edward IV*, ed. Richard Rowland, The Revels Plays (Manchester and New York: Manchester University Press, 2005).

36 Heywood, *Edward IV*, ed. Rowland, 19.

37 Anthony Chute, *Beawtie Dishonoured* (1593), quoted in Heywood, *Edward IV*, ed. Rowland, 44.
38 Bevington, *Tudor Drama*, 242.
39 McLuskie, *Dekker and Heywood*, 88.
40 Daryl W. Palmer, 'Edward IV's Secret Familiarities and the Politics of Proximity in Elizabethan History Plays', *English Literary History*, 61 (1994), 300.
41 Heywood, *Edward IV*, ed. Rowland, 56.
42 Ivo Kamps, *Historiography and Ideology in Stuart Drama* (Cambridge: Cambridge University Press, 1996), 169.
43 Susannah Brietz Monta, 'Mental Discord and Political Discord: Reconsidering *Perkin Warbeck*', *Studies in English Literature*, 37 (1997), 392.
44 Quotations from John Ford, *Perkin Warbeck*, ed. Donald K. Anderson Jr, Regents Renaissance Drama Series (London: Edward Arnold, 1966).
45 Wikander, *Play of Truth and State*, 69.
46 Philip Edwards, *Threshold of a Nation: A Study in English and Irish Drama* (Cambridge: Cambridge University Press, 1979), 185.
47 Anne Barton, ' "He that plays the king": Ford's *Perkin Warbeck* and the Stuart History Play', in Marie Axton and Raymond Williams (eds), *English Drama: Forms and Development* (Cambridge: Cambridge University Press, 1977), 80.
48 Ibid., 81.
49 Lisa Hopkins, 'We Were the Trojans: British National Identities in 1633', *Renaissance Studies*, 16 (2000), 37.

Chapter 6 Tragedies of Tyrants

1 Scott Colley, '*Richard III* and Herod', *Shakespeare Quarterly*, 37 (1986), 451–58.
2 Quoted in William Armstrong, 'The Elizabethan Conception of the Tyrant', *Review of English Studies*, 22 (1940), 164.
3 Ibid., 164.
4 Quoted in Rebecca Bushnell, *Tragedies of Tyrants. Political Thought and Theater in the English Renaissance* (Ithaca, N.Y.: Cornell University Press, 1990), 65.
5 Quoted in ibid., 48.
6 Philip Sidney, *An Apology for Poetry*, ed. Geoffrey Shepherd, revised by R. W. Maslen (Manchester and New York: Manchester University Press, 2002), 98.
7 Thomas Heywood, *An Apology for Actors* (1612), sig. F4v.
8 Bushnell, *Tragedies of Tyrants*, 9.
9 Ibid. 159.
10 Quoted from Daniel C. Boughner, 'Sejanus and Machiavelli', *Studies in English Literature*, 1 (2) (1961), 84.
11 James I, *The Political Works of James I*, ed. C. H. McIlwain (Cambridge, Mass. and London: Harvard University Press, 1918), 66.
12 Martin Butler, 'Romans in Britain: *The Roman Actor* and the Early Stuart Classical Play', in Douglas Howard (ed.), *Massinger: A Critical Reassessment* (Cambridge: Cambridge University Press, 1985), 142.
13 J. W. Lever, *The Tragedy of State: A Study of Jacobean Drama*, new edn (London and New York: Methuen, 1987), 61.
14 Stephanus Junius Brutus, *Vindiciae contra Tyrannos. A Defence of Liberty against Tyrants*, with historical introd. by Harold J. Laski (London: Bell, 1924), 182.
15 Ibid. 140.
16 Matthew Wikander, ' "Queasy to be Touched": The World of Ben Jonson's *Sejanus*', *Journal of English and Germanic Philology*, 78 (1979), 346.

17 Robert Miola, 'Julius Caesar and the Tyrannicide Debate', Renaissance Quarterly, 38 (1985), 284.
18 Ibid., 298.
19 Annabel Patterson, ' "Roman-cast Similitude": Ben Jonson and the English Use of Roman History', in P. A. Ramsey (ed.), Rome in the Renaissance (Binghampton, N.Y.: Center for Medieval and Early Renaissance Studies, 1982), 382.
20 Ben Jonson, ed. C. H. Herford and Percy Simpson, 11 vols (Oxford: Clarendon, 1925), I, 141.
21 Ibid., 36.
22 Quotations from the play are taken from Ben Jonson, Sejanus his Fall, ed. Philip J. Ayres, The Revels Plays (Manchester and New York: Manchester University Press, 1990).
23 John G. Sweeney, 'Sejanus and the People's Beastly Rage', English Literary History, 48 (1981), 75.
24 Jonathan Goldberg, James I and the Politics of Literature: Jonson, Shakespeare, Donne and their Contemporaries (Stanford, Calif.: Stanford University Press, 1989), 182.
25 Butler, 'Romans in Britain', 143.
26 Jonson, Sejanus, ed. Ayres, 9 .
27 By Ayres, Sejanus, and Wikander, ' "Queasy to be Touched" '.
28 Wikander, ' "Queasy to be touched" ', 365, quoting Geoffrey Hill, 'The World's Proportion', in John Russell Brown and Bernard Harris (eds), Jacobean Theatre (London: Arnold, 1960), 124.
29 Lever, Tragedy of State, 68.
30 Arthur Marotti, 'The Self-reflexive Art of Ben Jonson's Sejanus', Texas Studies in Language and Literature, 12 (1970), 213.
31 Dollimore, Radical Tragedy, 137.
32 Lever, Tragedy of State, 68.
33 Bushnell, Tragedies of Tyrants, 173.
34 Quotations from The Plays and Poems of Philip Massinger, ed. Philip Edwards and Colin Gibson, 5 vols (Oxford: Clarendon, 1976), III.
35 Bushnell, Tragedies of Tyrants, 179.
36 Butler, 'Romans in Britain', 150.
37 Ibid., 154.
38 Quotations from The Second Maiden's Tragedy, ed. Anne Lancashire, The Revels Plays (Manchester: Manchester University Press, 1978).
39 Quotations taken from Dramatic Works in the Beaumont and Fletcher Canon, IV (Valentinian), III (The Maid's Tragedy).
40 Bushnell, Tragedies of Tyrants, 167.
41 Samuel Taylor Coleridge, Coleridge on the Seventeenth Century, ed. Roberta F. Brinkley (Durham, N.C.: Duke University Press, 1955), 656.

Chapter 7 Reading Revenge

1 Quotations taken from Henry Chettle, The Tragedy of Hoffman 1631, ed. Harold Jenkins, Malone Society Reprints (Oxford: Oxford University Press, 1951).
2 Fredson Bowers, Elizabethan Revenge Tragedy 1587–1642 (Princeton: Princeton University Press, 1940, 1966), 45.
3 Gordon Braden, Renaissance Tragedy and the Senecan Tradition: Anger's Privilege (New Haven, Conn.: Yale University Press, 1985), 107.
4 Ronald Broude, 'Revenge and Revenge Tragedy in Renaissance England', Renaissance Quarterly, 28 (1) (1975), 47.
5 Mervyn James, Society, Politics and Culture. Studies in Early Modern England (Cambridge: Cambridge University Press, 1986), 309.

6 Katherine Eisamen Maus, 'Introduction', in Katherine Eisamen Maus (ed.), *Four Revenge Tragedies* (Oxford: Oxford University Press, 1995) ix.

7 Quotations from *The Spanish Tragedy* taken from the edition by J. R. Mulryne, New Mermaids (London: Ernest Benn, 1977).

8 Broude, 'Revenge', 53.

9 Quotations from *The Atheist's Tragedy* taken from the edition by Irving Ribner, The Revels Plays (Cambridge, Mass.: Harvard University Press, 1964).

10 Thomas Nashe, *Works*, ed. R. B. McKerrow, vol., 1 (Oxford: Blackwell, 1958), 186.

11 Quotations from *The Jew of Malta* taken from *Complete Works of Christopher Marlowe*, IV, ed. Roma Gill.

12 A misquotation from Terence, *Andria*, 4.1.12, meaning 'no one is nearer to me than I myself'.

13 Katherine Eisamen Maus, *Inwardness and the Theater in the English Renaissance* (Chicago and London: University of Chicago Press, 1995), 35.

14 Jonathan Bate, 'The Performance of Revenge: *Titus Andronicus* and *The Spanish Tragedy*', citing James I, *Political Works*, ed. McIlwain, 181, in *The Show Within: Dramatic and Other Insets, English Renaissance Drama 1550–1642*, ed. Francois Laroque (Montpellier: Université Paul-Valery, 1992), II, 274.

15 Clark, *Women and Crime*, 34.

16 Charles Dale Cannon (ed.), *A Warning for Fair Women: A Critical Edition* (The Hague: Mouton, 1975), 227.

17 Bate, 'Performance', 278.

18 Alison Findlay, *A Feminist Perspective on Renaissance Drama* (Oxford: Blackwell, 1999), 49.

19 Chapter 4, 'Journalistic Plays', *supra*, n. 20.

20 Joy Wiltenberg, *Disorderly Women and Female Power in the Street Literature of Early Modern England and Germany* (Charlottesville and London: University of Virginia Press, 1992).

21 Quotations from *Antonio's Revenge* taken from the edition by G. K. Hunter, Regents Renaissance Drama Series (London: Edward Arnold, 1966).

22 Barbara J. Baines, '*Antonio's Revenge*: Marston's Play on Revenge Plays', *Studies in English Literature*, 23 (2) (1983), 277–94.

23 Ibid., 290.

24 Quotations from *The Revenger's Tragedy* taken from the edition by R. A. Foakes, The Revels Plays (London: Methuen, 1966).

25 Gentillet, *A Discourse . . . Against Nicholas Machiavel* (1608), trans. Simon Patericke, Part 3, max. 6, quoted in Bowers, *Elizabethan Revenge Tragedy*, 52.

26 Scott McMillan, 'Acting and Violence: *The Revenger's Tragedy* and its Departures from *Hamlet*', *Studies in English Literature*, 24 (1984), 277, quoting Jonas Barish.

27 Ibid., 284.

28 John Peter, *Complaint and Satire in Early English Literature* (Oxford: Clarendon Press, 1956), 262–4.

29 McMillan, 'Acting', 275, citing Howard Felperin, *Shakespearean Representations: Mimesis and Modernity in Elizabethan Tragedy* (Princeton: Princeton University Press, 1977).

30 Bowers, *Elizabethan Revenge Tragedy*, 109.

31 Ibid., 140.

32 Braden, *Renaissance Tragedy*, 113.

33 Bowers, *Elizabethan Revenge Tragedy*, p 146.

34 Quotations taken from *The Plays of George Chapman: The Tragedies. A Critical Edition*, general editor Allan Holaday (Cambridge: D. S. Brewer, 1987).

35 *The Cardinal*, ed. E. M. Yearling, The Revels Plays (Manchester: Manchester University Press, 1986), 8. Quotations from the play are taken from this edition.

36 Butler, *Theatre and Crisis*, 236.

37 Deborah G. Burke, ' "This sight doth shake all that is man within me": Sexual Violation and the Rhetoric of Dissent in *The Cardinal'*, *Journal of Medieval and Early Modern Studies*, 26 (1) (1996), 152.

Chapter 8   Comedy and the City

Chapter epigraphs from Laurence Manley, *London in the Age of Shakespeare: An Anthology* (London: Croom Helm, 1986), 37–8, 36.

 1 Richard Rawlidge, *A Monster Late Found Out. And Discovered. Or, The Scourging of Tiplers* (1628), 2.
 2 sig. *3.
 3 A. L. Beier and Roger Findlay (eds), *London 1500–1700: The Making of the Metropolis* (London: Longman, 1986), 3.
 4 Manley, *London*, 50.
 5 Lawrence Stone, *The Crisis of the Aristocracy, 1558–1614* (Oxford: Clarendon Press, 1965), *passim*.
 6 Manley, *London*, 242.
 7 F. J. Fisher, 'The Development of London as a Centre of Conspicuous Consumption in the Sixteenth and Seventeenth Centuries', *Transactions of the Royal Historical Society*, 4th ser., 30 (1948), 37–50.
 8 Gail Kern Paster, *The Idea of the City in the Age of Shakespeare* (Athens, Ga.: University of Georgia Press, 19850), 155.
 9 Thomas Dekker, *The Seven Deadly Sinnes of London*, ed. H. F. B. Brett-Smith (Oxford: Basil Blackwell, 1922), 9.
10 Manley, *London*, 287.
11 Jean-Christophe Agnew, *Worlds Apart: The Market and the Theater in Anglo-American Thought, 1550–1750* (Cambridge: Cambridge University Press, 1986), 50.
12 Ibid., 54–5.
13 Rowland, 'Introduction', in Heywood, *First and Second Parts of King Edward IV*, ed. Rowland, 15.
14 Douglas Bruster, *Drama and the Marketplace in the Age of Shakespeare* (Cambridge: Cambridge University Press, 1992), 34; Anne Barton, 'London Comedy and the Ethos of the City', *The London Journal*, 4 (2) (1987), 158.
15 Manley, *London*, 285.
16 Bruster, *Drama*, 30.
17 Quotations from *The Alchemist* are taken from *Complete Plays*, ed. Wilkes, III.
18 R. L. Smallwood, 'Immediacy and Theatricality in *The Alchemist'*, *Review of English Studies*, n.s. 32, no. 126 (1980), 148.
19 Quotations taken from *Dramatic Works in the Beaumont and Fletcher Canon*, ed. Bowers, I.
20 Quotations taken from *Plays and Poems of Philip Massinger*, ed. Edwards and Gibson, IV.
21 Dekker, *Lanthorne and Candle-light* (1608), in *The Non-Dramatic Works of Thomas Dekker*, ed. A. B. Grosart, 5 vols (London,1885, reissued New York: Russell & Russell, 1963), III, 267.
22 Janette Dillon, ' "Is not all the world Mile End, mother?": The Blackfriars Theatre, the City of London, and *The Knight of the Burning Pestle'*, *Medieval and Renaissance Drama in England*, 13 (2000), 129–41 .
23 Quotations taken from *The Dramatic Works of Thomas Dekker*, ed. Bowers, II.
24 Ibid., I.
25 Quotations taken from *Eastward Ho!*, ed. C. G. Petter, New Mermaids (London: Ernest Benn, 1973).
26 Ibid. 74.

27 Quotation taken from *A Critical Old Spelling Edition of The Works of Edward Sharpham*, ed. Christopher Gordon Petter, The Renaissance Imagination, vol. 18 (New York and London: Garland Publishing, 1986).

28 Jonathan Haynes, *The Social Relations of Jonson's Theatre* (Cambridge: Cambridge University Press, 1992), 43.

29 Quotation taken from *Complete Plays of Ben Jonson*, ed. Wilkes, IV.

30 Agnew, *Worlds Apart*, 112.

31 Ronda A. Arab, 'Work, Bodies and Gender in *The Shoemakers' Holiday*', *Medieval and Renaissance Drama in England*, 13 (2000), 183.

32 Quotations taken from *A Chaste Maid in Cheapside*, ed. Alan Brissenden, New Mermaids (London: Ernest Benn, 1968).

33 Quotations taken from *Plays and Poems of Philip Massinger*, ed. Edwards and Gibson, IV.

34 Stone, *Crisis*, esp. ch. 4.

35 Brian Gibbons, *Jacobean City Comedy. A Study of Satiric Plays by Jonson, Marston and Middleton*, 2nd edn (London and New York: Methuen, 1980), 141.

36 Theodore Leinwand, *The City Staged. Jacobean Comedy, 1603–1613* (Madison: University of Wisconsin Press, 1986), 53.

37 Haynes, *Social Relations*, 115.

38 Anne Barton, *Ben Jonson, Dramatist* (Cambridge: Cambridge University Press, 1984), 143.

39 Haynes, *Social Relations*, 120–1.

40 Quotations taken from *Complete Plays of Ben Jonson*, ed. Wilkes, IV.

41 Gibbons, *Jacobean City Comedy*, 149.

42 Bruster, *Drama*, 42.

43 Karen Newman, *Fashioning Femininity and English Renaissance Drama* (Chicago and London: University of Chicago Press, 1991), 134, 136.

44 Leinwand, *City*, 140.

45 Michelle M. Dowd, 'Leaning Too Hard upon the Pen: Suburb Wenches and City Wives in *Westward Ho*', *Medieval and Renaissance Drama in England*, 15 (2002), 235.

46 Bernard Capp, *When Gossips Meet: Women, Family, and Neighbourhood in Early Modern England* (Oxford: Oxford University Press, 2003), 67.

47 Newman, *Fashioning Femininity*, 138.

48 Sandra Clark, '*Hic Mulier, Haec Vir*, and the Controversy over Masculine Women', *Studies in Philology*, 82 (1985), 166.

Chapter 9 The Place of Shakespeare

1 Russ McDonald, *Shakespeare & Jonson / Jonson & Shakespeare* (Brighton: Harvester, 1988), 95.

2 E. A. J. Honigmann, *Shakespeare's Impact on his Contemporaries* (London: Macmillan, 1982), 88–9.

3 James Shapiro, *Rival Playwrights: Marlowe, Jonson, Shakespeare* (New York: Columbia University Press, 1991), 86.

4 Ibid., 91.

5 Harold Brooks, 'Marlowe and the Early Shakespeare', in Brian Morris (ed.), *Christopher Marlowe*, Mermaid Critical Commentaries (London: Ernest Benn, 1968), 70.

6 Jonathan Bate, *The Genius of Shakespeare* (London: Picador, 1997), 113–14.

7 *As You Like It*, ed. Juliet Dusinberre, The Arden Shakespeare (London: Thomson Learning, 2006), 36–46.

8 David Riggs, *The World of Christopher Marlowe* (London: Faber & Faber, 2004), 347.

9 Park Honan, *Shakespeare. A Life* (Oxford: Oxford University Press, 1998), 252.

10 Ruth Morse, ' "What City, Friends, Is This?" ', in Mehl et al., *Plotting Early Modern London*, 179.
11 Shapiro, *Rival Playwrights*, 141; Honigmann, *Impact*, 102.
12 Honigmann, *Impact*, 107.
13 Quotations taken from *Complete Plays of Ben Jonson*, ed. Wilkes, I.
14 Anne Barton, *Ben Jonson*, 69.
15 James P. Bednarz, *Shakespeare and the Poets' War* (New York: Columbia University Press, 2001), 181.
16 *The Second Part of The Return from Parnassus*, in *The Three Parnassus Plays*, ed. J. B. Leishman (London: Nicholson & Watson, 1949), ll. 1769–73, 337.
17 McDonald, *Shakespeare*, p.7.
18 Bednarz, *Poets' War*, 32.
19 Honan, *Shakespeare*, 256.
20 David Riggs, *Ben Jonson: A Life* (Cambridge, Mass. and London: Harvard University Press, 1989), 56.
21 Andrew Gurr, 'A Jibe at Shakespeare in 1606', *Notes and Queries*, 49(2) (2002), 245. Quotations from *The Woman-Hater* taken from *Dramatic Works in the Beaumont and Fletcher Canon*, ed. Bowers, I.
22 Sandra Clark, *The Plays of Beaumont and Fletcher: Sexual Themes and Dramatic Representation* (Hemel Hempstead: Harvester Wheatsheaf, 1994), 97–100.
23 Honan, *Shakespeare*, 375.
24 Philip Finkelpearl, *Court and Country Politics in The Plays of Beaumont and Fletcher* (Princeton: Princeton University Press, 1990), 152.
25 Katherine Duncan-Jones, *Ungentle Shakespeare: Scenes from his Life* (London: Thomson Learning, 2001), 233.
26 Ibid., 233.
27 King *Henry VIII*, ed. McMullan, 66.
28 *The Two Noble Kinsmen*, ed. Lois Potter, The Arden Shakespeare (London: Thomson Learning, 1997), 32.
29 Ibid., 32.
30 E.g. Brian Vickers, *Shakespeare, Co-author* (Oxford: Oxford University Press, 2002), 491–500.
31 Douglas Bruster, *Quoting Shakespeare. Form and Culture in Early Modern Drama* (Lincoln, Nebr., and London: University of Nebraska Press (2000), 170.
32 Vickers, *Shakespeare*, 500.
33 D. J. McGinn, *Shakespeare's Influence on the Drama of his Age, Studied in 'Hamlet'* (New Brunswick: Rutgers University Press, 1938), 133–226.
34 T. A. Dunn, *Philip Massinger: The Man and the Playwright* (London: Thomas Nelson, 1957), 203.
35 Quotations taken from *Plays and Poems of Philip Massinger*, ed. Edwards and Gibson, II.
36 Michael Neill, 'Massinger's Patriarchy: The Social Vision of *A New Way to Pay Old Debts*', in Michael Neill (ed.), *Putting History to the Question: Power, Politics and Society in English Renaissance Drama* (New York: Columbia University Press, 2000), 74.
37 Quotations taken from *'Tis Pity She's a Whore*, ed. Derek Roper, The Revels Plays (Manchester: Manchester University Press, 1975).
38 Richard A. McCabe, *Incest, Drama and Nature's Law 1550–1700* (Cambridge: Cambridge University Press, 1993), 238.
39 Roslyn Lander Knutson, *The Repertory of Shakespeare's Company 1594–1613* (Fayetteville: University of Arkansas Press, 1991), 177.
40 Quoted from *Norton Shakespeare*, 3359.
41 Honigmann, *Shakespeare's Impact*, 45.

42 Peter Blayney, 'The Publication of Playbooks', in Cox and Kastan, *New History*, 383–422.

43 Lukas Erne, *Shakespeare as a Literary Dramatist* (Cambridge: Cambridge University Press, 2003), 14.

44 David L. Frost, *The School of Shakespeare. The Influence of Shakespeare on English Drama 1600–1642* (Cambridge: Cambridge University Press, 1968), 11.

45 Honigmann, *Shakespeare's Impact*, 45.

46 Ibid., 22.

Epilogue

1 Agnew, *Worlds Apart*; Steven Mullaney, *The Place of the Stage: License, Play and Power in Renaissance England* (Chicago and London: Chicago University Press, 1988).

2 Richard Wheeler, 'Introduction', in C. L. Barber, *Creating Elizabethan Tragedy: The Theater of Marlowe and Kyd* (Chicago: University of Chicago Press, 1988), 8.

3 Ibid., 9.

Further Reading

Introduction

English Professional Theatre, 1530–1660 (2000), edited by Glynne Wickham, Herbert Berry and William Ingram is a useful anthology of contemporary documents relating to the stage in this period, which supplements rather than supersedes E. K. Chambers, *The Elizabethan Stage*, 4 vols (1923). G. E. Bentley's two volumes, *The Profession of Dramatist in Shakespeare's Time 1590–1642* (1971) and *The Profession of Player in Shakespeare's Time 1590–1642* (1984), put together in discursive form the kind of material found in *English Professional Theatre* and *The Elizabethan Stage*. Andrew Gurr's books, *The Shakespearean Stage, 1574–1642* (2nd edn, 1982) and *Playgoing in Shakespeare's London* (1987), are both mines of information, the latter with a useful appendix detailing actual playgoers in the period. Richard Dutton's *Mastering the Revels: The Regulation and Censorship of English Renaissance Drama* (1991) gives an important account of the functioning of the Revels Office in the Jacobean period. Martin Butler's *Theatre and Crisis 1632–1642* (1984) is the definitive study of theatre in this period, overturning many old assumptions about the Caroline stage. Jeremy Lopez, *Theatrical Convention and Audience Response in Early Modern Drama* (2003), takes off from earlier work by Muriel Bradbrook (*Themes and Conventions of Elizabethan Tragedy*, 1960, and *The Growth and Structure of Elizabethan Comedy*, 1955) to examine how plays utilize and manipulate audience awareness.

Monarchy and the Stage

Of the many recent books on the regulation and censorship of the stage, Dutton, *Mastering the Revels*, and Janet Clare, *'Art Made Tongue-tied by Authority': Elizabethan and Jacobean Dramatic Censorship* (1990) complement one another in approach and often conclusions, but Clare makes a broader chronological survey of the period. Annabel Patterson, *Censorship and Interpretation: The Conditions and Reading and Writing in Early Modern England* (1984), discusses ways in which theatrical texts might be coded to escape censorship. Richard Burt's article, ' "Tis Writ by Me": *The Roman Actor* and the Politics of Reception in the English Renaissance Theatre', *Theatre Journal* (1988), critiques these works. Margot Heinemann, *Puritanism and Theatre: Thomas Middleton and Opposition Drama under the Early Stuarts* (1980), makes a case for the drama as critical of Stuart absolutism. Philip Finkelpearl, '"The Comedians' Liberty": Censorship of the Jacobean Stage Reconsidered' (*English Literary Renaissance*, 16, 1986), takes an interestingly sceptical view of the effectiveness of theatrical censorship. Two books on the cult of Elizabeth, Helen Hackett, *Virgin Mother, Maiden Queen: Elizabeth I and the Cult of the Virgin* (1995), and Michael Dobson and Nicola J. Watson, *England's Elizabeth: An Afterlife in Fame and Fantasy* (2002), relate the staging of Elizabeth's reign in the early seventeenth century to broader contexts. Philippa Berry's challenging feminist study, *Of Chastity and Power: Elizabethan Literature and the Unmarried Queen* (1989), relates the cult of Elizabeth to explorations of female power in the work of Lyly and other writers of the period. Sandra Billington, *Mock Kings and Medieval Society in Renaissance Drama* (1991) relates dramatic depictions of monarchy and rebellions against it to the festive phenomenon of mock kings in court revels and pageantry, with a well-detailed historical background. R. Malcolm Smuts, *Court Culture and the Origins of a Royalist Tradition in Early Stuart England* (1987), although not concerned with theatre as such, fills in the cultural and historical background for the Stuart period lucidly and effectively.

Sex, Marriage and the Family

Lawrence Stone, *The Family, Sex and Marriage in England 1500–1800*, has been challenged in certain respects, but remains immensely useful for the background in social history. Other social historians, such as Bernard Capp, *When Gossips Meet: Women, Family and Neighbourhood in Early Modern England* (2003), and Laura Gowing, *Domestic Dangers: Women, Words, and Sex in Early Modern London* (1996), provide material which often challenges assumptions about the conditions of patriarchy at this time. Joy Wiltenberg, *Disorderly Women and Female Power in the Street Literature of Early Modern England and Germany* (1992), also enlarges our notions of gender relations, and contributes to the debate as to whether they were in crisis. Mary Beth Rose, *The Expense of Spirit: Love and Sexuality in English Renaissance Drama* (1988), is particularly helpful on theories of marriage. Kathleen McLuskie, in her feminist study, *Renaissance Drama* (1989), relates issues of sex and gender to stage representation in a way not often done. Richard McCabe, *Incest, Drama and Nature's Law 1550–1700* (1993), discusses his topic in a context which includes classical tradition, changing concepts of natural law, and also theories of family development. Christine Peters, in 'Gender, Sacrament and Ritual: The Making and Meaning of Marriage in Late Medieval and Early Modern England', *Past and Present* 169 (2000), pp. 63–96, gives a detailed and helpful overview of marriage in relation to religious change in the period.

Journalistic Plays

H. H. Adams, *English Domestic or, Homiletic Tragedy, 1575 to 1642* (1943) was the standard study of most of these plays, and remains valuable, but his rather old-fashioned moralistic approach needs to be tempered by more modern views, particularly in the light of feminist criticism. Frances Dolan, *Dangerous Familiars: Representations of Domestic Crime in England 1550–1700* (1994), and Sandra Clark, *Women and Crime in the Street Literature of Early Modern England* (2003) both discuss domestic plays in relation to current ideas about gender relations and the household. Lena Cowen Orlin, *Private Matters and Public Culture in Post Reformation England* (1994), takes the murder of Arden of Faversham as a starting point for an intensely detailed account of the changing culture of the public and the private in the period. Diane Purkiss, *The Witch in History: Early Modern and Twentieth-Century Representations* (1996), gives a closely documented discussion of the witchcraft plays in their contemporary context. Finally, the research represented in C. J. Sisson, *Lost Plays of Shakespeare's Age* (1936), illuminates the whole topic of journalistic plays and has never been superseded.

History Plays

Given the current interest in English nationalism in the period, history plays represent an area of much ongoing research. Richard Helgerson, *Forms of Nationhood: The Elizabethan Writing of England* (1992), has set many of the terms of the current debate, and has been challenged, for instance by Phyllis Rackin, *Stages of History: Shakespeare's English Chronicles* (1990). Helgerson's concern with nationhood was usefully anticipated by Philip Edwards in *Threshold of a Nation: A Study in English and Irish Drama* (1979). Matthew Wikander, *The Play of Truth and State: Historical Drama from Shakespeare to Brecht* (1986), considers reasons for the failure of the history play as a genre in the seventeenth century, while Ivo Kamps, *Historiography and Ideology in Stuart Drama* (1996), takes issue with Wikander, discussing specific examples of the later history play to demonstrate that it still dealt with living concerns. David Bevington, *Tudor Drama and Politics: A Critical Approach to Topical Meaning* (1968), remains essential for consideration of the earlier history plays. Judith Doolin Spikes, 'The Jacobean History Play and the Myth of the Elect Nation', *Renaissance Drama*, n.s. 8 (1977), drew attention to the Protestant polemic in the Foxean history plays and has been followed in this by Julia Gasper, *The Dragon and the Dove: The Plays of Thomas Dekker* (1990). Richard Rowland's extensive introduction to his edition of Heywood's *Edward IV* (2005) is very stimulating on contemporary attitudes to history, as well as on the place of London in the development of English national identity. Two articles in the *Huntington Library Quarterly* 68 (2005), Ian Archer, 'Discourses of History in Elizabethan and Early Stuart London', and Richard Dutton, ' "Methinks the Truth Should Live from Age to Age": The Dating and Contexts of *Henry V*', which usefully fill out the background on changing view of the function of historiography in the period, might be a good place to start.

Tragedies of Tyrants

Much ground-breaking work on concepts of tyranny was done in William Armstrong's two articles, 'The Elizabethan Conception of the Tyrant' (*Review of English Studies*, 22, 1946) and 'The Influence of Seneca and Machiavelli on the Elizabethan Tyrant' (*Review of English Studies*, 24, 1948). Rebecca Bushnell, *Tragedies of Tyrants: Political Thought and Theater in the English Renaissance* (1990), builds on Armstrong but relates tyrant plays to the changing discourses of tyranny in the period, with useful discussions of the relationship between tyranny and sexuality. J. W. Lever's concise book, *The Tragedy of State* (1971), was ahead of its time in focusing on the political dimension of Renaissance tragedy and its critiques of the monarchy. Jonathan Dollimore, *Radical Tragedy: Religion, Ideology and Power in the Drama of Shakespeare and his Contemporaries* (1984), gives provocative readings of a range of tragedies as evidence of a contemporary crisis of order centred on absolutism. Matthew Wikander, ' "Queasy to be Touched": The World of Ben Jonson's *Sejanus*' (*Journal of English and Germanic Philology*, 78, 1979) relates the play to anxieties over the growth of Stuart despotism, and Martin Butler does the same for Massinger's *The Roman Actor* in 'Romans in Britain: *The Roman Actor* and the Early Stuart Classical Play' (in Douglas Howard, ed., *Philip Massinger: A Critical Reassessment*, 1985). Robert Miola, '*Julius Caesar* and the Tyrannicide Debate' (*Renaissance Quarterly*, 38, 1985) relates this play and others of Shakespeare to the contemporary debate over the ethics of tyrannicide, which forms the background to many of these plays.

Reading Revenge

Fredson Bowers, *Elizabethan Revenge Tragedy 1587–1642* (1966), is the starting point for any study of this genre, with its unparalleled coverage of the period. Ronald Broude's article, 'Revenge and Revenge Tragedy in Renaissance England' (*Renaissance Quarterly*, 28, 1975), relates the plays to power struggles going on all over Europe, and covers a huge amount of ground. Mervyn James, *Society, Politics and Culture. Studies in Early Modern England* (1986), gives a historical background in changing attitudes to honour and chivalry at this time, which is illuminating for these plays. Gordon Braden, *Renaissance Tragedy and the Senecan Tradition: Anger's Privilege* (1985), examines revenge plays in terms of classical ideas about selfhood and identity, and later developments in Renaissance Europe. Katherine Eisaman Maus, *Inwardness and the Theater in the English Renaissance* (1995), is especially good on the figure of the Machiavel. Her essay, '*The Spanish Tragedy*, or, The Machiavel's Revenge' (in Stevie Simkin, ed., *Revenge Tragedy*, 2001) explores themes of agency and retaliation in revenge drama in relation to contemporary cultural issues. Jonathan Bate, 'The Performance of Revenge: *Titus Andronicus* and *The Spanish Tragedy*' (in *The Show Within*, ed.

François Laroque, 1992), and Barbara J. Baines, '*Antonio's Revenge*: Marston's Play on Revenge Plays' (*Studies in English Literature*, 23, 1983) are both interesting on the meta-theatricality of plays in this genre. John Kerrigan's monumental study, *Revenge Tragedy: Aeschylus to Armageddon* (1996), locates the plays within a long and evolving tradition, and is stimulating at every point.

Comedy and the City

The study of city comedy as a genre began with Brian Gibbons, *Jacobean City Comedy* (1968), and the essays in *Plotting Early Modern London* (ed. Dieter Mehl et al., 2004) position themselves in relation to it as re-examinations of the plays in the light of historical contexts such as early modern capitalism and urban culture. Much has been written on early modern London recently; A. L. Beier and Roger Findlay's anthology of essays, *London 1500–1700: The Making of a Metropolis* (1986), and Ian Archer, *The Pursuit of Stability: Social Relations in Elizabethan London* (1991), are both very useful here. Douglas Bruster, *Drama and the Marketplace in the Age of Shakespeare* (1992), goes on from Jean-Christophe Agnew's seminal book, *Worlds Apart: The Market and the Theater in Anglo-American Thought, 1550–1750* (1986), to explore how drama handles the implications of fluid capital and the idea of the placeless market. Theodore Leinwand also examines the importance of money and trade in London in *Theatre, Finance and Society in Early Modern England* (1999); his earlier book, *The City Staged: Jacobean Comedy, 1603–13* (1986) attends to more formal considerations in the plays. Jonathan Haynes, *The Social Relations of Jonson's Theatre* (1992), is interesting on the formulation of urban social types in Jonson's comedy, perhaps taking a cue from Anne Barton, *Ben Jonson, Dramatist* (1984), who remarks on Jonson's almost novelistic detail. Such attention to detail is illuminatingly discussed by R. L. Smallwood in 'Immediacy and Theatricality in *The Alchemist*' (*Review of English Studies* n.s. 32, 1980). Ronda A. Arab, 'Work, Bodies and Gender in *The Shoemakers' Holiday*' (*Medieval and Renaissance Drama in England*, 13 (2000), makes connections between the three elements of her title in a way that might be extended to other plays.

The Place of Shakespeare

Shakespeare's intricate relationship to Jonson is the subject of Russ McDonald's very accessible book, *Shakespeare & Jonson / Jonson & Shakespeare* (1988), which looks at the creative intersections in the lives of the two playwrights, and also, in part, of James P. Bednarz, *Shakespeare and the Poets' War* (2001), which examines Shakespeare's involvement with Jonson and others in this fin-de-siècle phenomenon. James Shapiro, *Rival Playwrights: Marlowe, Jonson, Shakespeare* (1991), views the relationship of the three as essentially a competitive one, but differentiates interestingly between Shakespeare's attitude to Jonson and Jonson's to him. E. A. J. Honigmann, *Shakespeare's Impact on his Contemporaries* (1982), makes a convincing case for the recognition of Shakespeare's significance from early on. In the recent spate of biographical books about Shakespeare, Park Honan, *Shakespeare: A Life* (1998), and Katherine Duncan-Jones, *Ungentle Shakespeare: Scenes from his Life* (2001), glance at his relationships with other playwrights, but are more concerned with re-evaluating his reputation. Brian Vickers, *Shakespeare, Co-Author* (2002) makes a detailed examination of the evidence for Shakespeare as a collaborative playwright in specific instances at all stages of his career. David Riggs's biographies of Jonson (1989) and Marlowe (2004) see their subjects in relation to Shakespeare, but also, obviously, to their literary and cultural contexts more broadly. The most stimulating account of Shakespeare's place in English cultural life is Jonathan Bate's *The Genius of Shakespeare* (1997).

Editions and Primary Texts

[*Arden of Faversham*] *The Tragedy of Master Arden of Faversham*, ed. M. L. Wine, The Revels Plays (London: Methuen, 1973).

Averell, William, *A Dyall for Dainty Darlings, rockt in the cradle of Securitie* (1584).

Beaumont, Francis, and John Fletcher, *The Dramatic Works in the Beaumont and Fletcher Canon*, general editor Fredson Bowers, 10 vols (Cambridge: Cambridge University Press, 1966–).

Bentley, G. E., *The Jacobean and Caroline Stage*, 7 vols (Oxford: Clarendon Press, 1941).

Bullough, Geoffrey, *Narrative and Dramatic Sources of Shakespeare*, 8 vols (London: Routledge & Kegan Paul, 1957–75).

Chamberlain, John, *The Letters of John Chamberlain*, ed. Norman Egbert McLure, 2 vols (Philadelphia: American Philosophical Society, 1939).

Chambers, E. K., *The Elizabethan Stage*, 4 vols (Oxford: Clarendon Press, 1923).

Chapman, George, *The Plays of George Chapman: The Tragedies. A Critical Edition*, general editor, Allan Holaday (Cambridge: D. S. Brewer, 1987).

Chettle, Henry, *The Tragedy of Hoffman 1631*, ed. Harold Jenkins, Malone Society Reprints (Oxford: Oxford University Press, 1951).

Dekker, Thomas, *The Dramatic Works of Thomas Dekker*, 4 vols, ed. Fredson Bowers (Cambridge: Cambridge University Press, 1953).

Dekker, Thomas, *The Gull's Hornbook*, in *Thomas Dekker: Selected Writings*, ed. E. D. Pendry (Cambridge, Mass.: Harvard University Press, 1968).

Dekker, Thomas, John Ford and William Rowley, *The Witch of Edmonton*, ed. Arthur F. Kinney, New Mermaids (London and New York: A&C Black and W. W. Norton, 1998).

Ford, John, *Perkin Warbeck*, ed. Donald K. Anderson, Jr, Regents Renaissance Drama Series (London: Edward Arnold, 1966).

Ford, John, *'Tis Pity She's a Whore*, ed. Derek Roper, The Revels Plays (Manchester: Manchester University Press, 1975).

Gayton, Edmund, *Pleasant Notes upon Don Quixot* (1654).

[*Gorboduc*] *Gorbuduc*, ed. Irby B. Cauthen, Jr (London: Edward Arnold, 1970).

Harington, John, *The Letters and Epigrams of Sir John Harington*, ed. N. E. McClure (Philadelphia: University of Pennsylvania Press, 1930).

Heywood, Thomas, *An Apologie for Actors* (1612).

Heywood, Thomas, *The First and Second Parts of King Edward IV*, ed. Richard Rowland, The Revels Plays (Manchester and New York: Manchester University Press, 2005).

Heywood, Thomas, *If You Know Not Me, You Know Nobody*, Part 1, ed. Madeleine Doran, Malone Society Reprints (Oxford: Oxford University Press, 1935).

Heywood, Thomas, and Richard Brome, *The Late Lancashire Witches*, ed. Laird Barber (New York and London: Garland Publishing, 1979).

[*Jack Straw*] *The Life and Death of Jack Straw*, ed. Kenneth Muir, Malone Society Reprints (Oxford: Oxford University Press, 1957).

Jonson, Ben, *Ben Jonson*, 11 vols, ed. C. H. Herford and Percy Simpson (Oxford: Clarendon Press, 1925–63).

Jonson, Ben, *The Complete Plays of Ben Jonson*, ed. G. A. Wilkes, 4 vols (Oxford: Clarendon Press, 1981–2).

Jonson, Ben, *Sejanus his Fall*, ed. Philip J. Ayres, The Revels Plays (Manchester and New York: Manchester University Press, 1990).

Jonson, Ben, John Marston and George Chapman, *Eastward Ho!*, ed. C. G. Petter, New Mermaids (London: Ernest Benn, 1973).

Kyd, Thomas, *The Spanish Tragedy*, ed. J. R. Mulryne, New Mermaids (London: Ernest Benn, 1977).

Lyly, John, *The Complete Works*, ed. R. W. Bond, 3 vols (Oxford: Oxford University Press, 1902).

Marlowe, Christopher, *The Complete Works of Christopher Marlowe*, 5 vols, ed. Edward J. Esche et al. (Oxford: Clarendon Press, 1998).

Marston, John, *Antonio's Revenge*, ed. G. K. Hunter, Regents Renaissance Drama Series (London: Edward Arnold, 1966).

Marston, John, *The Dutch Courtesan*, ed. M. L. Wine, Regents Renaissance Drama Series (Lincoln, Nebr.: University of Nebraska Press, 1965).

Marston, John, *The Fawn*, ed. Gerald A. Smith (Lincoln, Nebr.: University of Nebraska Press, 1965).

Marston, John, *The Malcontent*, ed. Bernard Harris, New Mermaids (London: Ernest Benn, 1967).

Massinger, Philip, *The Plays and Poems of Philip Massinger*, ed. Philip Edwards and Colin Gibson, 5 vols (Oxford: Clarendon Press, 1976).

Middleton, Thomas, and William Rowley, *The Changeling*, ed. N. W. Bawcutt, The Revels Plays (Manchester: Manchester University Press, 1970).

[Middleton, Thomas] *The Revenger's Tragedy*, ed. R. A. Foakes, The Revels Plays (London: Methuen, 1966).

Middleton, Thomas, *Women Beware Women*, ed. J. R. Mulryne, The Revels Plays (Manchester: Manchester University Press, 1975).

Nashe, Thomas, *Works*, ed. R. B. McKerrow, 5 vols (Oxford: Blackwell, 1958).

Niccholes, Alexander, *A Discourse of Marriage and Wiving, and of the greatest Mystery contained, How to choose a good Wife from a bad* (1615).

[*Parnassus Plays*] *The Three Parnassus Plays*, ed. J. B. Leishman (London: Nicholson & Watson, 1949).

[*Second Maiden*] *The Second Maiden's Tragedy*, ed. Anne Lancashire, The Revels Plays (Manchester: Manchester University Press, 1978).

Shakespeare, William, *The Norton Shakespeare*, ed. Stephen Greenblatt et al. (New York and London: W. W. Norton, 1997).

Shakespeare, William, *As You Like It*, ed. Juliet Dusinberre, The Arden Shakespeare (London: Thomson Learning, 2006).

Shakespeare, William, *King Henry VIII*, ed. Gordon McMullan, The Arden Shakespeare (London: Thomson Learning, 2000),

Shakespeare, William, *Titus Andronicus*, ed. Jonathan Bate, The Arden Shakespeare (London and New York: Routledge, 1995).

Shakespeare, William, and John Fletcher, *The Two Noble Kinsmen*, ed. Lois Potter, The Arden Shakespeare (London: Thomson Learning, 1997).

Sharpham, Edward, *A Critical Old Spelling Edition of The Works of Edward Sharpham*, ed. Christopher Gordon Petter, The Renaissance Imagination, vol. 18 (New York and London: Garland, 1986).

Shirley, James, *The Cardinal*, ed. E. M. Yearling, The Revels Plays (Manchester: Manchester University Press, 1986).

[*Thomas of Woodstock, or King Richard the Second, Part One*], ed. Peter Corbin and Douglas Sedge, The Revels Plays (Manchester: Manchester University Press, 2002).

Tourneur, Cyril, *The Atheist's Tragedy*, ed. Irving Ribner, The Revels Plays (Cambridge, Mass.: Harvard University Press, 1964).

[*A Warning for Fair Women*] *A Warning for Fair Women: A Critical Edition*, ed. Charles Dale Cannon (The Hague: Mouton 1975).

Webster, John, *The Selected Plays of John Webster*, ed. Jonathan Dollimore and Alan Sinfield (Cambridge: Cambridge University Press, 1983).

Wickham, Glynne, Herbert Berry and William Ingram (eds), *English Professional Theatre, 1530–1660* (Cambridge: Cambridge University Press, 2000).

Wilkins, George, *The Miseries of Enforced Marriage*, 1607, The Malone Society Reprints (Oxford: Oxford University Press, 1964).

Yarrington, Robert, *Two Lamentable Tragedies*, 1610, Students' Facsimile Edition (Amersham: John S. Farmer, 1913).

[*Yorkshire Tragedy*] *Three Elizabethan Domestic Tragedies*, ed. Keith Sturgess (Harmondsworth: Penguin Books, 1969).

Index